ROOTED SORROWS

PSYCHOANALYTIC PERSPECTIVES ON CHILD PROTECTION, ASSESSMENT, THERAPY AND TREATMENT

ROOTED SORROWS

PSYCHOANALYTIC PERSPECTIVES ON CHILD PROTECTION, ASSESSMENT, THERAPY AND TREATMENT

Being: Papers given to a conference for judges and mental health professionals at the Dartington Hall Conference Centre, Dartington Hall, Totnes, Devon, between 22 and 24 September 1995, together with a record of the discussions taking place in the plenary sessions of the conference and additional papers on related subjects.

Edited and with an Introduction by

THE HON MR JUSTICE WALL

with a Foreword by

THE RT HON THE LORD LLOYD OF BERWICK

ff **Family Law**
1997

Published by
Family Law, a publishing imprint of
Jordan Publishing Limited
21 St Thomas Street
Bristol BS1 6JS

© 1997 Jordan Publishing Limited
Reprinted March 1997
Reprinted May 1997

British Library Cataloguing-in-Publication Data
A catalogue record for this book is available from the British Library.

ISBN 0 85308 396 7

Phototypeset by Mendip Communications Ltd, Frome
Printed in Great Britain by Hobbs The Printers Ltd of Southampton

CONTRIBUTORS

The Rt Hon Lord Justice Thorpe

Brian Jacobs, Consultant Child and Adolescent Psychiatrist, Maudesley Hospital

Dr Judith Trowell, Consultant Psychiatrist, Tavistock Clinic

The Hon Mr Justice Wall

Anne Zachary, Psychoanalyst and Consultant Psychotherapist, Portman Clinic

Dr Roger Kennedy, Consultant Psychotherapist, Family Unit, the Cassel Hospital

Trudy Klauber, Consultant Child Psychotherapist, Donald Winnicott Centre, Queen Elizabeth Hospital for Children, London

Donald Campbell, Consultant Psychotherapist, Portman Clinic

Dr Clifford Yorke, formerly Psychiatrist-in-charge, the Anna Freud Centre, and Consultant Psychotherapist to the Psychiatric Unit at Watford General Hospital

J Hodges, B Williams, C Andreou, M Lanyado, A Bentovim and D Skuse, Behavioural Sciences Unit, Institute of Child Health, University of London, London

The Rt Hon Lady Justice Butler-Sloss

Dr Patrick Gallwey, Consultant Forensic Psychiatrist, Nuffield Hospital, Exeter

Brian Waller, Director of Social Services, Leicestershire County Council

Macbeth:

How does your patient, Doctor?

Doctor:

                              Not so sick, my Lord,
As she is troubled with thick-coming fancies,
That keep her from her rest.

Macbeth:

                              Cure her of that:
Canst thou not minister to a mind diseas'd,
Pluck from the memory a rooted sorrow,
Raze out the written troubles of the brain,
And with some sweet oblivious antidote
Cleanse the stuff'd bosom of that perilous stuff
Which weighs upon the heart?

Doctor:

                              Therein the patient
Must minister to himself.

Macbeth:

Throw physic to the dogs; I'll none of it.

                    Macbeth, Act V, Scene III, lines 37 to 47

FOREWORD

Dartington Hall Conference

22–24 September 1995

At Dartington Hall, in September 1995, there took place a multi-disciplinary conference which included judges, psychiatrists and other professionals concerned with the protection of children within the family justice system. This book is the result.

Dartington Hall has played host to many such conferences in the past. What made this conference unique was the attendance of so many judges coming to discuss with mental health professionals the almost insoluble problems which they face every day in court.

The conference was not quite the first of its kind. Eighteen months ago a similar conference was held at Cumberland Lodge, which focused on the criminal justice system, and especially on the problems of dangerousness. But having attended both conferences, I can say that the Dartington Hall conference was, if anything, even more successful.

Thirty or forty years ago such an event would have been almost unimaginable. The fact that the conference took place at all shows how far we have moved. That it was such a success was due to the inspiration and careful planning of Lord Justice Thorpe and his team. The Department of Health and the Judicial Studies Board are to be warmly congratulated on supporting the conference financially.

Much of the benefit of any conference lies in the informal discussion which takes place between sessions. The Dartington Hall conference was no exception. Miss Florence Baron QC in her commentary had done well to capture something of the atmosphere in print. But the main purpose of this book must be to give permanence to the papers prepared for the conference in advance. They seem to me to be of an exceptionally high standard. I hope that the book will have as wide a circulation as possible, not only among judges, but also among all those who are concerned with the protection and care of children in need. I hope also that in due course there will be other conferences along the same lines. It was an experiment well worth repeating.

THE RT HON THE LORD LLOYD OF BERWICK
House of Lords

CONTENTS

EDITOR'S INTRODUCTION

The structure of this book follows the programme of the conference, about which a word needs to be said. With one exception, all the papers were collected, printed and sent to each participant in early August 1995, some seven weeks in advance of the conference. The object of enabling everybody to read and absorb all the papers in advance was, of course, to maximise the time for syndicate and plenary discussion. None of the papers was, accordingly, formally delivered at the conference. Ten minutes were allocated in each session for authors to introduce their papers: the conference then broke up into eight syndicates each containing a maximum of four judges. Syndicate discussion, which lasted an hour, was then followed by a plenary session lasting slightly longer. None of the syndicates was chaired by a judge; nor were the plenary sessions, with the exception of the final session, which took the form of a conference review and which was chaired by Lady Justice Butler-Sloss. The conference programme is printed at Appendix I (p. 143), and a list of those who attended is printed at Appendix II (p. 145).

The manifest advantage of the programme as so structured was that the discussion both in the syndicates and in the plenary sessions was fully informed and wide-ranging. The conference was also fortunate to have as its *rapporteuse* Florence Baron QC, and I echo Lord Lloyd's praise for the manner in which she has captured the essence of the discussion in the plenary sessions. To give the full flavour of the conference therefore, each of the papers printed is preceded by a summary of the introduction given by its author, and is followed by a note of the plenary discussion.

After the conference, all the authors were given the opportunity to revise their papers in the light of the discussion which had taken place. All did so. In relation to my own paper, a group of the doctors met to produce an agreed response to the questions which I had raised in the three specific case histories annexed to the paper. That response, and a further individual response from the viewpoint of a psychoanalyst and consultant adult psychotherapist, Dr Anne Zachary, are published in the chapter immediately following my paper.

In addition, the conference steering group agreed to publish a paper by Dr Patrick Gallwey entitled *Bad Parenting and Pseudo Parenting* which had been delivered to a Western Circuit conference of judges at Dartington on 18 September 1995. This paper seemed to the group to complement in particular Dr Roger Kennedy's paper on *Assessment of Parenting* from the perspective of a consultant adult forensic psychiatrist. Finally, the group agreed to publish Brian Waller's short paper written subsequent to the conference and entitled *A Social Services View of the Dartington Conference*.

Brian Waller makes the point – a concern echoed informally during the conference, both by judges and by other non-psychodynamically trained professionals – that the focus of the conference was narrow in that it was directed to, and therefore concentrated on, the psychodynamic approach to assessments and decisions in the family justice system. However, I am struck, on re-reading the papers and preparing them for publication, both by the breadth of the subject matter addressed and by an absence of dogmatism or any sense that a particular model for understanding the complexities of the human psyche has a monopoly of wisdom or appropriateness. As Brian Jacobs said in introducing his paper:

> 'When considering any framework of thinking about the human mind it is worth remembering that there are many conceptual frameworks that can be used. Psychodynamic models form some perspectives, but there are others which can be helpful. Different frames provide different slants on the same problem, but we should remember that whatever perspective is taken, it is the same human individual or relationship that is being described.'

I am also struck by the down-to-earth practicality of approach demonstrated in the papers by Judith Trowell, Roger Kennedy, Donald Campbell and Trudy Klauber. Each has a message of direct relevance to the non-medical family law practitioner. Brian Jacobs and Clifford Yorke provide introductions to psychodynamic theory which are models of clarity and practical wisdom. Jill Hodges and Bryn Williams in their paper again combine practicality of objective with strong academic discipline in analysing a subject of growing concern to all agencies in the multi-disciplinary family justice system. Readers of this book need have no fears that they are being led in only one direction, or that they are looking at the issues raised only from a narrow or blinkered perspective.

The general consensus was that the conference was a remarkable event. Too often the information and enthusiasm generated by such conferences are retained only in the minds of those who attended. For this reason, the steering group determined from an early stage that, if possible, the papers presented to and the discussions taking place at the conference should be published. We were delighted when Jordans readily agreed with us. I have often heard it said that conference papers are the kiss of death to publishers. But this book is not just a collection of conference papers: it was conceived as an attempt to traverse the issues of child protection, assessment, therapy and treatment within the family justice system. I believe this is what it achieves. The reader will agree or disagree after reading the book. But even if the reader disagrees, I am in no doubt that he or she will emerge from the reading both wiser and better informed. That, certainly, was how I am sure most of us felt as we left Dartington.

A further fruit of the conference has been the formation of the President's Inter-Disciplinary Committee, which had its first meeting on 30 April 1996 in the President's Chambers at the Royal Courts of Justice. Appropriately, it was chaired by Sir Stephen Brown, the President of the Family Division. A list of the members of the committee is printed as Appendix IV (p. 149).

Two final expressions of appreciation are due. The first is to Mathew Thorpe, supported throughout by Carola who was solely responsible for securing Clifford Yorke's participation. Although there was an informal steering group, the organisation of the conference fell almost exclusively on Mathew, aided by his indefatigable clerk, Roger Kennerley. Secondly, the conference could not have taken place without the funding jointly provided by the Judicial Studies Board and the Department of Health. I hope this book is a fitting reflection of the imagination and far-sightedness shown by these two bodies in agreeing to fund such a pioneering and worthwhile event.

NICHOLAS WALL
Royal Courts of Justice
Strand
London WC2
1996

FIRST SESSION

THE IMPACT OF PSYCHOANALYTIC PRACTICE ON THE FAMILY JUSTICE SYSTEM

Mathew Thorpe[1]

SECTION 1

Introduction

Between the family justice system and child psychiatry there is a crucial interdependency. The task of the Family Division judge in modern times would be intolerably burdensome without the contribution of the forensic child psychiatrist, particularly in public law cases. It is worth noting that it was less than 30 years ago that case-law first recorded the role of the forensic psychiatrist, but that was in wardship judgments in the Chancery Division. The huge evolution that has been achieved to arrive at Children Act 1989 jurisdiction applied at all levels of the family justice system, has gone largely unconsidered and unrecorded in reported cases. The evolution is the child of practice rather than statute or rules. The best modern judgment on the role of the forensic expert is that of Mr Justice Cazalet in *Re R (A Minor) (Experts' Evidence)*[2] in 1991. But it was provoked by an irresponsible medical contribution in a physical abuse case and is therefore not specific to child psychiatry.

To what extent is the value of the forensic child psychiatrist doubted or questioned? Judges have expressed vexation at the number of experts or the unnecessary dispute between experts in particular cases. But those are faults of poor case preparation and management. Looking back on four years of service on the Family Proceedings Rules Committee, my only memorable achievement was to contend successfully for the provision that experts might not be instructed in Children Act proceedings without leave of the court. So court control should ensure that experts are not instructed unnecessarily and that any who are instructed are bound to discuss their respective opinions well in advance of the trial. These propositions are now obvious and clearly stated in reported judgments, particularly *Re G (Minors) (Expert Witnesses)*[3]; *Re C (Expert Evidence: Disclosure: Practice)*[4]; and *Re AB (Child Abuse: Expert Witnesses)*[5]. But it is amazing to me how often they continue to be ignored. Wall J has drawn attention to the limitations of our system for disseminating judgments on practice[6]. But preparation of cases is for the lawyers and they have no excuse for not reading the specialist law reports. For doctors there is the excellent book, *Child Psychiatry and the Law* (1991) by Black, Wolkind and Hendricks, that spells out good practice from first instruction through to the court room appearance for the guidance of medical experts. Although in a relatively straightforward public law case, one medical expert, preferably instructed by the guardian ad litem, is likely to be sufficient, there are difficult and finally balanced cases in which it is extremely helpful to have several medical experts expressing a range of opinions. The perspective that results is invaluable and it is often possible to extract elements from more than one opinion to construct a composite plan for judgment and therapy.

Other professions concerned with child health and welfare have questioned the status of the child psychiatrist's opinion at the trial. Why is it accorded such weight? Why should it have any

---

[1] At the time this paper was written, Mr Justice Thorpe was a judge of the Family Division of the High Court. He was appointed a Lord Justice of Appeal on 2 August 1995.

[2] [1991] 1 FLR 291, where only the open court judgment is reported. For a full report, including the judgment given in chambers, see [1991] 1 FCR 193, where the case is reported under the name *Re J (Child Abuse: Expert Evidence)*.

[3] [1994] 2 FLR 291, [1994] 2 FCR 106.

[4] [1995] 1 FLR 204, [1995] 2 FCR 97.

[5] [1995] 1 FLR 181, [1985] 1 FCR 280.

[6] See 'Publicity in Children Cases – A Personal View' (1995) 25 Fam Law 136, 138.

greater validity than the opinion of the social worker who has perhaps devoted innumerable hours over several years to working with the child? The answer seems to me to lie in the profundity of the training and clinical experience that precede the acquisition of consultant status as well as the accumulation of expertise while in post, clinically and probably forensically. Furthermore, it is not by chance that the qualification and subsequent forensic practice are acquired. The freshly qualified doctor who chooses to specialise in psychiatry is expressing a fundamental interest in and concern for the mental, emotional, and psychological processes and disturbances of fellow human beings. Likewise, the subsequent election for child and adolescence psychiatry indicates a fundamental concern for children. Thereafter, the decision to take on court work reflects an interest in and commitment to the justice systems despite their many demands and frustrations.

Of course the greatest demand that the court puts on the forensic child psychiatrist is to evaluate the future and to select which of the available disposals is likely to prove least harmful. That is a province that inevitably contains speculative ground. Any of us may speculate but our speculations are only of value if founded on expertise, experience and wisdom. Of particular importance is an understanding of the adult psyche, since the safety and well-being of children depend upon adult commitment and consistency. That is not a field in which a judge has any expertise. Furthermore, within the unconscious lie the springs and forces of sexuality and dangerousness often unrecognised or denied by the conscious and sometimes elaborately and skilfully concealed by the external presentation. Similarly, it follows that the evaluation of the risk that an adult presents to children in his or her care is made most profoundly by the forensic psychiatrist. This ultimately is the justification for the respect the court invariably pays to the evaluations of the forensic child psychiatrist, especially one in whom the court has learned to trust over previous shared cases.

This expertise is, of course, not the exclusive property of child psychiatry. It may be found anywhere within the broader field of psychological medicine and, indeed, in paediatrics. Winnicott was a paediatrician and developmental paediatricians, such as Dr Bamford, have individually made outstanding forensic contributions to the family justice system. Nor is this expertise confined to the medically qualified. Clinical psychologists as well frequently develop forensic practices and it may well be that in a particular care centre the essential forensic contribution comes from the psychologists and not the child psychiatrist. Equally, an individual social worker may have a qualification in psychology or psychotherapy. Over the past four years the Portman Clinic has developed a course in forensic psychotherapy and this conference is the offspring of that development. The course offers a demanding training to medical and non-medical applicants alike. Initially the response came from those working exclusively in the criminal justice system but applicants from the family justice system are now coming forward.

It is not easy for a judge to assess the methodology of differing schools within the psychological medical field. That is an issue that I do not intend to address in this paper. My own preference is for the psycho-dynamic approach essentially because it seems to me to survey more profoundly the unconscious, an exercise that is just as vital as an evaluation of more patent issues. That is of course a rationalisation and it perhaps disguises predispositions and prejudices to which judges are as prone as any other group.

SECTION 2

The relationship between psychoanalysis and family law

Nothing in my introduction suggests any relationship between psychoanalysis and family justice. Perhaps direct relationship is not to be expected. Therapy rather than forensic assessment is the province of the psychoanalytically trained. The very nature of their work, with its concentration on the unconscious and with the special quality of the relationship developed between the therapist and the patient, disinclines if not disqualifies them from forensic participation. Their adoption of language that, like the lawyers', does not readily admit the outsider renders intercommunication more difficult. What evidence, therefore, is there of intercommunication and interaction between the judges and psychoanalytic thinking?

Judges communicate publicly from the Bench. In the reported cases, there is nothing specific. As far as I know, there is not a single dictum upon the relevance of the psychodynamic approach to assessments and conclusions affecting outcome in Family Division cases. Considering that psychoanalytic thinking has now been available for a century and that it has markedly influenced so many aspects of our culture, that seems to me remarkable. I cite only two judgments that I know that specifically consider a challenge to the role of the child expert, if only to illustrate the limited territory that they cover. The more important is the first instance decision of Cross J in *Re S (Infants)*[7]. The expert, Dr S, is described as 'consultant physician at a London hospital who specialises in child guidance'. The quotations from his report suggest that he was properly concerned to make a profound assessment of the family dynamics beneath the surface of superficial appearances. His involvement was opposed by the Official Solicitor on the argument then fashionable that since Howard 'seemed a very normal boy any introduction to psychiatric processes would tend to have the reverse effect and make him a psychiatric case'. Of course that submission confuses the forensic, clinical and therapeutic roles of the psychiatrist and it is inconceivable that it would be advanced today. But, in 1966, it convinced even as shrewd a judge as Geoffrey Cross. He developed an intellectual analysis that destroyed Dr S's argument and refused leave. However, he concluded by laying down very sensible guidelines that no expert might be instructed without leave and that any instructions should come from a neutral source. It is a pity that the adoption of the latter rule has still not been universally achieved 30 years later.

The subsequent case of *B(M) v B(R)*[8] is significant only in that the Court of Appeal approved the guidelines set by Cross J in *Re S*. The expert unilaterally instructed by the appellant to provide fresh evidence was a paediatrician. He emphasised the risk of harm in shifting a 7½-year-old child from the placement which had served her since birth. However, we can see from these words of Willmer LJ in rejecting that opinion how far he was removed from a psychodynamic approach:

> '... any of us would readily recognise that it is almost a necessary consequence of the Judge's order that, for the time being at any rate, the child will necessarily be disturbed and upset. How long that disturbance and upset will last, and how much it will in the long run affect the child, is quite a different matter. In this case it is not unimportant to note the fact that this is a well adjusted child, not showing any particular signs of nervous habits. It may very well be that, unpleasant shock as it may be for the child in the first instance, she will be able to show plenty of resilience and will soon recover from it'.

In fact, he was the only one of the three judges of the court who had sat in the Probate, Divorce and Admiralty Division. But, in those days, it was possible for a judge to sit in that Division without gaining much experience of child placement.

The judicial approach illustrated by these two reported cases was the conventional one 30 years ago. Of course, there has been a huge change in that approach over the last 30 years. The responsibility for deciding custody and wardship disputes was unified in the Probate, Divorce and Admiralty Division in 1970 and it was renamed the Family Division. In 1991, came the revolution of the Children Act 1989. The policy of appointing judges from general or even specialist practices in other fields has been abandoned in favour of the more rational choice of either leading silks from the ranks of the Family Bar, or others with specialist experience. The creation of a corps of specialist judges in the county court has produced huge benefits at relatively little administrative cost. All these developments have individually contributed to this profound change. Judges have also seen the need for inter-disciplinary exchange and in the main have proved effective at it. So it is statute, administrative reforms, and practice that have achieved beneficial change. Precedent has made no significant contribution.

Nor is there any evidence that psychoanalytic thinking has made any direct contribution to this evolution in judicial approach. Teaching and the dissemination of new ideas within that field are primarily confined within its own ranks by books and by papers published in specialist journals or offered at meetings that may be public but which are not widely targeted and make little public appeal. The process seems individualistic if not competitive and the language is highly

---

[7] [1967] 1 All ER 202.
[8] [1968] 3 All ER 170, CA.

technical and apparently exclusive of those who have not an understanding of the fundamental concepts. Secondary teaching specifically directed to other professions and to the application of the theory to other professional tasks does not extend to lawyers or judges. There seems to have been very little published work that considers the relationship between psychoanalysis and law.

One exception to this rule is surely Anna Freud. In the 1960s, her collaboration with Yale University led to *The Family and the Law* by Goldstein and Katz (1965) and *Psycho-Analysis, Psychiatry and Law* by Katz, Goldstein and Dershowitz (1967). Then in 1973 came *Beyond the Best Interests of the Child* by Goldstein, Freud and Solnit. Joseph Goldstein was Professor of Law at Yale. Professor Solnit was head of the Yale Child Study Centre. The book was addressed to lawyers, although it may in the end have been more widely read by members of other disciplines concerned with child placement. The book was remarkable in that it launched concepts many of which have since become axiomatic. It contended that court proceedings relating to child placement should not be dominated by consideration of adult rights but by the interests and needs of the child as demonstrated by psychoanalytic knowledge. It contended that in all such proceedings children should be separately represented. It contended that the court's search should not be for the best interests of the child but for the least detrimental alternative. It emphasised the distinction between the biological and the psychological parent and argued that where there was a conflict between the two the needs and interest of the child would ordinarily be for the psychological parents. It offered three guidelines for child placement decisions:

(a)   continuity of the basic child–parent relationship;
(b)   the child's sense of time;
(c)   the limits of the law, by which was conveyed the notion that once a placement has been ordered there should be no re-litigation except in pursuit of child protection.

In relation to this important and fruitful collaboration, it is to be noted that English lawyers played no part. I wonder how many Family Division judges read this book when it appeared in the 1970s? I note that the Supreme Court Library does not possess a copy.

In 1979 the same trio published *Before the Best Interests of the Child*. They then embarked on *In the Best Interests of the Child*, incomplete at Anna Freud's death in 1982 but subsequently completed with the help of Sonja Goldstein and published in 1986[9].

On any historic review of psychoanalytic communication the outstanding public communicator seems to me to have been Donald Winnicott. For the benefit of judges may I record the milestones:

1896	His birth
1923	Appointed Consultant Paediatrician
1935	Admitted to membership of the British Psychoanalytic Society
1956–9)	President of the British Psychoanalytic Society
1966–8)	
1971	His death

At the outbreak of war in 1939, he, together with Dr Bowlby, drew public attention to the dangers of evacuating children between the ages of 2–5 without their mothers. In 1940, he was appointed psychiatric consultant to the Government evacuation scheme in the county of Oxford. The psychiatric social worker appointed to the scheme was Claire Britton and she later became his second wife. Perhaps this collaborative partnership made inter-disciplinary communication even more natural. Certainly, he spoke to many professional groups including social workers, midwives, doctors and teachers. Masud Khan wrote of him:

> 'For every one lecture that Winnicott was asked to give to one of the so-called learned professional societies, he gave at least a dozen to gatherings of social workers, child care organisations, teachers, priests, etc'[10].

In 1943, as a result of an article on delinquency research distributed by the Institute for the Scientific Treatment of Delinquency, he entered into correspondence with a Norfolk Chairman

---

[9] All three titles are shortly to be republished by Yale as a single volume with more recent case examples.
[10] See *Winnicott* by Adam Phillips: Fontana Modern Masters (1988) at p 24.

of Quarter Sessions on the management of juvenile offenders. The exchange was later published. In 1946, he presented to magistrates a paper, subsequently published, entitled *Some Psychological Aspects of Juvenile Delinquency*. Of course these efforts to instruct justices were essentially directed to offending and punishment within the criminal justice system. But he also broadcast widely, in 1945 specifically to parents and foster-parents who were struggling to cope with the strains of evacuation and return. Whilst his writings were perhaps primarily in psychoanalytic language for other psychoanalysts, he was also published for a wider audience: *The Child Family Outside World* and *Home is Where We Start From*.

For a glimpse of Donald Winnicott's interdisciplinary work in later life, I am grateful to Lucy Faithfull for this vignette. Knowing how attached he and Claire Britton were to Oxford, she offered them a weekend's hospitality every other month in return for a supervision session. On Friday evenings, she assembled her social work team and difficult cases or particular problems were brought for general discussion under his guidance, all sitting round on the floor. From this followed an arrangement sustained over 10 years under which two social workers spent two days a week at the Tavistock Clinic for further training.

I have not found any evidence that he thought about or contributed to family law as it then was or addressed family lawyers and judges as they then were. It is easy to forget how different the system was in the life of someone who still seems so vivid a presence. There was then no recognisable family justice system. The statutes regulating child care and protection then in force now seem archaic. In 1945 there were only five Family Division judges and they were dealing with divorce, probate and admiralty. In the Division of that day there was little common ground between the work of the High Court judge and Dr Winnicott. Nor was the culture yet right for this inter-disciplinary exchange. The judge remained a remote figure who could only be communicated with from the witness box which he controlled. There was a judicial attitude that expressed itself in thought if not in words thus: 'I am a father and a grandfather. I have had a wide experience of life and I have observed most facets of human behaviour both as an advocate and a judge. I am quite confident of my ability to reach commonsense conclusions about the welfare of children'. That attitude precluded a readiness to learn, certainly from a starting point of due humility. Hopefully it is rare if not extinct in present times. Certainly if Dr Winnicott were living now, I am convinced that he would see and seize the plentiful opportunities for inter-disciplinary exchanges in the family justice system, and would write for and lecture to specialist family judges in the way that he taught social workers and magistrates when in his prime. I am equally convinced that the majority of specialist family judges would recognise the quality of his understanding and experience and by learning from him expand their potential to do good work.

Another instance of a psychoanalyst whose influence on thinking and practice in child care spread across the professional boundaries was surely Dr John Bowlby (1907–1990). He was Director of the Department of Child and Families at the Tavistock Clinic and author of *Attachment and Loss* (1969) and, for the World Health Organisation, *Maternal Care and Mental Health* (1951), subsequently published in 1953 by Pelican Books in abridged form as *Child Care and the Growth of Love*. Charles Rycroft in *Psychoanalysis and Beyond* wrote in a review of his work:

> '… his findings are of vital importance to all who have the care of children, who are members of any of the helping professions, and indeed to all those of us who have attachments …'

He influenced social policy about child care in a very direct way. His conclusions as to the importance of the child–mother attachment led to very practical developments, for instance in hospital visiting policies. The dissemination of his work through James Robertson's classic films reached a wide audience and affected the approach and training of other professions.

My final instance of collaboration for external communication is *Children's Welfare and the Law* by Michael King and Judith Trowell published in September 1992. Michael King is an academic lawyer and Judith Trowell needs no introduction. The book offers a robust criticism of the role of the family justice system in child protection and placement. It seems to me that some at least of the criticisms raised were in the process of being rectified by administrative changes that followed upon the Children Act 1989. But I will be interested to hear Judith's assessment of the impact of the book and its achievement.

If I have seemed to criticise the psychoanalytically trained for generally preferring their ivory tower, have the lawyers been more extrovert? I think not. In my professional life there has been one outstanding Family Division judge who was unbounded in his thinking and unequalled in his influence[11]. But the majority have been individuals who may have curbed their individuality in the interests of contributing to a system that users could recognise as consistent, uniform and predictable within the wide bounds that must inevitably be allowed to the exercise of a judicial discretion. Our system offers a level of training for judges which I believe to be quite inadequate. Although there have been significant improvements in judicial training there is still no continuing training for Family Division judges after their appointment. Such judicial training as the budget allows is sensibly concentrated on preparing part-time or full-time judges for new responsibility or for the expansion of existing responsibility. As far as I know, those child psychiatrists or child psychologists who work psychodynamically have not participated in judicial training. Nor has the voice of child psychotherapy been heard. Outside the gates of official training, the individual judge may of course pursue his or her own preference. The demands of the job are considerable and ever-increasing. Limits have to be set on extra-curricular activity. Furthermore, the judge draws on the well of accumulated court experience and must be wary of developing and then relying on theories or principles that have not been introduced in evidence.

Therefore, it is my conclusion that the influence of psychoanalytic thinking probably reaches the specialist family judge at one remove. His concepts and premises are influenced and evolved through other disciplines contributing to the decision making process, particularly experts who have by qualification or subsequent training absorbed the psychodynamic approach. Furthermore, in modern times influence is not only exercised through reports in the witness box but through inter-disciplinary exchanges at forums and conferences.

I firmly believe that there should be a closer relationship between our two disciplines. We have only to look back to see that perhaps the three most significant influences on the development of our understanding of child welfare in the last half century have been Donald Winnicott, John Bowlby and Anna Freud, all psychoanalysts. For reasons, some good and some not so good, none had any direct impact on the family justice system. Creativity springs from the union of opposites. Winnicott's collaboration with Britton and Anna Freud's with Goldstein were so fruitful because each imported distinct qualifications and perspectives. In the present, I am sure that the contributions that Mervyn Murch and Douglas Hooper have made to the development of the family justice system would not have proved so influential had they shared the same speciality.

In addition, what judges stand to gain is greater understanding of:

(a)   adults whom they judge; and
(b)   children whose placements they determine; and
(c)   themselves.

The importance of the dimension that the psychodynamic practitioner brings to the assessment of adults I have already expressed in the first section of this paper. The importance of a psychodynamic approach to evaluating the interests and needs of children is perhaps the foremost single theme of *Beyond the Best Interests of the Child*. Whilst that basic lesson has now been generally learned, the Children Act 1989 poses new questions with its emphasis on the wishes and feelings of the child and its requirement to judge the sufficiency of the understanding of the child. The judge's need for self-understanding is less often discussed, at least by judges. But, in our system, the decision that may determine the course of a child's upbringing throughout his minority is taken by a single individual whose discretionary conclusion is not easy to appeal, so long as he has applied himself conscientiously to the task. There is an obvious risk that the decision may be dictated or distorted by a predisposition. Of course, if the judge is aware of his prejudice, he will guard against its operation. The danger is the prejudice of which he is unaware. The greater his understanding of the unconscious and its power, the better he is equipped to judge others.

---

[11] Roger Ormrod, a judge of the Probate, Divorce and Admiralty Division, subsequently a Lord Justice of Appeal.

What the psychoanalytic discipline stands to gain from a more direct relationship with the judges is perhaps not for me to define. But it seems enough to make the obvious point that all who care about children, one of the most vulnerable sections of society, have an immediate concern for the quality of judicial determination and an interest in contributing to its improvement.

The remarkable advances in inter-disciplinary communication in the family justice system over the last five years enhance the prospects for the forging of closer links. Surely there is goodwill on both sides. The National Council for Family Proceedings exists in large part to promote inter-disciplinary exchange. Perhaps the psychotherapy section of the Royal College of Psychiatrists might join its corporate membership. I believe that this conference is of great significance and potential. It is the first time that the Judicial Studies Board has agreed to finance inter-disciplinary training for specialist family judges. It is the first time that the Judicial Studies Board has shared the funding of a conference with the Department of Health. It is remarkable that both the Judicial Studies Board and the Department of Health have given a working party of judges and doctors carte blanche to select the topics, the speakers and the programme. When we look back in years to come, I hope that we will see this conference as a sowing from which grew a considerable harvest rather than an experiment that was not repeated.

BIBLIOGRAPHY

Black, Wolkind and Hendricks (1991) *Child Psychiatry and the Law* (Gaskell)
Bowlby, J (1969) *Attachment and Loss*: Vol 1 *Attachment* (Penguin)
Bowlby, J (1973) *Attachment and Loss*: Vol 2 *Separation, Anxiety and Anger* (Penguin)
Bowlby, J (1988) *A Secure Base: Clinical Applications of Attachment Theory* (Routledge)
Bowlby, J (1953) *Child Care and the Growth of Love* (Pelican Books)
Goldstein and Katz (1965) *The Family and the Law* (Collier-Macmillan)
Goldstein, Freud and Solnit (1973) *Beyond the Best Interests of the Child* (Collier-Macmillan)
Goldstein, Freud and Solnit (1979) *Before the Best Interests of the Child* (Free Press)
Goldstein, Freud and Solnit (1985) *In the Best Interests of the Child* (Free Press)
Katz, Goldstein and Dershowitz (1967) *Psychoanalysis, Psychiatry and the Law* (New York Free Press)
King, M and Trowell, J (1992) *Children's Welfare and the Law* (Sage)
Rycroft, C (1985) *Psychoanalysis and Beyond* (Chatto and Windus)
Winnicott, D (1946) *Some Psychological Aspects of Juvenile Deprivation and Delinquency* (Tavistock Publications (1984))
Winnicott, D (1964) *The Child, The Family and the Outside World* (Penguin Books)
Winnicott, D (1987) *Home Is Where We Start From* (Pelican Books)

ACKNOWLEDGEMENT

I am particularly indebted to Ray Shepherd for the material covering the life and work of Dr Winnicott.

SOME ASPECTS OF THEORIES OF THE MIND: A PSYCHODYNAMIC PERSPECTIVE. HOW MIGHT THEY HELP A JUDGE?

Brian Jacobs

INTRODUCTION TO HIS PAPER

By way of introduction to his paper, Dr Jacobs said that there is a need to recognise how unconscious processes impact upon our conscious, 'logical' thinking. Psychodynamic concepts may aid those working in the legal field in thinking about these matters. Additionally, judges and others in the court will be subject to powerful emotions and psychological pressures, only some of which they will be aware of. Some processes occur quite below the level of conscious awareness. Sometimes one can get an inkling of this by the emotions quickly stirred up in one that do not feel as though they belong to your immediately preceding state of mind or what you are thinking about.

When considering any framework of thinking about the human mind, it is worth remembering that there are many conceptual frameworks that can be used. Psychodynamic models form some perspectives but there are others which can be helpful. Different frames provide different slants on the same problem but we should remember that whatever perspective is taken, it is the same human individual or relationship that is being described.

FIRST SESSION

SOME ASPECTS OF THEORIES OF THE MIND: A PSYCHODYNAMIC PERSPECTIVE. HOW MIGHT THEY HELP A JUDGE?

Brian Jacobs*

Throughout this paper you will be asked to consider aspects of being human from different perspectives. No perspective is static; each model alters with time and becomes more complex with changing internal consistencies and inconsistencies as our access to empirical data changes. The nature of such empirical data is itself altered by the context in which it is observed. Perhaps the starkest example here is the data obtainable by observation of infant and child behaviour in experimental situations in the 'laboratory' or at home and the data obtainable from adults in a talking therapy such as psychoanalysis.

For the former case, we are largely left to our observations of complex interactions between the infant and his mother. The infant does not have the tool of language to describe his experience. In the latter case, we have very detailed discussions of perceived feelings and associated thoughts together with the therapist's sense of the atmosphere and the unspoken. But it provides only a murky view backwards into a reconstructed childhood of the patient that will, hopefully, make subjective sense. This can only be a part of the objective truth of the child's historical experience. Both approaches have their place. We should remember that the human being under discussion is the same animal, whether infant or patient. What we get is a tangential cut of reality in every theoretical approach that attempts to describe the human condition and its development in individuals.

Any theory of the mind has to account for human thought, feeling and activity. Different theories have emphasised different aspects of the human condition as being the driving force behind all other aspects of development. The account that follows is necessarily simplified for brevity.

Facets of human development to be accounted for include

- development of thinking – cognitions
- development of feelings – affect
- development of interpersonal relationships – object relations
- moral development – superego
- psychosexual and gender development.

It was about one hundred years ago that Freud, a neurologist in Vienna, and a respected physician, Breuer, described a series of cases of hysteria that then led one of them, Sigmund Freud, to develop his first model of the mind and of psychological development. During the course of his life, he then reworked this model producing two subsequent models of the mind. In the course of writings, which collected extend to 24 volumes, it is inevitable that there are contradictions and enthusiasms that at other times get dropped, and that there are inconsistencies.

Freud came to the conclusion that much of our thinking as humans occurs outside conscious experience and beyond our awareness. It follows different rules of thought than that of conscious everyday experience and is based on more primitive modes of thought. He proposed that one could access these unconscious influences on our so-called 'rational' thought through free association and through dreams. By free association, he meant the stream of thought that passes through our minds before editing and selection. He arrived at these conclusions from the treatment of several patients by a new treatment method that he invented for the purpose of

---

* Consultant child and adolescent psychiatrist, Maudesley Hospital.

understanding the workings of the mind; psychoanalysis. His version of this treatment has many characteristics that are still applied by psychoanalysts today but also many differences.

Freud developed a theory in which the link between an infant and his mother was driven by instinctual needs for gratification and satiation. He suggested that the infant would seek satisfaction through different bodily zones depending on his stage of development. This produced the well-known sequence of oral, anal and genital phases of development as the infant grew to a toddler and then to a slightly older child. He had the idea that children are sexual beings from the start of life, not in an adult way but that the drives are every bit as imperative. He later came to modify these ideas as comprising two streams of drive at each stage of development, the life-related or libidinal force and the destructive or aggressive component.

Freud thought that psychological systems would seek for a state of minimum stimulation and conflictual thought. Conflict between a wish and a thought forbidding the wish would lead to a demand for psychological work and the mobilisation of psychological defence mechanisms leading to repression of wishes. They are 'lost' into the unconscious. With these ideas, he came to postulate a variety of defence mechanisms which are there to protect the psychic apparatus; to prevent it becoming overwhelmed with powerful conflict-ridden emotions and guilt.

Freud came to think that certain aspects of this model were unsatisfactory. In his later work, he developed the structural model of the mind in which there were essentially three layers of the mind in each of which thinking and feeling could take place, the id, the ego and the superego. The rules governing the processing of such thought and feeling differ according to which part of the mental apparatus is operating at that moment.

Very simplistically, we might divide up these three theoretical areas of the mind as follows the id contains unconscious instincts and is the source of psychological energy derived from these instincts. It also contains wishes, feelings and thoughts which operate according to *primary process thinking*, the sort of 'crazy' logic that seems to operate in dreams and, according to Freud, in madness.

The ego, crudely speaking, functions as the part of the mind that interfaces with external reality and uses what is called *secondary process thinking*. This is the type of logic with which we are more familiar in our everyday lives. The trap, however, is the following. What we think of as our logical thinking is not so. It is affected by the processes of the id and the demands of the superego. In effect, this means that the ego, our everyday thinking and feeling part of the mind, has to distort or expel from its conscious area (our awareness) those wishes, thoughts and feelings that do not fit, that for psychological reasons are intolerable. They are either massaged to a view, then supported by secondary logic (rationalisation) which is acceptable to conscious thought and feeling, or they are simply expelled from the conscious area of our minds into the unconscious. In simple terms, we forget them. However, these thoughts and feelings do not cease to exist in memory. Indeed, they exist as memories associated with intense feeling states. They affect our everyday thinking but we are unaware of their subtle influence.

The superego is a complex area of the mind in Freud's model. Again, in simple terms, it acts as a judge, a censor (Laplanche and Pontalis, 1980) which is the place where conscience, self-observation and the formation of ideals occurs. It operates according to a mixture of primary process (wish fulfilling and prohibition-led thinking) and secondary ('everyday') logic. It seems to be the area of the mind in which identification with the teachings of our parents by their words and example in moral matters is located. *But* it is distorted by demands on us to think, feel and behave in 'ideal' ways which are unsustainable in real life. It carries in it thoughts and feeling states that are associated with a threat to us of punishment and shame. It is imperative in its demands. It has no forgiveness. According to Freud, it is often far more terrifying than our actual parents.

Freud suggested that, at about five years old, the superego is formed from wishes of possession of the opposite sex parent and obliteration of our same sex parent (*the Oedipus complex*). There is then postulated a terrified reaction to the (imagined) revenge of our same sex parent. The realisation that these wishes might lead to the child's destruction was suggested as the root of the identification with parents – a placatory phenomenon. But the nascent superego is left

Some Aspects of Theories of the Mind: A Psychodynamic Perspective. How Might They Help a Judge? 11

FIRST SESSION

redolent with the unconscious terrifying threats. To a greater or lesser extent, these threats are processed by our ego reality thinking selves. These thoughts can lead to a frightened, anxious or even terrified child or one in which such terrors have had to be 'obliterated' from the mind, which is thought to lead to conscience-less behaviour, thought and feeling – if you like, a burnt-out moral telephone exchange.

Again, it must be emphasised that this model was derived by psychotherapeutic work with adults and to a lesser extent, from children. It was not empirically derived from infants and toddlers.

For many, this framework has been very important. For others, it has been seen as unsatisfactory in various aspects. This has led to other formulations of psychoanalytic models of the mind. Many of these have wanted to emphasise the early psychological processes from infancy and pre-birth and their ebb and flow during childhood. They have emphasised the relationship with the mother and with others. They have modified the place of instinctual drives as the primary motivating forces. These formulations have nevertheless seen instincts as very important modifiers of feeling, thought and behaviour.

I cannot consider in detail all the theories that have arisen over the past 90 years and indeed to try would only lead to confusion. I will mention briefly the work of Melanie Klein, and the British School of psychoanalysis in that you, as judges in the United Kingdom, are likely to come across clinicians who use these frameworks in their thinking. Some of the other papers presented at this meeting use such frameworks of thinking.

Melanie Klein departed from Freud's developmental model. She developed a theoretical framework that described two rather different ways in which the mind manages anxiety and relationships. She came to envisage a primitive way of relating that she thought was present in infants in the earliest months of life. She called this, very confusingly for psychiatry, *the paranoid-schizoid position*. She thought that the infant later tended to a more mature way of managing thinking and feeling, in *the depressive position*.

To divert for a moment, the source of confusion in her dense writing is that she uses words that have specific meanings elsewhere in psychological and psychiatric writings to mean different things. In her paranoid-schizoid position, the infant can only relate to part-objects[1]. In each such part-object, the infant perceives something that can satisfy and soothe or something that will attack and destroy himself. These are postulated by Klein to be reflections of states of satiation alternating with states of overwhelming anxiety with feelings of disintegration. In this theoretical framework, the infant has few ways of managing such catastrophic fears. He can try to get rid of them wholesale into the mother or he can create a state of omnipotence in which he has no needs of others either for physical contact, feeding or anything else, a state in which he imagines himself to be wholly self-sufficient.

The mother's tasks include providing physically for the infant so that the perceived threat to continued existence does not become a real one. But her task is much more. In the Kleinian view, it is one of *containing* these mind-threatening anxieties and so processing them through her own mind and her actions that the infant can take the emotions back in a manageable way. Thus she will soothe her bawling infant with gentle words and stroke him in such a way that he begins to feel calm. If, on the other hand, she is quite fraught and shakes him and shouts at him, he is quite likely to experience this as confirmation of dangers lying somewhere between his mind and that of his breast/mother (part-object at this stage of infancy). He may become even more frantic or suddenly disengage and go to sleep. Sleep can be positive but observations suggest that it can also be like a fuse being blown in a household electricity mains circuit, a way of 'switching off'.

Repeated cycles in which the disaster does not occur are postulated by Klein to allow the infant gradually to move to the *depressive position*. Here the infant has moved to a mode of mental functioning in which the predominant way of interacting with the object (his mother) treats her

---

[1] A part-object is used by Klein to mean the function of a body part rather than its anatomy. For example the breast comes to be associated with experiences of feeding and nurturing or poisoning or choking depending on whether the experience of feeding is felt as good or bad.

now as a whole person (an object in this language). The infant can now bear to love and hate his mother or others simultaneously; he can hold both poles in mind and can experience ambivalence without having to keep the emotions apart. Klein postulates that we go through life having both ways of functioning as potentially within us. The earlier mode can be reactivated by great stresses. Some people never really progress into the depressive position. Again, this is a schematic presentation of these views.

Other attempts to provide what is called *an object relations view* of infant and child development have been made by members of The Middle Group of psychoanalysts which has come to be known as The Independent Group. It will not have escaped your attention that the theoreticians whose work is sketched above came from Continental Europe. Without in any way wishing to enter into the current debate as to whether this country is a European Nation in 1995, there has been a somewhat different tradition of approaches to thinking about the human condition. Eric Rayner discusses this succinctly (1990). He refers to the contrast between the British empiricism based on a dislike of the grand idea and the charismatic philosophical romanticism that he sees characterised in Continental European thought.

I will take the ideas of two psychoanalysts who have contributed from this tradition first, I will use the example of Winnicott. In his view 'there is no such thing as an infant'. He meant that one cannot consider the infant in isolation from his mother. He regarded the infant as being in a state of unintegration at birth. Through the mother's attention and in particular through her *primary maternal preoccupation* to which he drew attention, the mother allows the infant to feel that he is controlling and, indeed, creating his environment by her fitting in with his demands.

The feed appears as if by magic, conjured up by his omnipotent wish. By her graded failure to fit in with his wishes over time in the early months, the mother gradually introduces a sense of reality into his life. It is the sense that he can control his environment that allows the infant to create an increasingly robust sense of himself over this period. The mother's initial adaptation to him allows him to feel a person in safety. The mother's failures to fit in with the infant are vitally important in allowing differentiation but they must allow transient returns to a fused, fitting-in state so that the infant is not overwhelmed by a sense of being abandoned or alone or having to cope with an enraged carer. Each of these latter states are traumatic and impinge on the infant; they may interfere with the development of the *self* in Winnicott's view. The infant is likely to respond with overwhelming anxiety. He may retreat into what Winnicott viewed as a psychotic autistic state (again, a private use of words) or prematurely use whatever psychological resources are available to him to try to survive psychologically. This may produce *a false self* in which the child fits in with his carers in a compliant way but at a high cost to himself of a loss of creativity.

You may have noticed a similarity to some of Klein's views here. They were both working in London at the same time but there is also a major difference in their thinking. Klein envisages an infant with more complete if primitive phantasies and constitutional aggression. Winnicott refers more to environmental deficiencies resulting in traumatic responses.

My second example from The Independent tradition is of some aspects of the work of Bowlby. He became interested in the application of psychoanalysis and in ethological theory to explain human behaviour. From these dual interests, he emphasised that there was a discrepancy that often children's anxieties and sometimes their aggressive behaviours are in response to real trauma rather than the anxieties being driven by aggressive phantasies arising in the child. He developed the ideas of *attachment* as a biological system that is seen universally in primates and that becomes active in infants at about six months to three years of age. He realised that if children are deprived of opportunities for a reliable and secure relationship with a principal care-giver over a three-month period during this age range then the child will develop abnormally and will often later develop compulsive thieving (Bowlby, 1944). Bowlby worked with Mary Ainsworth to develop and classify attachment patterns. It has subsequently been shown that attachment patterns found at 12 to 18 months are robust and predict behaviour blindly rated in the classroom at five years, particularly in terms of peer relationships. Though not directly psychodynamic, this work has been very valuable in stimulating an enormous amount of research over the past 15 years or so. It has provided a model for possibly linking 'clinical facts' from the consulting room to developmental psychology research.

Some Aspects of Theories of the Mind: A Psychodynamic Perspective. How Might They Help a Judge? 13

FIRST SESSION

There are, of course, other theoretical frameworks within the psychodynamic field but I will not describe them. Further, the psychodynamic way of conceptualising human development is certainly not the only one. For example, *learning theory* suggests that much of the way we behave is directly learnt by the consequence of our actions (whether they are rewarding or punishing[2]), by example or is learnt by extrapolation. Such theories have no room for the unconscious. They are more easily amenable to 'scientific' experiment. However, I will not discuss their advantages and disadvantages as part of this paper. Suffice it to say that some phenomena are apparently well explained by such models but others are not. In addition, there may be hybrid explanations, eg for conduct disorder in childhood. We must all remember that it is the same child and parent that is being observed through different spectacles.

What of empirical research? How does it illuminate the value or otherwise of psychodynamic models of human development? I have already given one example in the work of John Bowlby. There are numerous others becoming available. One creative synthesis of this work is to be found in *The Interpersonal World of The Infant* (1985), a book by Daniel Stern who is both a developmental psychologist and a psychoanalyst. This book brings together a wealth of research that shows that the infant has some sense of his own boundary and a functioning memory from and before birth. Infants whose mothers have sung particular songs to them while they were still in the womb show a differential response to those tunes sung by their mothers a few weeks after birth. This immediately contradicts some aspects of some psycho-analytic formulations, those aspects that suggest a completely undifferentiated newborn infant. Stern elegantly demonstrates that infants in the first two months of life are very sensitive to new learning; they are not completely unintegrated as in some psychoanalytic formulations. They are tuned to take sensory information in through one sensory system and translate it into the recognition of similar sensory information through another sensory system. They are also tuned to so-called vitality affects. These are not the usual emotional states that we talk about, laughter, anger (categorical affects), but they comprise the pace of onset and fading of an emotion containing response and its amplitude and rhythm – if you like the music of an emotion. So that a chuckle will be monitored by the infant in its interaction with its mother for its loudness, tone, length and pace, and also for any accompanying acts such as a stroke or tickle or a bounce on a parent's knee. The pace of such acts, the giggle and the tickle, tend to fit with the emotional response of mother and infant. I will not go on but I hope that you will understand the complexity of information already being processed and patterns being discerned by the newborn. The ideas of Winnicott are amended and given more definition.

From about two months, there is a change in the level of complexity of information processing and interpersonal interactions between the infant and his care-giver. To quote Stern, 'They seem to approach interpersonal relatedness with an organising perspective that makes it feel as if there is now an integrated sense of themselves as distinct and coherent bodies, with control over their own actions, ownership of their own affectivity, a sense of continuity and a sense of other people as distinct and separate interactants'. This sense of self is still at a basic level. Mutual gaze is sought by the infant. He shows a preference for the human face. When things are going well, the infant and his mother adapt their behaviours to keep the level of stimulation optimal for that particular infant. Less than optimal stimulation and the infant loses interest. Overstimulation leads to gaze aversion, etc. The social interactions focus on levels of excitation and on emotions, not on knowledge or learning-based tasks. The infant develops a sense of agency, of authorship of his own actions, eg reaching for an object and of cause and effect in interactions with his mother and others. This forms an early sense of self-coherence and of recognition of others, eg photographs of their mothers are preferentially attended to.

Stern describes a model of how memory develops and how emotional states become so bound up with this process. He talks of 'Representations of Interactions that have been Generalised' (RIGs). By this he means that repeated cycles of events or images become averaged and remembered with their emotion-related state as a single instance, but one that has never actually happened. This can then be compared with new instances of similar cycles to look for novelty or difference. A baby shown photographs of a series of faces 'recognises' most strongly

---

[2] Things that adults see as punishing may be rewarding in their effect. If a child receives no attention and is desperate for it then even an angry response from a parent is better than nothing.

a face that is the average of all these photographs but not one it has actually seen before. To take the feeding paradigm, repeated episodes of feeding easily will become generalised as a satisfying event with sights, smells and touch so that contrasting unsatisfying events, eg feeding with a blocked nose and not being able to breathe whilst attempting to feed, will produce a very different set of memories with associated affects.

Stern gives many examples of the qualitatively different effect on the infant's experience of being involved in interactions with others, principally his mother. He sees the mother as crucial in helping the infant regulate intense emotions, in achieving a sense of security, of feeding, of making the transition to sleep and in regulating curiosity, etc. The adult will help the child decide if a strange face is to be feared or chuckled at. These 'self with other' episodes also get incorporated into RIGs. They form the basis of 'the evoked companion'. As judges, you will recognise that the evoked companion may be very supportive or neglectful or frankly abusive. These working models of what to expect are taken into the mind and form the basis for the infant's and later the child's expectations of those around them. They are hard to unlearn.

Through the vitality affects and categorical affects the mother will begin to modulate the child's own sense of himself. This seems to occur through the mother's mind. The mother comes to associate aspects of her infant in her mind with others important to her in her inner world. So a baby that is temperamentally boisterous may be associated in her mind with Uncle Jack who would always take crazy risks. She will find that her responses to her infant will tend to dampen the child's responses or show disapproval.

At somewhere between seven and nine months old the infant begins to discover and demonstrate that he has a sense that he has a mind and that others around him have one as well. This means that the infant becomes aware that he can share experience without words with another person. The infant can now become aware of his mother's sensitivity to him rather than just being subject to it. It allows for psychological intimacy. What is the evidence for this stage? I cannot describe it in detail but let me give a few examples. The infant begins to point at objects whilst looking at the mother. He will follow the mother's line of gaze if she looks at something other than himself. Thus joint attention on a something external to both is achieved. The beginning of private jokes without words seems to start between siblings from about this age. Similarly, some teasing, a state that requires some sense of the effect of one's actions on another person's mind, begins. The infant learns to use mother's expression of affect as a key to what he should feel. In experiments with a visual cliff where a child aged 12 months is encouraged to crawl across a sheet of reinforced glass plate placed over a small drop to reach a favourite toy he will look to his mother for her expression. If she smiles; he will take the risk; if she shows distress; he will hesitate and may cry himself.

These momentous developments become the medium of interpersonal meanings that are mutually created between mother and infant. They provide the infant with a sense of what is shareable experience and what somehow is received on stony ground or ignored. All this is occurring before the medium of language becomes available to the young child.

Stern quotes an example from his clinical work in which a mother consistently seemed not to match the enthusiasm of her 10-month-old son in any interactions with him. This was odd as in all other settings she was a vivacious woman. When they questioned her about this she was aware that she did this but only vaguely so. An articulate woman, she found herself struggling to find words. She was gradually able to realise that she wanted to under-respond to her son because she was wanting to play second fiddle to him. She felt that if she were to match his behaviour in enthusiasm then he would watch her more than vice versa. When asked what was wrong if the initiative passed to her some of the time, she came to realise that her worry was that he was too like his father who was passive and quiet. She had to be the spark in the family. This had become a largely unconscious organising principle in her interactions with her son. Without alteration, it would have achieved exactly the opposite of her intentions. I will not discuss the formation of language or its effect on the interactions. However, I hope that the above account gives a flavour of how mother–infant observations are illuminating another perspective on child development.

HOW ARE THESE CONCEPTS USEFUL TO A JUDGE?

Perhaps this issue can most usefully be addressed by suggesting questions that judges may already ask themselves. Such questions might be illuminated by these models of the mind. For example

- What is the stage of development of this infant or child?
- What might be the consequences for developing a sense of dependable security of past likely actions?
- How long a time frame is there to establish stability for this child? Where might the child be on his developmental trajectory?
- How do the temperaments of the child and those of the main caregivers interact?
- Is history repeating itself across the generations? If so, can, and should this be interrupted?
- How can a judge avoid the traps of idealisation and denigration?
- Even if the main parent has had an awful personal childhood, is there a sense in which he or she is psychologically sensitive and aware of the needs of the child?
- The court, witnesses and professionals alike can be affected by unconscious processes. One aspect of this might be a sympathy stirred up for the child's plight or that of the parent that may lead to irrational decisions. Are strong emotions being created in the Court or are they absent when they might be appropriate?
- What might be destroyed or hazarded by a particular decision? In addition, what does this child stand to gain by my action?
- Is this person somebody who is fighting for the real needs of the child or for something that remains unresolved for themselves?
- Truth – Witnesses can deceive themselves and convince themselves of their distortions. They can then be completely convincing of themselves. This can be a particular problem in abuse cases when innocence is claimed.
- When should a judge recognise that whatever the justice of a situation he or she is actually powerless to achieve the desirable solution?
- It is so easy to identify with one's own 'tribe'. This is a process that can distort the assessment of professionals, including judges. The two dangers are of a reaction of sympathy and understanding or an over-reaction in the opposite direction in an attempt to avoid identification with the adult, or child, concerned.
- When the heat is on, how do I remain child needs and development centred?
- Empathy – think of the effect of interviewing the child – are they asking to see you? How might the child understand the interview you offer? There is the example of a child who said that he wants to see his father when interviewed by the kind judge, having previously been adamant that he did not want to do so. It later transpired that the child was scared that if he did not say 'yes' the judge would 'send him away' from home. It is very difficult to know what the child might fantasise. He may not tell you.

These and other questions may be illuminated by a framework that is sensitive to what we know of child development and what we can learn of the powerful psychological forces that affect us during development and into adulthood.

REFERENCES

Bowlby, J (1944) 'Forty-Four Juvenile Thieves' *International Journal of Psycho-Analysis* 25 19–52, 107–127.

Laplanche, J and Pontalis, J-B (1980) *The Language of Psycho-Analysis* (The Hogarth Press, London)

Rayner, E (1990) *The Independent Mind in British Psychoanalysis* (Free Association Books, London

Stern, D (1985) *The Interpersonal World of the Infant* (Basic Books, New York)

Other useful books include

Brazelton, TB and Cramer BG (1991) *The Earliest Relationship – Parents, Infants and the Drama of Early Attachment* (Karnac Books, London)

Greenberg, J and Mitchell, S (1983) *Object Relations in Psychoanalytic Theory* (Harvard University Press, Cambridge, Mass.)

Hinshelwood, RD (1989) *A Dictionary of Kleinian Thought* (Free Association Books, London)

Rutter, MR (1980) *Developmental Psychiatry* (William Heinemann Medical Books, London)

Tyson, P and Tyson, RL (1990) *Psychoanalytic Theories of Development – an Integration* (Yale University Press, New Haven and London)

FIRST PLENARY SESSION

DISCUSSION

THE 'UNCONSCIOUS PROCESS' AND ITS IMPORTANCE

It was accepted that unconscious processes were at work in every courtroom setting. As a simple illustration, it was accepted that most judges would react differently to witnesses of differing appearance. Examples given were 'an attractive lady witness in a tight dress' and 'a man with a pony-tail'. Taken further, most judges would be influenced by parents acting 'impeccably' in the witness box as contrasted with those who 'went berserk' in court. These vignettes demonstrated obvious, but elementary, factors which could affect a judge's mind. However, at a deeper level, it had to be accepted that there were in-built prejudices, factors of background and the unconscious processes at work, all of which would affect a judge's evaluation of evidence. Naturally, judges and psychodynamic practitioners, by the very nature of their work, had acquired skills and had developed an 'insight' born of experience and collected professional expertise. But all judges needed to be cautious and should be made aware of their own fallabilities – many of which are unconscious. A greater understanding of the unconscious mind and its power was therefore an important tool for the judiciary because, when coupled with a basic knowledge of the psychodynamic theories, it enabled a judge to make more informed decisions.

In the light of this, there was unanimous consensus that it was important for every judge deciding family cases to acquire a good working knowledge of the teaching methods/basic concepts used by psychodynamic practitioners. On a personal level, this was important because there was a need for self-understanding – in order to avoid the obvious risk that a decision may be dictated/distorted by a personal pre-disposition. On a professional level, it was essential to assist with the evaluation of expert evidence.

It was also agreed that psychodynamic practitioners benefited from an interchange of ideas because they could better understand the legal process and the areas of their work which assisted the judiciary.

An inter-disciplinary conference (such as this) was an important and valuable tool for all professionals. Accordingly, this meeting should be the first of many, as the learning/ethos absorbed by all would lead to a better informed judiciary and other professionals more attuned to the Court process.

THE EVALUATION OF EXPERT WITNESSES

It was recognised that the bulk of expert reports were brought into being before the facts of the case had been established and so were often premised upon a wrong factual base. Given this difficulty, it was accepted that the contents of all expert reports had to be analysed carefully so as to ensure that they contained 'findings' rather than a 'rationalisation of the conclusions' which an expert sought to propound. It was agreed that judges required a good working knowledge of underlying psychodynamic theories employed, so they could more easily discern when the latter was occurring.

FEEDBACK ON DECISIONS

Both the judge and the forensic expert would not (in the normal course of events) hear anything more of the case once it was completed. However, the clinician and the local authority (as appropriate) would remain in touch with the participants. It was confirmed that it would be possible to undertake specific research for the assistance of the judiciary. This work might be undertaken by academics or might be done, on a more informal basis, by local authorities who could be asked to provide the judge with details (for example, some 12 months after the case had ended) of the outcome/progress in the light of the decision made. Local authorities were accustomed to providing information for the Youth Courts and, at a local level, often liaised with the Designated Judge in an informal way.

The judges felt that it would be of assistance to know, in general terms, what had occurred as a result of the decisions which they had made.

JUDICIAL INTERVIEWING OF CHILDREN

It was accepted that the guidelines were clear and that a judge would not normally interview a child, save in special circumstances where, for example, an older child particularly wanted to see the judge. A careful balance had to be struck between 'empowering of the child' in a helpful way and enabling the child to 'run the family'. It was agreed that judges should refuse to see children who were using or attempting to use their position of 'power' or who were seeking to manipulate the situation to their own advantage.

SECOND SESSION

CHILD SEXUAL ABUSE

Dr Judith Trowell

INTRODUCTION TO HER PAPER

Dr Trowell stated that she was impressed by the ability of the judiciary to analyse evidence placed before them and, whilst they may not have been trained to analyse their own unconscious mind on a fundamental level, they were undertaking this task on a regular basis. She saw 'context' as the fundamental distinction between the work of a lawyer and a doctor. Judges were accustomed to dealing with specific instances, for example, child sexual abuse, whereas psychiatrists had to deal with children in a much broader context in order to understand their difficulties within the totality of the circumstances. In that sense, she saw a measure of conflict in the tasks which the lawyers and medical practitioners were trying to perform. She pointed to the fact that there were many cases which never reached the courts and that, many of those which did were distorted because the issues under scrutiny were not the fundamental underlying problems of the family.

Psychodynamic practitioners were accustomed to living with and tolerating uncertainty, whereas lawyers did not like it. Accordingly, all child professionals needed to meet on a more regular basis so that they could compare their reactions to a given sets of problems.

Psychodynamic practitioners had to deal with very powerful feelings and painful experiences when interviewing children who had been abused. This type of work directly affected the practitioner and could affect the analysis which resulted. It was important for judges to understand the reasons for this phenomenon.

CHILD SEXUAL ABUSE

*Judith Trowell**

Child Sexual Abuse (CSA) is now recognised as a major mental health problem. Considerable resources are involved in identifying and investigating cases in civil and criminal legal interventions; lesser resources, but hopefully an increasing amount, in prevention, early intervention and treatment of identified cases[1]. There do remain problems in considering child sexual abuse because of lack of agreement on definition, for example:

(a) contact and non-contact abuse and 'talking about sexual things in an erotic way';

(b) on the age limit (14 years, 16 years, given developmental differences);

(c) peer abuse (what behaviour is considered as abuse when the age gap is less than five years?)

(d) the 'Gracewell' inclusion of illegal fantasies.

The prevalence of child sexual abuse therefore remains uncertain (see *Child Abuse Review*, 'Prevalence of Child Sexual Abuse'[2]). The authors highlight two studies in particular that are worthy of serious consideration. Russel (1983)[3], considered first only contact sexual abuse: 16% of 930 women reported intra-familial sexual abuse before the age of 18 years; 12% had been abused before the age of 14 years. When non-contact sexual abuse was included, 38% had experienced intra-familial abuse before the age of 18 years.

Wyatt (1985)[4] considered Afro-American and White American women and included contact, non-contact intra- and extra-familial abuse; 62% of women reported at least one incident before the age of 18 years; 57% Afro-American and 67% White American. When non-contact abuse was excluded the prevalence fell to 45% (total sample: 248 women).

Finkelhor et al (1990)[5] did a national telephone survey of adults in the USA. Twenty-seven per cent of females gave a history of child sexual abuse prior to 18 years – contact and non-contact abuse – and 16% of men gave a history of sexual abuse. These are all community samples; the prevalence in clinical populations is known to be higher.

Why does it matter and what do we know of the consequences? It is important to be clear. Childhood sexual abuse is not an illness. It is an event that occurs. There are, therefore, problems about commenting on the outcome because the consequences depend very much on the context in which the abuse took place. We know the outcome depends on the severity of the abuse, the duration over which it took place, the degree of coercion and the response of those to whom the victim discloses. It also seems likely that the emotional context, the family relationships and caretaking that the child has received prior to the abuse mean that the child can be a vulnerable child or a resilient child, and this influences the outcome.

---

* Consultant psychiatrist, Tavistock Clinic, MBBS, DPM, DCM, FRC Psych.

[1] *Child Protection: Messages from Research*, (HMSO (1995)) Dartington Research Unit.

[2] Pilkington B and Kremer J, 'A Review of Epidemiological Research on Child Sexual Abuse: Community and College Student Samples' (1995) Child Abuse Review, Vol 4: No 2.

[3] Russell D, 'The Incidence and Prevalence of Intrafamilial and Extrafamilial Sexual Abuse of Female Children' (1983) Child Abuse and Neglect 7: pp 133–146.

[4] Wyatt S, 'The Sexual Abuse of Afro-American and White American Women in Childhood' (1985) Child Abuse and Neglect 9: pp 507–519.

[5] Finkelhor D, Hotaling G, Lewis I A and Smith C, 'Sexual Abuse in a National Survey of Adult Men and Women: prevalence, characteristics and risk factors' (1990) Child Abuse and Neglect 14: pp 19–28.

There have recently been reviews of follow-up studies of children who have been sexually abused. Beitchman et al (1991)[6] looked at 42 studies for short-term effects. In brief, they concluded:

1. Victims of child sexual abuse are more likely to develop some form of inappropriate sexual or sexualised behaviour.
2. The frequency and duration of sexual abuse is associated with more severe outcome.
3. CSA involving force and/or penetration is associated with greater subsequent psychopathology.
4. Sexual abuse perpetrated by the child's biological or stepfather is associated with greater psychological problems.
5. Victims of CSA are more likely than non-victims to come from families with a higher incidence of marital separation/divorce, parental substance abuse and psychiatric disorder.

In an allied review, Beitchman et al (1992)[7], in relation to long-term effects, concluded that there are three major sets of sequelae.

1. In comparison with women not reporting CSA, women who do report a history of CSA more commonly show evidence of anxiety and fear, and depression and depressive symptoms, which may be related to force or threat of force during the CSA. They also show evidence of re-victimisation experiences, suicidal ideas and behaviour.
2. There is insufficient evidence to show a relationship between CSA and a specific post-sexual abuse syndrome; however, there is evidence to show a link between multiple personality disorder and borderline personality in adults and a history of childhood physical and sexual abuse.
3. Looking at the relationship between facets of abuse and particular or specific outcomes: more evidence exists to support a traumatic impact of post-pubertal than pre-pubertal abuse; longer duration of abuse is associated with greater impact; the use of force or threat of force is associated with negative outcome; penetration (oral and vaginal) is associated with greater long-term harm; abuse involving father or step-father is associated with greater long-term harm.

This review considers work up to 1987; more recent papers indicate that there may be more links emerging (Ogata et al, 1990[8]; Brown and Anderson, 1991[9]; Zanarini et al, 1989[10]). This work has been summarised by Cotgrove and Kolvin (1993)[11] who conclude that there are four main long-term associations with CSA:

1. Psychological symptoms consisting of depression, anxiety, low self-esteem, guilt, sleep disturbance and dissociative phenomena.
2. Problem behaviours including self-harm, drug use, prostitution and running away.
3. Relationship and sexual problems – social withdrawal, sexual promiscuity and re-victimisation.
4. Psychiatric disorders particularly eating disorders, sexualisation, post-traumatic stress disorder and borderline personality disorder.

We recognise that the above problems are more likely to be reported by clients in long-term therapy or referrals to psychiatric or social services, and it remains unclear how widespread the

---

[6] Beitchman J H, Zucker K J, Hood J E, Da Costa G A, Akman D, 'A Review of the Short-Term Effects of Child Sexual Abuse' (1991) Child Abuse and Neglect Vol 15: pp 537–556.

[7] Beitchman J H, Zucker K J, Hood J E, Da Costa G A, Akman D, Cassavia E 'A Review of the Long-Term Effects of Child Sexual Abuse' (1992) Child Abuse and Neglect Vol 16: pp 101–118.

[8] Ogata S N, Silk K R and Goodrich S 'The Childhood Experience of the Borderline Patient' *Family Environment and Borderline Personality Disorder* (1990) (ed P Links) American Psychiatric Press, Washington DC.

[9] Brown G R and Anderson B, 'Psychiatric Morbidity in Adult Inpatients with Childhood Histories of Sexual and Physical Abuse' (1991) American Journal of Psychiatry, 148: pp 55–61.

[10] Zanarini M, Gunderson J G, Marino M F, 'Childhood Experiences of Borderline Patients' (1989) Comprehensive Psychiatry Vol 30: pp 18–25.

[11] Cotgrove A J and Kolvin I, 'The Long-Term Effects of Child Sexual Abuse' (1993) Hospital Update.

associations are in non-selected community samples of sexual abuse victims (Trowell, Berelowitz and Kolvin (1995))[12].

ASSESSMENT

As indicated, it is very important always to consider the family context in which the abuse has taken place. The child's physical and emotional care prior to the abuse is important to consider. Frequently, sexual abuse occurs alongside physical abuse or neglect. Very often, sexual abuse allegations can present in a 'problem' family where agencies have been concerned for years and where there are large, fat files.

Despite all this, it is very important to ensure that there is a full assessment. Clearly the first step is a strategy meeting as decisions need to be made about the child's safety and arrangements need to be made which may involve the law, if need be, to ensure that the child remains in the home or is placed somewhere that can keep the child safe. Usually this will be at home with the non-abusing parent but it may be that he or she will be placed with substitute carers with the help of an EPO or an interim care order. Police, Social Services, the GP and Community Health are likely to be involved at this stage. An interview with the child will have been held, using the Memorandum of Good Practice Guidelines, and the allegation discussed with the child's carer. The alleged abuser is likely to have been interviewed by the police and the child will have had a medical examination.

There is a need then to proceed to an overall assessment, if the allegations of abuse are sufficiently serious. These are cases where abuse appears to have definitely taken place or where abuse probably has occurred. Some of the 'possible' cases may also proceed.

After an allegation, cases at this early stage can usually be divided into *definite* abuse, probable abuse, possible abuse, no abuse.

These are a menu of possible assessment interventions:

Child
Investigative Interviews
Developmental Status
Mental State
Family Relationships and Interaction
Social Relationships
A Full Medical, Psychological and Social History
Health Record Inspection
School Functioning

Parents
Individual History
Mental State
Developmental Status/Level of Functioning
Substance Misuse
Parenting Capacity

Family
Parent/Child Relationship (each parent)
Sibling Relationships
Family Interaction and Dynamics
Family History – Agencies involved

Adults (Any other adult involved)
Individual History
Assessment of Developmental Level, Mental State, Substance Misuse
Police Screening of all the Adults

---

[12] Trowell J A, Berelowitz M and Kolvin I, 'Design and Methodological Issues in Setting Up a Psychotherapy Outcome Study with Girls who have been Sexually Abused' (1995) *Research Foundations for Psychotherapy Practice* (Eds M Aveline and D A Shapiro).

Foster-Parent Information

Other Children in the Family
Individual Assessment

ROLE OF CHILD AND ADOLESCENT PSYCHIATRIST

Where does the psychiatrist with child and adolescent psychiatric expertise come in?

There are a number of ways in which such a person can be involved.

(a) Consultation

Frequently when cases of child sexual abuse emerge there are very considerable anxieties and concerns. If the case involves several children and perhaps several adults, ie organised abuse, feelings of panic can easily develop. Agencies can feel overwhelmed. If a case involves important, high status individuals in the community this can also cause considerable concern. If abuse is discovered in an institution again there can be anxiety, fear and panic.

The professionals involved need to think and plan carefully. It is important they do not rush in or act in an impulsive way desperate to rescue the children.

Consultation at this early stage can be very useful. There may have been longstanding conflicts between agencies, or within agencies, between workers and management, or between different teams in the same agency.

Time spent in trying to understand these issues is vital. Child sexual abuse cases stir up great emotions; rage, fear, disgust, shame and excitement. The staff need to have been helped to understand the dynamics and to have worked on pre-existing conflicts so they can proceed with the work in a thoughtful rational way. The consultant needs a good grasp of organisations and group process, and of the interaction and dynamics that can take over all too easily.

Hopefully, the Area Child Protection Committee will have already in place, policies and procedures on how to respond to child sexual abuse whether they are individual cases or organised or group cases (institutional abuse). The consultant can ensure that these documents are referred to, along with the nationally agreed policies (*Working Together, Memorandum of Good Practice*).

Part of the consultation will involve trying to ensure that there are good management arrangements in place, that the communication between agencies will go through specified channels and that supervision will be available for the professionals doing the work. As well as management supervision, where decision making occurs, professionals need case supervision and may need personal supervision. Case supervision looks at the material emerging in the interviews and tries to help the professional understand what is being communicated. Given that there are likely to be very powerful feelings being expressed, this can be very important. It provides a space for the professional to form a more objective view and not be swept along by the feelings. Some professionals find a case touches something inside themselves and they may then need personal supervision to explore this, and may need to be helped to seek counselling or therapy for themselves.

A skilled consultant can help by raising all these issues and ensuring that the agencies are clear about their task and the structures they need in place to deal with the work in order not to be overwhelmed by feelings and become unthinking. The consultant needs a good grasp of the impact of abuse and what is required for these cases, as well as an understanding of organisational dynamics and processes.

(b) Training

At all levels where cases of sexual abuse emerge some professionals are likely to need training. Hopefully, basic awareness training has been done and the specialist workers have had additional training. But there may be some middle and senior managers who become involved in the case who do not have sufficient training, perhaps when other staff are on leave or off sick. Purchasers also may not understand the sudden demand for resources, and yet need to be involved.

It is particularly important that senior staff understand the emotional impact of child sexual abuse. They need to be aware of the impact on staff, the tensions that can arise within and between agencies and the very powerful feelings that can be provoked. The splits, denial and projections experienced by the child and the family all too easily spread to involve the professionals. Unless this is fully grasped, the need for considerable management time and staff supervision and even personal support will not be appreciated.

If this training is provided by someone with a good grasp of the emotional impact of abuse and the dynamics that are provoked it can be particularly helpful.

(c) Clinical work

Child and adolescent psychiatrists used to be involved in many of the initial abuse assessments. This is no longer the case; the training and skills of other professionals have been developed.

It is appropriate that most of the face-to-face work is done by social workers and police as the statutory agencies, and by GPs, teachers and community nurses. Complex or difficult cases are then referred to secondary or tertiary services. Child and family mental health services provide most of this expertise, but there are in addition tertiary specialist centres.

What sort of complex cases need a child and family mental health view?[13]

Child

1. Very young children – six years and under – often need specialist interviewing.
2. Children with developmental delay and learning difficulties.
3. Children with severe chronic illness or physical disability particularly deaf children.
4. Severely deprived children.
5. Children where there are questions about mental state, mental illness.
6. Abusing children and young people.

Adults

1. Assessing parenting capacity where there are mental health problems, learning difficulties or substance misuse.
2. Assessment where abuse arises in a matrimonial dispute.
3. Assessment of abusers.

THE CONTRIBUTION OF PSYCHOANALYTIC UNDERSTANDING

Understanding the impact of sexual abuse is important if the assessment process is to be conducted in a useful and helpful way.

Child sexual abuse affects the mind at different levels. If we use the old-fashioned model of the mind, conscious, preconscious and unconscious, it can be helpful.

Many abuse survivors present with Post Traumatic Stress Disorder (PTSD); that is they have a number of problems and difficulties. They may have re-experiencing phenomena; memories may keep coming into their minds of the abusive experience(s); they may have repeated dreams where the event is happening. They may have 'flashbacks' where the abuse is felt to be happening, there at that moment. They may find themselves very distressed if anything reminds them of the abuse or they may be hyper-aroused, becoming easily sexually excited, wanting to talk about sex, tell dirty jokes, look at or touch their own or other children's genitals. Or there may be a persistent avoidance or numbing, with the child refusing to think about the abuse,

---

[13] Kolvin I and Trowell J A, 'Advances in Child Sexual Abuse' *Sexual Deviation* (Ed I Rosen) (Oxford University Press (1995)).

pushing thoughts and feelings out of their minds. They may avoid everything that might remind them of the abuse and this can result in *psychogenic amnesia*. The child can no longer recall all or part of what happened. But if asked, they are aware there are aspects of their experiences they cannot remember.

It seems likely that this process is going on in the mind at the conscious and preconscious levels. Cognitive behavioural treatments and debriefing work, target this area and can be of considerable benefit in giving the child relief.

However, the sexual abuse can also penetrate and have an impact on the unconscious inner world of the child. This can mean the sexual abuse becomes part of unconscious fantasies. Mechanisms are activated to protect the child from possible distressing or frightening thoughts and feelings entering their minds. These are mainly splitting, denial, projection and introjection (projective and introjective identification). The mechanisms are an attempt to eliminate awareness of the abusive experiences from deep inside the internal world (the unconscious). These processes all too often become transmitted to, and involve, professionals. Often all the family members are functioning in this manner and the professionals can become caught in the splits and projections going on in the child and family.

Why is it that sexual abuse has such a profound impact on survivors? There are resilience factors. Children who have had good enough early parenting can be much less traumatised. Children who find an adult who believes them, supports them and tells them it is not their fault can often survive surprisingly well even though the abuse continues. Children who use telephone helplines and are supported often manage to survive.

Sexual abuse, because it involves a violation of the body, because of the power imbalance and because of the fear and secrecy, does have a particular impact. But does this fully explain it? It is necessary to move the level of thinking and understanding to a deeper level if we are to try and grapple with why sexual abuse can be so damaging in some cases.

As part of normal child development, children have very intense emotions, many fantasies and many conflicts in their internal world. Little children have to struggle with their wish, their longing to be the centre of the universe, to be omnipotent. Normally this is gradually relinquished, but while it is very strong they believe that they are responsible for whatever happens. So if anything goes wrong there is a belief that they caused it to happen, it is their fault and they are responsible.

PSYCHOSEXUAL DEVELOPMENT OF CHILDREN

In order to understand why sexual abuse can be so disturbing, one needs to consider the process of psychosexual development, a process that occurs in all of us.

Infancy

Infants come into the world with a primitive sense of self, capable of very powerful emotions: Love, and in opposition to this, Hate and Envy. Hopefully they learn quite soon that no one is all good, to be given all the love; and others all bad, to be hated, envied, against whom all the anger and aggression should be directed. They bring the two sides together and realise painfully we are all shades of grey, to be loved and hated, and are both loving and hating.

Alongside this it seems, from the beginning, there is an awareness of sexuality and sexual differences. Little boys are aware of their penis as a source of pleasure and excitement (the erections when their nappies are changed) and are also aware of desire to thrust forward, penetrate, a wish to get inside.

Little girls are likewise aware of sexual pleasure, both from their external genitalia but also have a sense of something valuable; an awareness of their insides, of a space that is important, and a wish to be entered. Both, it seems, are aware of an incompleteness, and there is a turning to others due to this awareness of differences; equal but different. This then is the beginning of infantile sexuality.

We need to consider psychosexual development in the pre-school phase, at primary school age and then secondary school age. This does not include biological and physiological developmental changes, but focuses on the emotional development. How this assists our understanding of children and the impact on them of sexual abuse will be explored.

Pre-school children

Children of this age are dominated by a sense of omnipotence that they control and rule the world. Giving this up is a slow, painful process. They have magical thinking, believing that a thought is translated into action. They have animistic thinking, their own understanding of time and they lack impulse control, finding frustration difficult to tolerate, wanting immediate gratification. Their sexual feelings and interest are very intense. They have intense sexual feelings for both parents.

Boys wish to enter their mother and fear father's rivalry. They also wish to be entered by fathers to have babies. Girls wish to be entered by father and have babies. They fear rivalry with mother. They also wish to enter mother and make babies. These fantasies are normal in all small children.

Also, both boys and girls, I think, are aware of the goodies, the 'source of life' inside mother. The major anxiety is not, as Freud suggested, in boys the fear of castration, and in girls the acceptance of their lack of a penis. It is, I think, a recognition of Mother as the powerful one. Mother, who has inside her the womb, the father's penis and all the babies. Boys and girls fear mother (woman). Boys fear their penis will be trapped inside mother (vagina dentate) and girls fear that mother's envy will lead her to attack them as potential rivals.

How this fear and anxiety is dealt with depends on:

(a)   the mother's capacity to go on loving, despite the child's rage and fear;
(b)   the father's capacity appropriately to support the child and support the mother;
(c)   the children's sense of mother and father as nurturing, caring and supporting each other, *not* attacking or destroying each other. The implications for children with warring parents, or a single isolated unsupported parent, are obvious at once;
(d)   the child's capacity to tolerate being left out of the parental couple's relationship, usually turning to masturbation with fantasies of a simple kind.

These young children have a number of confusions which are entirely normal arising from all this. They are:

1.   How are babies made? Does the penis enter the mouth, anus, wee wee hole or where, which is the vital one?
2.   Are babies made from food and therefore are they really rubbish – pooh?
3.   Boys and girls believing they can make babies all by themselves and therefore not need anyone else.
4.   Boys longing to have babies, girls longing for their penis to grow.

Given that all this is normal, it is not surprising that child sexual abuse in these small children and babies can be emotionally seriously dangerous (never mind the physical damage). To be subjected to actual sexual experience can lead to emotional chaos. Boys and girls sexually abused by their father, stepfather or elder brother do not have the maturational space to do all the developmental work required to be ready to move ultimately to normal adult sexuality.

Oral or anal penetration fits in with, and reinforces some of these confusions. Actual vaginal penetration in girls is an attack, not a loving acceptance. Anal intercourse can lead on to homosexuality for boys. If it is violent the boy may become passive or identify with the violence and become very aggressive. Their fantasies and longings, if actually enacted, leave them stuck with their magical thinking and omnipotence.

But perhaps the most damaging aspect for these children is linked with their belief/perception that mother's wish to attack or destroy something precious and potentially rivalrous (particularly for girls), leaves them with a sense that the sexual abuse was in some way done on behalf of or with mother's agreement. She wanted it to happen and could have prevented it. I am in no way wanting to diminish the responsibility of the adult male for his actions, just trying to understand how the child perceives it.

We see this particularly clearly in children in foster placement, who in treatment become increasingly enraged, defiant and difficult with the foster-mothers, to the extent that placements break down unless the child and foster-mothers can be helped to handle this fury.

The perception of mother's involvement in their abuse by men is of course as nothing compared with the cases of sexual abuse *by* women. These do seem to be particularly damaging to children's emotional development. If the mother is the central emotional figure and she herself actively abuses, the experience then can only be described as mind-blowing. There is nothing to hold on to, no possibility of help, of rescue, or of being protected.

I am aware that the literature does not describe severe emotional consequences following sexual abuse in the pre-school years. I would suggest that this is because children who still lack verbal capacities have difficulty in thinking about what has happened. What they are left with are sensations and feelings. Working with clinical samples, it is only late in treatment that they begin to develop an awareness and an understanding of these sensations and feelings that have troubled them, perhaps for years, without being able to clarify what caused them or put them into words.

Katie, 4½ years – An actual session from a pre-school child who had cut off contact with reality

She had experienced oral sexual abuse; older siblings had also been abused.

Katie had been in three foster homes. There was great concern in the day nursery and current foster home as she was unable to learn, appeared not to know where she was, and no one was able to get through to her. The day nursery and foster home felt unable to keep her.

Initially, she tried hard to write – numbers, letters, etc. Then, I encouraged her to use the animals, dolls, plasticine, etc.

She tipped out the animals and dolls. The animals were in a zoo and the family of dolls (mummy, daddy, sisters, brothers, babies) all went to visit together with grandmother who was central.

The animals were dangerous and bad. The people had magic milk and could fly and so avoided the fierce animals. Then Katie turned from being very afraid of the animals and quite violently attacked and killed the animals, then hurled them around the room.

She went on to talk about Night Bears and nightmares: I was confused at first. Night Bears have huge teeth and claws and come and attack in the night in order to eat her up. Nightmares were less clear. What was so terrifying? Daddy, John, the man next door, it varied. She went on to talk about magic. I said the people dolls had magic milk. She said John had magic – a magic gun and a magic willy. He lets her suck it and she has the magic milk from him. She has magic too – her red nail varnish. She got angry when I didn't understand; then angrily told me I was dead – she had killed me. She had also killed Mummy. They were bad – only John is good. She and John kill off everyone. She then went behind a chair and emerged, saying she was John. I had to call her John, ask where Katie was and then 'John'. Katie attempted physically to attack me. She refused to speak if I called her Katie. John and Grandmother are the only good ones in her family. He/she hoped Mummy was gone, she/he wanted to see Daddy. She took a roll/sausage of plasticine with her. I had to fight to remove it as she held it in front of her genitals and advanced on me. It felt as though I was about to be raped for a few seconds until I took a deep breath and saw the small child in front of me (it seems possible that she was playing out an experience she had herself had).

Junior school age children

These children are rapidly acquiring skills and gaining considerable satisfaction from this. They have logical concrete thinking and have learnt impulse control. However, their emotions, although hidden beneath a calmer exterior, are very intense and powerful. They are capable of a greater range of emotions as well as love, hate and envy – they experience joy, hope, concern, depression, shame and guilt. Their sexual identity is more developed. Doubts and fears are dealt with by 'rude' jokes, sniggering or by sublimation, eg football, bikes, etc.

The responses of the adults to them and their function as role models as a basis for sexual identity remains very important. These children masturbate frequently and have elaborate private fantasies. The direct link to their own parents is displaced onto Prince Charming, Superman, a Princess, Superwoman, or some other cartoon or 'real' super-hero or heroine.

There is a vulnerability about children of this age as they struggle to tolerate/accept differences between boys and girls, men and women, children and adults (the generational gap). If it is mishandled by those around it is very easy for these children to tip over into derision, hostility, contempt and then sadism, or an increased vulnerability, offering themselves up as victims, ie masochism with the loss of self-esteem, self blame and acceptance of guilt that we see so often.

Therefore, sexual abuse in this age group can very easily lead to the child adopting a masochistic victim position and, particularly in the boys, a sadistic attitude and a frightening identification with and wish to emulate the abuser. Their sexual development can be halted or they may espouse a homosexual orientation.

Susan, 9½years – Who had cut off her cognitive capacity

Susan was referred by SSD. One of four children, her mother left when Susan was small. The older two were in one foster home. Susan and her youngest brother (about 18 months) were placed in another foster home. It was a family with six foster-children, the parents being full-time foster carers. A short-term foster-child, a girl, there whilst her mother was in hospital, when back at home told her father about Mr X, the foster-father, touching her, Susan and other girls. Father told SSD. The children were removed.

Mr X began touching Susan when she was small, soon after she arrived. Initially, it was masturbation of her, then mutual masturbation, then intercourse over the last few years.

Susan was in a school for children with moderate learning difficulties. She was moved after nursery class: no reason had been found for her quite serious learning difficulties.

Assessment showed a very flat, unresponsive child. She had hearing problems – but how much was she hearing, how much was subnormality or was she depressed? Recurrent ear infections had left her virtually completely deaf in her right ear and partially deaf in the left. She was unable to cope in a group, unresponsive to counselling in school and would not speak to the new foster-parents.

She was offered twice weekly treatment. She was brought by the foster-mother once and by school once; SSD paid the taxi. There were weeks of saying very little, with apparently no response, then I became aware of her eyes which were quite alert, watchful, usually hidden by her hair. She never appeared to look at me and still looked stupid. I was aware of feeling more and more depressed and said this – how hopeless it all felt.

She began to talk with rage and hatred about her ex foster-mother; the terrible food, the hours slaving away doing work in the house and garden, the terrible pain in her ears and never being taken to the doctor.

At times she was very hostile and suspicious of me. She had further ear infections and told me I was there in the night hitting her about the head, making her vomit, forcing burnt food on her, standing over her until she ate it. She had difficulty in sorting out me in her dreams and me at the Clinic. It seemed I was seen as the cruel foster-mother.

Towards the end of the first year, she began to talk about her foster-father. She wept a great deal. He hadn't been cruel. She had felt bad, dirty, knew it was wrong but it was also good, being held, being touched, stroked; no one else did, except she and her brother, but hardly ever. The inside bit was awful and all the mess and the smell. She thought everyone could smell it, knew it, everyone at school. Now he was in trouble and she felt sad, but glad it had all stopped. She sort of missed him. He had a terrible time with Mrs X; she was a right cow.

Now she was sobbing for her natural mother. Where was she, why had she walked out? To a lesser extent, why hadn't their father kept them? (She still saw him.) She began to learn – to ask questions – and started to read and write her name. We drew family trees. She began to read books about families and animals, and later began to use small numbers and add up.

Susan developed a real talent for drawing and painting and using clay, making animal models, and she was a real star in the kitchen. She loved cookery. She began to read in earnest – recipes and the instructions on the kiln at school.

We went over and over the sexual abuse now, her sexual feelings for girls and women, her shame, her longing for babies. Was she normal – could she have them? Would she ever have a normal relationship with men?

My reactions were very powerful and at times difficult to cope with. Despair, fear, guilt, anger, the seduction of being the good, idealised, abandoning mother – the ease with which I could have been the cruel sadistic foster-mother.

Secondary school age children: 11–16 years

The sexual development of girls faces a crucial phase, I believe somewhere between 10–12 years. With the onset of puberty and emerging genital sexuality, girls having been close to their fathers during the activities of primary school, move into a phase when they are very close to their mothers. The onset of menstruation must inevitably have immense consequences. As I have indicated earlier the fear of their mother's attacks on their insides was a concern in their early years, and now it re-emerges. If a girl is to successfully pass through this phase, her mother needs to be very sensitive and supportive. Girls seem particularly to need the 'blessing' on their emerging sexuality from their mothers. They need their mother's approval, pride and pleasure in their daughters. This means mothers have to accept there may shortly be two sexually active women in the house at the same time, and also a recognition by mother of their daughter's ascendency and their own inevitable decline. Mothers also have to help fathers admire their daughter and let her go.

Boys are rivals with their fathers, and mothers may be possessive, but usually both parents take pride and pleasure in their son's developing physique and prowess.

In both sexes, there is extensive masturbation. The peer group is important but in early adolescence the masturbatory fantasies are usually directed at older adolescents or 'superstars' e.g. pop figures. Sexual experimentation, homosexuality, love and hate, very intense relationships, with peers of both sexes and other adults are the norm.

Sexual abuse at this stage in a vulnerable young person can grossly distort and stop the normal experimentation and evolution of their sexual identity. It can drive young people to take up a homosexual position, become sexually indiscriminate or retreat into mind-blowing activities – alcohol, substance abuse, suicidal behaviour and violence or anorexia.

If girls experience sexual abuse around the time of the onset of menstruation they have considerable problems in negotiating this phase because the damage of the sexual activity and the 'bleeding' leave external reality and internal fantasies in a confused muddle.

Phillipa, 14 years – Cut Off Her Feelings

History

Phillipa was referred by an outside psychiatrist for treatment. She was doing extremely well at school, spending hours there and was reluctant to leave. She was very friendly with teachers. She was very small and uncared for. CSA was discovered when she talked to the Deputy Head saying her father came to her room at night.

She was the eldest of three children with a younger brother and then a sister. Since her sister's birth, ie when Phillipa was five years, mother and father had been having problems. Mother adored the younger brother and sister. Phillipa had to help in the house, run errands, and give father his meals as her mother was busy with other two children. Phillipa was very fond of her father. Mother was thought to be very depressed. Father began to cuddle Phillipa a lot, then visit her bedroom for cuddles, then got into the bed. Intercourse was, at the start anal, then vaginal for about three years.

She was fostered by a teacher at school. Phillipa was very angry. Why did she need to come? She only came because she was made to. What did I know, what could I do? Nothing. I hadn't been abused, had I? I was totally useless, no point, etc etc. I arranged to see her once weekly. Contempt, derision, sarcasm, denigration went on and on. She knew more than I did about everything. She was more intelligent than I was, sneering, mocking, relentless. Then she began to flaunt her sexual knowledge and be quite provocative. It felt as though she could get inside my pants and masturbate me with her words. I began to dread her visits, her words, and to dislike her intensely. And yet, here was this small vulnerable child/woman who seemed to desperately need help. I felt ground down and useless. Her foster-mother felt she couldn't get near her. The foster-father felt extremely uncomfortable.

I began to talk about her mother and she became more and more repulsive. She resembled a poisonous snake. I began to talk about terror and fear and panic and feeling trapped. This latter produced an electrifying response. She began to talk and talk about her terror and sense of being trapped in her family, in her bed, with her father.

She had coped by pulling the sheets up to her chin, putting her arms and head out of the top and not knowing what went on below. She insisted she had completely cut off. She began to have terrifying night terrors – reliving action replay dreams of the abuse. She talked about her father coming home drunk, how he hated himself, how she was left to get him undressed and into bed, how one day she couldn't support him and he fell and injured himself. She was very upset but relieved. With me, she began to weep. For several weeks, she wept and wept. She was turning to her foster-mother but when she wept for three weeks almost continuously, I think everyone wondered what I was doing to her.

Around this time, she started to have symbolic dreams. Nightmares of her father in a coffin; either he was dead and it was her fault, or he was being buried alive and only she knew it.

She wept for her father, finding it hard to be in touch with any anger, or rage and a wish to kill her father. They were both victims. He should not have done it, but her hatred of her mother was intense, vitriolic.

She also still woke up frequently at night screaming, having felt something hard pressing against her and feeling terrified; an action replay non-symbolic dream. She became aware that it was her father beside her and his erect penis, and that she 'knew' intercourse would follow. We understood these dreams as 'memories', whereas the other dreams were more usual symbolic dreams which we could struggle to understand at the different levels of meaning. She had become a person, not a walking mind, but the pain and despair were very powerful and at times she raged at me for having done this to her. I had put her in touch with feelings, tortured her. Finally, she was able to rage at her father. She had some compassion for her mother who she realised didn't know, and had probably been quite depressed.

The effects on the child

Where children have had good enough parenting early on and there is a reasonable degree of integration, the personality is formed but immature, the encapsulated area of the child's mind does not appear to be obvious. Sexual abuse for example involving a step-father, a relative, or a family friend that was of brief duration can be survived, and the child's psychosexual development may not be too distorted. But there are almost invariably changes in self-esteem, in the level of functioning and in the capacity to relate, and establish intimacy. Children may become aggressive and defiant, or timid, isolated and withdrawn. It needs to be stated that in the main these children have to cope as best they can. If they are fortunate, they are offered a community resource, an educative group, short-term group therapy, or individual counselling, and many do well enough or manage. But there are numbers of children who are profoundly traumatised, in need of specialist help, who present serious management problems. These children are the ones whose lives were in emotional chaos if not material chaos, where there has been persistent emotional abuse, deprivation or neglect. The sexual abuse may have been violent or of long duration, or both. The child's early parenting was almost certainly erratic and inconsistent, not meeting their basic needs. Or the child may be of itself a vulnerable child. Their psychological development and emotional development were erratic with some areas that were static and some area of pseudo maturity. Their psychosexual development was overtaken by actual sexual knowledge, leaving them no space to explore, experiment, in order to discover themselves. These children present in a range of ways. The splitting and denial can affect different aspects of functioning.

First, the child can switch off feelings to avoid any close emotional relationships, the refrigerator child no one can get through to. They can be quite competent, do well academically and use this as a means of escape. But many coping this way are out of touch, detached, drifting, isolated and aimless. They can, when provoked, erupt into unexpectedly violent behaviour over which they have little insight. Or they may wrist-slash, overdose or prostitute themselves.

Secondly, the child can switch off its mind, its intellect, and behave as 'stupid' not knowing, unable to learn anything. A number of children with learning difficulties or assessed as mildly or seriously learning disordered, if investigated have been sexually abused.

Thirdly, the child retreats – does not have contact with reality for part of the time, living in a world of his/her own. However, often the fantasies they live with have monstrous terrifying qualities which can lead to violence to others or their fear of a violent attack on themselves. So there is little chance of escape, or real peace for the child preoccupied with their fantasies.

The way to understand the impact of sexual abuse is, I am suggesting, to see it as an impingement, the child's (unconscious) mind is penetrated, regardless of what happened in the actual sexual abuse – what actually happened to their bodies.

In the external world the child has to handle a split. The apparently normal, perhaps caring adult; and then the bizarre experience of the intrusion, the secrecy, the fear, the lack of acknowledgement of what is happening. There is a 'madness'. The abuser forces the split, the 'madness', into the child. The unconscious fantasies that dominate the child will depend on which stage the child has attained at the time of the abuse, and how they and those around them react to the events. These secret experiences are split off in the unconscious and can become encapsulated. How much of the child's mind is taken over depends on the combination of the state of the child developmentally, as well as the severity, duration and degree of coercion. The child therefore may not 'know about', be aware of, or be able to recall the abusive experiences. Or they may remember in part and have forgotten (split off) other aspects of the above. The split off part can become very deeply embedded and difficult to contact. We call this encapsulated 'madness'. This is not a psychiatric diagnosis but describes as well as we can with inadequate words the bizarre, distorted, world of the child, with these experiences. In CSA the child may be forced to believe that what is happening is 'normal'. Not surprisingly, there can also be interference in thought, in thinking, making links and in remembering.

Gender identity

Infantile sexuality has only been acknowledged in the last one hundred years and was one of Freud's most significant contributions. By this is meant the recognition that children themselves have sexual feelings and sexual sensations that are focused on particular body areas; mouth, anus and genitals.

As the children grow and develop, their feelings change and evolve and the area of the body they find most pleasurable also changes. Children have to negotiate, therefore, a path through an emotional and physical highly charged minefield. By the time the emotional and mental work is well developed, their bodies bound them into adolescence and the whole process is reworked repeatedly until adulthood is attained with mature sexuality. The topics that have to be tackled include 'am I male or female', both a bodily recognition of gender and also a mental recognition of maleness or femaleness. Next, there needs to be exploration of possible sexual objects, the other one might turn to for sexual satisfaction; this may be same sex, opposite sex or both – heterosexual, homosexual or bisexual. There is then further work on more specific matters, the type of person and also age – older, same age group or much younger – children (paedophilia which can be heterosexual or homosexual). The remaining work to be done is around intimacy over a prolonged period and the development of ideas, thoughts and feelings about having one's own children – becoming a parent.

What does infantile sexuality and the psychosexual development tell us that helps understand childhood sexual abuse?

For all children, there are vicissitudes. Their psychosexual development and emergence of gender identity ebbs and flows as other aspects of development take more or less emotional and mental time and energy. There may also be external events that intrude or deflect events such as bereavements, physical or mental illness in family members, life events of all sorts.

Why it is important to consider these matters, is because some children traumatised by child sexual abuse can behave or react emotionally in ways that are puzzling and confusing. The children's perceptions of themselves can disturb those around them.

The child may be confused himself about male and female orifices, and the links between oral abuse and eating disorders are known. Other problems to do with the mouth, and taking in, are dental anxiety and asthma. The child who is highly sexualised and masturbates is well known; as sadly are the children whose sexual excitement leads them to engage in sexual activity with other children. But children whose premature sexualisation takes more bizarre forms are less easily understood. Some children retreat into a cut off state without any obvious external sexual activity and they can too easily be labelled as learning disabled or developmentally delayed.

It is important when considering the child's capacity to give an account of abusive experiences to be aware that the child's thinking, functioning and behaviour may well have been disturbed or driven up a developmental cul-de-sac. Clarifying what preceded the abuse and what is post-abuse trauma can be helped by an understanding of the normal developmental processes.

False memories/recollected memories

An important issue now, with the need for evidence and the appearance of 'false memory syndrome', is to think about the forgetting that affects some of these children. What I have tried to convey is how the forgetting can be at different levels in the mind[14, 15, 16].

Psychogenic amnesia is an aspect of PTSD and happens when the child pushes thoughts, feelings, and memories out of his mind – the conscious and preconscious mind. Unconscious not knowing is when experiences are split off and denied *unconsciously*. The child is *not* aware of this process. These two sorts of 'forgetting' do enormously increase the complexity of the assessment of childhood sexual abuse. But in only a few children does the forgetting seem to be complete. Most of the children are aware of some of the abuse and are aware they have forgotten much of it (psychogenic amnesia). Much more emerges during therapy. What is not remembered may never be remembered or may emerge later, at puberty, their first sexual experience, when pregnant, with the birth of the child, when the child reaches the age they were or when they are grandparents.

When child sexual abuse has entered into the unconscious, the internal world of the child, the child may have no awareness of what occurred. But usually the child does have some capacity to recall some aspects of the situation. What they are out of touch with are their emotions that went with the abuse, the fear, the shame, the excitement, the rage, the terror. It is these emotions that have felt unbearable, and have been split off and incorporated into unconscious fantasies. What is important in helping a child remember seems to be a person whom they can trust, who is able to listen and hear, to give sufficient time and a recognition that only partial recall is likely at any one time.

Adults who recall abuse in their childhood generally are recollecting abuse. When there is no detail, no capacity to provide any confirmation from any other source, then false memory is a possibility.

---

[14] Benedek E R and Schetky D H, 'Problems in Validating Allegations of Sexual Abuse: Part 1 Factors Affecting Perception and Recall of Events' (1987) American Journal of Child and Adolescent Psychiatry Vol 26: pp 912–915.

[15] Benedek E R and Schetky D H, 'Problems in Validating Allegations of Sexual Abuse: Part 2 Clinical Evaluation' (1987) American Journal of Child and Adolescent Psychiatry Vol 26: pp 916–921.

[16] Jones D and McGraw J, 'Reliable and Fictitious Accounts of Sexual Abuse of Children' (1987) Journal of Interpersonal Violence 2: pp 25–45.

SECOND

Treatment issues

Seeing children individually has its problems. First, there is the sex of the therapist. I think male and female therapists can do this work, but I would always respect the wishes of a child and not impose a therapist of the sex they categorically said they did not want. Second, does an individual session with an adult repeat the 'secret' experience of the sexual abuse? It is important to be aware of this, and explain to the child what will be shared and what is confidential. But I do find that for some of the really damaged children this is an effective way to help where groups and family work have proved insufficient.

Some children are unable to talk in front of others. Other children are so confused and troubled that they need slow, patient, child-led therapy to help them gradually make sense of their experiences. Where the child's internal world has become distorted and there are inappropriate, bizarre or frightening fantasies, then psychoanalytic psychotherapy does provide a helpful approach.

SECOND SESSION

SECOND PLENARY SESSION

Mr Justice Wall

INTRODUCTION TO HIS PAPER

Mr Justice Wall accepted that judges were no exception to conscious/unconscious influences and were susceptible to their own prejudices. He made the point, however, that during his career at the Bar, he had been involved in many child abuse cases as an advocate. He had been instructed by local authorities seeking to prove abuse; he had been instructed by the Official Solicitor on behalf of the child; he had been instructed by parents who were alleged to have abused their children. In some cases, the allegations of abuse were well founded; in others they were not. The result of his experience was that he approached non-physical evidence of sexual abuse with a measure of scepticism. Consequently, he felt that the medical profession owed it to the judiciary in particular as well as to the parties to the litigation to explain the philosophy/methodology behind their work in order to justify their conclusions. In return for this, he felt that judges had to give the medical profession the proper amount of feedback; to explain how they operated and what was of value to them.

He acknowledged that a good deal of a judge's work was based on an intuition borne of many years of experience and was heartened by the recognition that many psychodynamic practitioners worked on a similar basis.

He considered it important that the judicial function was in the public domain and invited a detailed criticism of the propositions which he had put forward in his paper.

ISSUES ARISING FROM THE INVOLVEMENT OF AND EXPERT EVIDENCE GIVEN BY PSYCHIATRISTS AND PSYCHOLOGISTS IN PROCEEDINGS INVOLVING CHILDREN

Nicholas Wall[1]

'Given the multi-disciplinary nature of family law it is inevitable in my view that judgments have to deal with social work practice and medical issues, to give but two examples. The judge must tread warily here, for he is not a social worker or a paediatrician or an expert in the clinical methodology of child abuse investigation. But the judge has to decide the case: the local authority who wants to place a child in care because it asserts that he or she has been abused has to satisfy the court that the case has been properly investigated and that abuse is established. Professionals in the different disciplines must therefore approach their work on the basis that they have to satisfy a person who is not an expert in their field that their work is sound.

In my judgment, the corollary to this process is that the judges must tell local authorities, police, paediatricians and psychiatrists how we perceive their work and what is and is not forensically acceptable. If we do not do so, we cannot in my view legitimately continue to complain that the material placed before us is unacceptable. In my view, therefore, judgments in child protection cases are not just for the lawyers: they are also for the social workers and the doctors and the other professionals working in the field.'

(Extract from a paper given to a conference in Oxford in September 1994 and published at [1995] 25 Fam Law 136.)

(1) INTRODUCTION

The object and structure of this paper

The object of this paper is to identify issues for discussion. I propose to raise a number of topics under different headings. They are:

(1)   The respective functions of expert and judge in the family justice system;
(2)   The tension between judicial and clinical findings: the methodology of the investigation of child sexual abuse;
(3)   The role of the expert in the assessment of the credibility of a child or patient;
(4)   The expert's role in advising the court on the therapeutic treatment of a child and on the manner in which the judge should dispose of the case;
(5)   The expert's role in the concept of the 'assessment' of a child in the context of the investigation and treatment of sexual or emotional abuse.

To avoid extensive quotations from reported cases I have attached as Appendix 1 to this paper a summary I have prepared of the current judicial thinking on the subject of expert evidence in the Family Division. For those familiar with this material, its only virtue may be that it is all collected together in one place: for those to whom it is not familiar, its purpose is not just to demonstrate that the judges of the Division recognise the enormous contribution which expert evidence makes to their decisions. It is designed to show the efforts which the judges are making to define both the issues upon which the advice of the expert is sought and the proper boundaries for the role of the expert in proceedings relating to children. Furthermore, the material I hope demonstrates that we are doing our best to facilitate co-operation both between experts and the legal profession and between experts themselves. Finally, on a more mundane but none the less important practical level it shows how we are striving to accommodate the

---

[1] Nicholas Wall is a judge of the Family Division of the High Court.

professional needs of the expert witness by ensuring that attendance at court is only required when absolutely necessary and that when called the professional witness is timetabled so far as possible to suit his or her convenience.

Much of the work of the Family Division judge is concerned with the physical, emotional and sexual abuse of children. On a broad estimate, I would say that such work has comprised the vast bulk of my first instance sittings since I was appointed two years ago. We therefore have a direct and practical interest in the psychiatric and psychological issues which arise in the cases we try. Yet, speaking for myself and, I suspect, for others, I do not think we have a proper understanding of the scientific or philosophical thinking which underlies the methodology of the psychiatrist and the psychologist. One of the principal functions of this conference, therefore, viewed from my perspective is to enable the judges to achieve a greater understanding of that methodology so that we can apply to the resolution of our cases the knowledge and experience which experts in the field of child psychiatry and psychology bring to the difficult issues which we have to try.

I thus confess to an ignorance of the underlying philosophy of the psychodynamic approach which I look to the conference to rectify. My method of inviting instruction and debate is to provide a paper which raises practical as well as philosophical issues. I am conscious that the issues it raises are broad, and I have deliberately chosen at least two areas in which I have experienced differences of approach within the psychiatric profession. At the same time, I hope that the questions I pose will be of interest to all present, and that the capacity of the judges to grapple with the profound and emotive issues with which we are regularly faced will be enhanced by what I am confident will be a rigorous exchange of views.

This conference is also a manifestation both of the judiciary's recognition that family law is a multi-disciplinary activity and of its commitment to inter-disciplinary co-operation. Long gone are the days when judges stood outside the debate. We are now part of it. As the quotation from the head of this paper makes clear, our decisions in the field of child protection inevitably impinge on areas of psychiatric, psychological, medical and social work practice. We therefore need to have a proper understanding of these areas. Yet there are few opportunities for the exchange of information, and many areas of suspicion remain. We do not read each other's journals and, as a minor example of the difficulties of cross-disciplinary communication, a recent attempt by a consultant paediatrician and myself to publish a paper on the role of the expert witness in Family Division proceedings was met by a rejection from the *British Medical Journal*. So I regard a conference such as this as an ideal opportunity to exchange views and ask questions.

The method I have chosen is to take three cases which I have tried in the last 18 months which, in my view, have raised important issues of psychiatric practice. The summaries of the cases in question are contained in Appendix 3 attached to this paper (pp 59–62) and I will make further reference to them. I was very pleased that at the conferences the questions which I posed by reference to these cases were the subject of detailed discussion by a group of the experts present at the conference, and that detailed responses were subsequently provided. These are printed in the following chapter, immediately following the case histories themselves[1].

(2) THE RESPECTIVE FUNCTIONS OF EXPERT AND JUDGE IN THE FAMILY JUSTICE SYSTEM

The starting point for any discussion of the inter-relationship between the judiciary and the expert witness in Family Division proceedings has to be the simple proposition that Parliament has entrusted the actual decision about what should happen to a child to judges and magistrates. Thus the decision is one which is made by the judge, and the structure of the forensic process, properly applied, means that the judge is the only person who, at the conclusion of the evidence of the witnesses and the argument from the lawyers, is in possession of all the facts and in a position to weigh all the multifarious facets of a given case. The expert's evidence fits into and is

---

[1] There was also an individual response by Dr Anne Zachary, consultant psychotherapist at the Portman Clinic. Dr Zachary's paper is also printed in the following chapter. His Honour Judge Fricker and Dr Gerald Bridges (the latter not an attendee of the conference) also produced a response. This is commented upon in fn 2.

part of this decision-making process. There are cases, of course, when the expert's opinion is effectively determinative, but philosophically it is important in my view always to remember that it is the expert who advises and the judge who decides[2].

(3) THE TENSION BETWEEN JUDICIAL AND CLINICAL FINDINGS: THE METHODOLOGY OF THE INVESTIGATION OF CHILD SEXUAL ABUSE

Inevitably, from time to time, there is a tension between the process of investigation which results in a judicial decision and that which results in a clinical judgment. This is a tension which, since my early days at the Bar when I was instructed in my first sexual abuse case, has worried me, and it continues to do so. I sought to address it in the first of the cases where I have chosen as raising issues for discussion, which I have called *A and B (Minors)*[3]. I attach as part of Appendix 2 to this paper (pp 55–58) an extract from my judgment in the case in which I discuss these matters. I will not therefore repeat what is there set out, but proffer it for discussion and comment.

Whilst lawyers always strive for definition and certainty, I am constrained to acknowledge that the tension which I describe in *Re A and B (Minors)* can never be eliminated. But I believe that by codes of good practice it should be possible for it to be reduced. The question I therefore raise is whether or not it is possible to achieve accepted norms of clinical practice in the investigation of child sexual abuse. And on this point I would like to understand from our psychiatrist and psychologist colleagues why it is, in 1995 with our highly advanced technology and rapidly expanding scientific knowledge that we have such stark divergences of psychiatric practice and methodology as are demonstrated by *Re A and B (Minors) (No 1)*.

(4) THE EXPERT'S ROLE IN THE ASSESSMENT OF A CHILD'S CREDIBILITY

The corollary of the proposition that it is for the judge to decide what should happen to a child at the end of a case is the proposition that it is also the judicial function in a case involving a child

---

[2] This section of the paper provoked a response by HH Judge Fricker QC and Dr Gerald Bridge, the latter a consultant psychiatrist with experience as an expert witness in child and family dysfunction for the Family Court and High Court in New Zealand. Dr Bridge did not attend the conference. My proposition that 'the judge decides what should happen to a child' was described as 'an over-simplification and capable of being misunderstood'. The argument of the paper was that the judicial role under the Children Act was in fact much more limited. The judge did not have to make major decisions which change the life of a child. The judicial function was to decide what orders to make on issues brought before the court for decision: it was to decide who was to exercise parental responsibility and, in appropriate cases, how that parental responsibility was to be exercised. A final judgment under the Children Act – as contrasted with Wardship – could be compared to changing the points to send a train in one direction rather than another. Cases in which decisions with a critical outcome for the child had to be made were the exception. Reference was made to the restrictions placed by the Act on continuing judicial involvement in the lives of children subject to care orders. The role of the expert witness had to be seen in this context. The expert guided the court, but it was not his function to usurp the decision entrusted by Parliament to the court nor did the court when making an order remove from the doctor or the statutory authorities the responsibility to manage the child.

The paper also went on to argue that it would never be possible to achieve complete agreement of experts in developing methodology. Unanimity in a developing area of knowledge would be suspect, sterile and potentially dangerous. It was important also to acknowledge that any judge, however competent, may have unacknowledged perceptions, even agenda, which may result in his decision being to some extent subjective and reflecting his own personality. It argued that an appropriately trained and experienced psychiatrist would bring an amalgam of different models into his approach to an assessment or treatment and that rigid adherence to a single model will lead to an inflexibility of approach.

The paper also argued strongly for the admissibility of a doctor's opinion on the credibility of the child. To exclude it would be likely to obscure the validity of the expert's assessment.

I disagree with Judge Fricker's and Dr Bridge's assessment of the judicial role under the Children Act. In my judgment, courts at every level habitually make decisions of critical importance in the lives of individual children. It is not simply a question of the High Court judge deciding whether or not the life support machine is turned off. Where and with whom a child is to live, whether or not he or she is placed for adoption or remains within his natural family – even whether or not he or she should see particular members of the family are all crucially important decisions which effectively determine the course of children's lives.

[3] The judgment is now fully reported sub nom *Re A and B (Minors) (No 1) (Investigation of Alleged Abuse)* [1995] 3 FCR 389. The extract cited in Appendix 2 is at [1995] 3 FCR 395 to 398.

SECOND SESSION

to decide what, factually, has happened to the child[4]. However, unlike juries in criminal cases, judges in civil proceedings rarely, if ever, hear evidence from children. I certainly have never done so. Yet it is a commonplace of cases involving child sexual abuse for the child's credibility to be put in issue, either by adult denial that abuse has occurred or by a suggestion that the allegation of abuse has been implanted by the interviewer or reporter. Clearly, whether or not the child is accurately describing what has happened is relevant to the question of whether or not the child has been abused. It is therefore difficult to say that the child's credibility is irrelevant or unimportant. How, then, is the child's credibility to be assessed? In particular, is an assessment by a child psychiatrist or psychologist as to the child's credibility admissible in evidence? And if it is, what weight should the judge give it?

The judicial standpoint hitherto has traditionally been that issues of credibility are a matter for the court, not the expert witness. Thus an expert in the course of his assessment of a patient (adult or child) was entitled to express an opinion as to whether or not what the patient says was capable of being true or worthy of credit: what was perceived as inappropriate and inadmissible was an expert's direct expression of opinion that what the witness is saying was actually true. It was, however, accepted that this was a 'fine boundary'[5].

It is, of course, an unwise professional who ties his credibility to that of his client or patient. The advocate is trained never to express a personal view about the credibility of his client, and wisely so. The judicial perspective is thus that any prospect of a dispassionate and objective assessment is vitiated if it depends upon an uncritical acceptance of the patient's account of events.

I do not know (and should thus be grateful to learn) the extent to which, in cases where the issue is whether or not sexual abuse has occurred and there is no conclusive medical or scientific evidence of abuse (that is, most of the cases I try) clinical opinion either depends upon or is influenced by the clinician's assessment of a child's credibility. The traditional judicial perspective that a clinical opinion based on an assessment of credibility was inadmissible raises what I perceive to be a difficult question. If during the course of a clinical assessment the expert forms a professional opinion of his patient's (or of a child's) credibility which materially influences the assessment itself, is the expert not entitled to express an opinion based, as it is, at least in part on that assessment of credibility?

Although the purist judicial answer at the time of the conference was, I think, 'no', I invited comment upon it[6]. The alternative view is that an expert is entitled to express such an opinion provided:

(a) he or she makes it clear that the assessment *is* based at least in part on his or her assessment of the patient's credibility;

(b) the expert explains *how* he or she has assessed credibility and gives reasons within the framework of the particular expert discipline which can be scientifically or professionally justified for the basis of the assessment; and

(c) he or she recognises both that:

---

[4] This proposition has recently been reinforced by the decision of the majority in *Re H (Minors) (Sexual Abuse: Standard of Proof)* [1996] 2 WLR 8, [1996] 1 All ER 1, [1996] 1 FLR 80, in which the House of Lords held that in order to decide whether or not a child 'is likely to suffer significant harm' within the threshold criteria for a care order under section 31(2)(a) of the Children Act 1989, the court must make findings of fact on the balance of probabilities as to past and present events in order to be able to form the basis upon which the likelihood of future harm can be assessed. A similar approach has been held to be necessary in private law cases relating to children when the court, under section 1(3)(e) of the Act is deciding what harm the child has suffered or is at risk of suffering in the future: see *Re M and R (Child Abuse: Evidence)* [1996] 2 FLR 195.

[5] *Re S and B (Minors) (Child Abuse: Evidence)* [1990] 2 FLR 489, 498 per Glidewell LJ: ibid at p 499 per Stocker LJ: see the passages cited at Appendix 1, part 6 below at p 49.

[6] This paper was, of course, delivered before the recent decision of the Court of Appeal in *Re M and R (Child Abuse: Evidence)* [1996] 2 FLR 195 which decided that all the previous decisions of the Court of Appeal on the point had been decided *per incuriam*. However, it was remarkable, as Florence Baron's commentary makes clear, that the unanimous view of the conference was that the approach of Morritt and Hutchinson LJJs in *Re FS (Child Abuse: Evidence)* [1996] 2 FLR 158, CA (as to which see pp 50 and 51) was wrong. I cannot therefore but think that the views of the conference were influential in the approach subsequently adopted by the Court of Appeal in *Re M and R*, in which the judgment of the Court was delivered by Butler-Sloss LJ.

> (i) the danger of basing an opinion on credibility is the obvious one that extraneous facts may falsify the factual substratum of what the patient has told the expert; and
>
> (ii) that ultimately his assessment of credibility is subject to and liable to be overriden by the judge's own assessment.

Most judges are, I think, sceptical of a professional opinion from an expert witness which is based solely or largely on an expert's assessment of the patient's or child's credibility. I should be interested to hear the doctor's answer to the question: 'Is there a medically scientific way to measure credibility?' I suspect it is 'no'. The wise judge accepts that there is indeed no art to find the mind's construction in the face[7]: hence a judicial assessment of credibility is invariably based on the evidence of the witness being tested in cross-examination and by comparing it with and analysing it against the other evidence in the case. At the end of the day, however, I think most of us would acknowledge that in a difficult and finely balanced case, our assessment of credibility is both impressionistic and intuitive.

Clinicians, whilst they have the advantage of interviewing patients or children in a more informal setting outside the courtroom, and whilst they may (and should) have access to all relevant documentation, do not have the advantage which the judge has of seeing all the witnesses and of cross-examination. As the extract from my judgment in *Re A and B (Minors)* (Appendix 3, pp 59–62) makes clear, my view in that case was that the more readily acceptable clinical diagnoses in cases of child sexual abuse are those which most closely shadow the forensic process: that is to say: (1) they begin with an open mind and without any preconception either that abuse has occurred or that it has not occurred; and (2) an opinion is not formed until the investigative process is complete and the allegations of the child (and to that extent his/her credibility) can then be assessed in the light of all the available evidence. That is why, in *Re A and B*, I preferred the approach of Dr W.

At the time of the Dartington Conference, the latest judicial thinking on the question of the admissibility in evidence of a clinical assessment of credibility was the decision of the Court of Appeal in *Re FS (Child Abuse: Evidence)*[8] which I summarise at pp 49–50 of Appendix 1 to this paper. The Court of Appeal appeared in that case to be saying not only that it was inappropriate for the expert to be telling the judge what the decision ought to be (Butler-Sloss LJ) but that an opinion from an expert based on his assessment of the child's credibility was both inadmissible and capable of being highly prejudicial (Morritt LJ). Whilst nobody, I hope, would quarrel with the proposition advanced by Butler-Sloss LJ, and whilst everybody, I hope, would recognise the danger of prejudice arising from an incautious opinion as to credibility expressed by an expert, I invited comment on the proposition that a child psychiatrist who in the course of a professional assessment of a child formed a view as to the child's credibility which was either influential or determinative of his diagnosis that the child had been abused should not be permitted to say so[9].

The question which I therefore posed for discussion at the conference was: to what extent is it professionally: (a) desirable; and (b) appropriate, in a case where a child's credibility is in issue and there is no objective scientific evidence to support what the child is saying for an expert to base an opinion on whether or not the child has been abused on a clinical assessment by the expert of the child's credibility?

The question posed at the conference has since been definitively answered by the decision of the Court of Appeal in *Re M and R (Child Abuse: Evidence)*[10]. A number of extracts from the

---

[7] Macbeth, Act I, Scene IV line 12, spoken by Duncan of the previous Thane of Cawdor: 'He was a gentleman on whom I built An absolute trust'. A useful reminder, perhaps, of the dangers of an over-reliance on making assessments based on credibility.

[8] [1996] 2 FLR 158.

[9] For the result, see Florence Baron's commentary (post) and note 6 above.

[10] [1996] 2 FLR 195, CA. The judgment of the Court was delivered by Butler-Sloss LJ, the other members of which were Henry and Saville LJJ.

judgment of the court will be found at Appendix 1 to this paper, at pp 50–51. It is, on any view, an extremely important decision[11].

The facts of *Re M and R* are in no sense unusual within the context of proceedings in the Family Division. The mother in the case had six children aged respectively 14, 12, 10, 9, 2 and 1 by three different men. Allegations were made by the two oldest children against the mother and the father of the two youngest children, who was living with the mother. Four consultant psychiatrists were involved and gave evidence. The balance of the psychiatric evidence was unanimously to the effect that the children had been abused. The judge (Connell J) was not satisfied on all the evidence that abuse had occurred. He declined to make a full care order, and the local authority appealed. The primary ground of appeal was that he was plainly wrong not to have found the allegations of abuse made out. The question of the judge's directions to himself on the proper approach to the psychiatric evidence was raised in the appellant's skeleton argument but not pursued.

The Court of Appeal dismissed the appeal. It rejected the primary argument, stating robustly that once a judge has made a decision in a child case, it was not for the Court of Appeal to second-guess the judge, to trawl through the evidence on paper, to consider whether the judge had given sufficient weight to one matter or too great weight to another matter, nor to allow minor discrepancies to provide the opportunity for a rehearing of the facts and a fresh exercise of discretion.

When it came to the question of expert evidence, the Court of Appeal found a conflict between the decisions in *Re S and B* and *Re FS* (or rather what is described as the *obiter dicta* in those two cases) and section 3 of the Civil Evidence Act 1972, to which the court had not been referred in either case. The effect of section 3 is to render admissible in civil proceedings the opinion of an expert on any relevant matter on which he is qualified to give expert evidence. Citing the dictum of the then Lord Chief Justice, Lord Parker in *DPP v A & B Chewing Gum Limited*[12] that when dealing with children the court needs 'all the help it can get', the Court held that section 3 of the Civil Evidence Act 1972 permitted the court to receive expert opinion as to credibility, if credibility was an issue in the case. *Re S and B* and *Re FS* were held to have been decided *per incuriam*[13].

Speaking for myself (and I suspect for the delegates to the Dartington Conference) I welcome the decision in *Re M and R*. I agree with the general feeling of the judges at the conference that expert evidence can only be fully assessed by judges if they are fully appraised of the basis upon which the expert's opinion has been reached, and that in some cases this inevitably includes the expert's opinion of the credibility of a child. Moreover, judges are pre-eminently able to weigh evidence and reject that with which they do not agree. This process necessarily includes discounting or rejecting an expert opinion inappropriately based on credibility. The danger of prejudice to which Morritt LJ referred in *Re FS* is, accordingly, in my view thereby substantially diminished.

In *Re K (Minors) (Alleged Sexual Abuse: Evidence)*[14], to which the Court of Appeal in *Re M and R* refers, I was faced with an identical problem to that covered by the decision of the Court of Appeal in *Re S and B*. An eminent child psychiatrist, brought in by the Official Solicitor to assess two children aged four and two and to advise on whether or not they had been sexually abused by their father, expressed opinions about the father's alleged sexual behaviour towards his sister and step-daughter when the two women were children. The psychiatrist had interviewed both the sister and the step-daughter, who were, of course, now adults. Both alleged sexual assault by the father in the past. The father denied those allegations, and it was

---

[11] It is principally authority for the proposition that the approach to the assessment of risk under section 1(3)(e) of the Children Act 1989 ('any harm which he (the child) has suffered or is at risk of suffering') is similar to that set out by the House of Lords in *Re H (Minors) (Sexual Abuse: Standard of Proof)* [1996] 2 WLR 8, [1996] 1 All ER 1, [1996] 1 FLR 80, namely that in order to assess future risk the court must first make findings as to past and present facts on the balance of probabilities as a basis upon which the future risk can then be assessed. This subject is, however, outside the scope of the present paper.

[12] [1968] 1 QB at 165A.

[13] Ie a decision made in ignorance of a relevant statute or precedent, and thus a decision which need not be followed.

[14] [1996] 2 FCR 425.

for me to find on the balance of probabilities whether or not such abuse had occurred. I heard evidence from both women and, of course, from the father.

The psychiatrist's opinion that the father had indeed sexually assaulted his sister and step-daughter when children was, I found, based in a very large measure on her assessment of the women's credibility. I formed a different view of the two women. I also held, following *Re S and B* that the evidence of the psychiatrist on this point was not admissible, as it crossed the fine *S and B* boundary. I rejected the *per incuriam* argument based on section 3 of the Civil Evidence Act 1972, and like Johnson J in *Re B (Child Sexual Abuse: Standard of Proof)*[15] regarded myself bound by *Re S and B*.

However, in *Re K*, my principal reason for finding the child psychiatrist's evidence as to adult credibility inadmissible was that, in my opinion, it was not expert evidence at all. I took the view that whether or not the two women were telling the truth about what happened to them as children was an issue of fact, and one which did not call for expert opinion. I cited a passage from the judgment of Lawton LJ in *R v Turner* [1975] QB 834 at 841:

> 'An expert's opinion is admissible to furnish the court with scientific information which is likely to be outside the experience and knowledge of a judge or jury. If on the proven facts a judge or jury can form their own conclusions without help, then the opinion of an expert is unnecessary. ... The fact that an expert witness has impressive qualifications does not by that fact alone make his opinion on matters of human nature and behaviour within the limits of normality any more helpful than that of the jurors themselves ...'

Having thus found the doctor's evidence inadmissible, I left open the question of the admissibility in evidence of the opinion of a child psychiatrist (who may, for example, have specific expertise in child development and behaviour) as to the credibility of allegations made by a child whom the expert has seen and the judge has not. That is the issue which has, of course, now been resolved by *Re M and R*.

It is to be noted that whilst the Court of Appeal in *Re M and R* said I was wrong to reject the *per incuriam* argument and to rule the evidence inadmissible on that basis, I was not wrong to rule the evidence inadmissible on the basis that it was irrelevant. The Court of Appeal said:

> '... the expert's opinion must be a matter upon which he is qualified to give expert evidence. Thus a witness's evidence as to the right answer on the ultimate issue will often be inadmissible because he has no expertise on the final question, eg whether adult A's evidence should be preferred to adult B's. It would not (because of the Act) be inadmissible because it went to the ultimate issue or usurped the judge's function. But it would be inadmissible as not being relevant ...

> ... while Wall J was wrong in his construction of section 3, we have no reason to believe that he was wrong in holding the doctor's evidence on the credibility of the two women giving evidence of abuse of them when they were children dealt with an issue which did not require her expertise. The evidence was inadmissible because irrelevant, and not because it went to the ultimate issue in the case.'

The result of *Re M and R*, as I understand it, is that whilst it is the function of judges to make the ultimate decision, when they are of the opinion that the expertise of a particular witness is relevant to the decision and can thus assist them in reaching it, then judges can safely and gratefully rely on expert evidence, including, where appropriate, evidence as to credibility. The proviso is that the evidence in question must truly be expert evidence – that is evidence deriving from the witness's expertise.

As I have already said, I welcome this development in the law. It accords with common sense, and it avoids arcane distinctions rightly incomprehensible to non-lawyers[16].

At Appendix 2 to this paper, p 55, will be found the opinion of a paediatrician which was provided to me in a case which I tried earlier this year. I have little doubt that such a statement would now be admissible in evidence, although the weight I would place on it would depend upon my assessment of all the other evidence in the case.

---

[15] [1995] 1 FLR 904.

[16] This was the point which particularly troubled Ward LJ in *Re N (Child Abuse: Evidence)*, CA, in which he said: 'One cannot ... expect the subtleties of the law of evidence to be understood by the child psychiatrist and the child psychologist. Experience shows that the subtleties are not always understood by the legal practitioners'.

(5) TREATMENT AND DISPOSAL: THE EXPERT'S ROLE IN ADVISING THE COURT ON THE THERAPEUTIC TREATMENT OF A CHILD AND ON THE MANNER IN WHICH THE JUDGE SHOULD DISPOSE OF THE CASE

Thus far I have raised issues relating to expert evidence insofar as it affects the investigative process. The second area in which psychiatric/psychological evidence is of material assistance to the court is where it relates to the outcome of the case: that is, the decision which the court should make about what is to happen to the child.

It is, of course, accepted that prescriptive orders from the court that the child should receive treatment of a given nature are usually inappropriate and outwith both judicial competence and jurisdiction. But there are often cases in which the judge is faced with a choice of courses of action for a child, each of which depends upon a different psycho-therapeutic assessment and approach. An example of such an approach is the case of Len (Appendix 3, p 60) in which I was faced with a straight choice between two different psychiatric approaches. Another example is the case of Harriet (Appendix 3, p 61) where the child in question was not the subject of the proceedings before me, but in which her circumstances raised a series of questions all of which can and do arise in other cases[17].

There is an issue here which I would like to explore. To the non-medical mind, 'treatment' implies an illness or condition which falls to be treated. This in turn implies a diagnosis of the condition which is to be treated. In cases of non-accidental injury the problem does not usually arise in any acute form. A readily recognised illness can be diagnosed from well-established criteria and treated. Fractured limbs in a non-ambulant child can usually be readily identified. They may give rise to an argument about causation, but the argument can be pursued on largely scientific lines. It is when one comes to consider psychotherapy for a child that in my view the difficulties arise, and the critical questions on which I invite discussion and seek advice are:

    (a)   on what criteria do you assess the need for treatment?;

    (b)   when do you treat?; and

    (c)   how do you treat?

There are in my experience particular difficulties arising from the need for therapeutic treatment in the context of disputed issues of fact relating to the child in question. A particular dilemma which I have come across several times and which is illustrated by *Re A and B (Minors)* is the case where it is alleged that the child is a victim of sexual abuse, but where the issue of whether or not the child has been sexually abused is before the court for determination. It has been my view that it is inappropriate to treat the child as a sexually abused child until the fact of sexual abuse is determined by the court. I do not know if that view is one which would be generally accepted by the conference. The difficulty about it, which I readily acknowledge, is that the legal process is frequently unacceptably slow in delivering a verdict. The question which thus follows is whether or not it is acceptable for a child who may have been the victim of sexual abuse to wait sometimes up to or more than one year before 'treatment' in the form of psychotherapy is commenced?

If the object of psychotherapy is to help the child come to terms with what has happened to him or her, to assist in the process of re-establishing the child's self-esteem and to provide him or her with the opportunity to acquire a proper perception of human relationships in general and of adult sexuality in particular, it must surely follow that the therapist can only work on a solid foundation of fact, namely whether or not the child has or has not suffered the sexual abuse alleged. This is not to claim for judicial findings either an infallibility or a detail which they plainly cannot and do not deserve, but the underlying premise remains the same, namely unless and until there is clarity about the fact of abuse, unless it is established by the best means possible that there has been abuse, the damage caused by that abuse cannot be treated. And if the child has not in fact been sexually abused, is he or she not further damaged and confused by therapy based on a false premise?

---

[17] Harriet's case (the name is not her real one) is reported in part sub nom *Re M (A Minor) (Application for Care Order)* at [1995] 3 FCR 611.

Is emotional abuse in a different category? In Harriet's case there was a clinical finding that the child had suffered psychological abuse in June 1993. At that point she was six years old and living with foster-parents. The question whether or not she had specifically suffered sexual abuse had not been determined and was not one which was any longer susceptible to judicial investigation. She was made the subject of a care order in January 1994 on the basis that she would be placed for adoption, but she had still not been placed when the case relating to her came before me in February 1995. The questions which I raise in relation to her case are the following:

(1)   Once the local authority had a care order – or even before – how should Harriet have been treated given the findings by the clinical psychologist in June 1993?

(2)   Should she have been treated with psychotherapy and if so at what stage? Was 'play therapy' an appropriate course of action? What could thereby be achieved?

(3)   Is it common ground that 'play therapy' should never be used as an investigative clinical tool?

(4)   What is the psychiatric advice about the manner in which Harriet should be prepared for her move to prospective adopters? Should she be treated by psychotherapy before or after the move or both?

(4)   At what stage should there have been an investigation designed to eliminate any medical cause for the soiling and freezing episodes?

As far as Len's case is concerned, the question on which I seek further help is as to the underlying scientific or philosophical basis for disagreeing with the proposition that exploration of a child's 'internal problems' can only be properly addressed from a secure and permanent placement, given the premise that such an exploration is itself a profoundly painful process and needs to be conducted from an environment in which the child feels secure.

(6) THE EXPERT'S ROLE IN THE CONCEPT OF THE 'ASSESSMENT' OF A CHILD IN THE CONTEXT OF THE INVESTIGATION AND TREATMENT OF SEXUAL OR EMOTIONAL ABUSE

It is, I hope, common ground, that, as Dr David Jones put it in his evidence to the Cleveland Inquiry the position of providing treatment while attempting to gather information is untenable: 'adequate treatment cannot proceed in a vacuum ... it must be based on a formulation of what is being treated' (see *Cleveland* para 12.36).

I have, however, detected an increasing use of the term 'assessment' in cases where the index of suspicion that sexual abuse has occurred is high, but there has been no judicial finding, and as part of the quasi-investigative process the child is referred to a hospital or to an expert for 'assessment'. In my view the concept of 'assessment' in this context raises a large number of difficulties. It is not therapy. The assessor is being asked for advice about the future care of the child. But that process must inevitably involve a degree of investigation. How can the assessor advise on the care of the child if he or she does not know what has happened to the child?

The problem was, of course, addressed in the *Cleveland* report (see paras 12.18 and 12.19 which I reproduce at Appendix 2, pp 56–57). It also arose in *In Re M (Minors) (Sexual Abuse: Evidence)* [1993] 1 FLR 822, where children had been interviewed by Dr Jones at the Park Hospital in Oxford. The children had been referred to him by the local authority for 'assessment'. His interview with one child in particular, on which the judge relied, was criticised by counsel for the father. In the leading judgment in the Court of Appeal, Butler-Sloss LJ comments as follows:

> 'Dr Jones had certain difficulties which he explained in his evidence. He was asked to assess the children by the local authority for the purpose of advice as to their future care. This involved a need to elicit if possible whether any, and if so, what abuse had occurred. He was interviewing the children 6 months after the allegations were first made and after they had already been interviewed by the police. As [counsel] put it, the trail was cold. Dr Jones acknowledged that he had used some "facilitation" at certain stages of his interviewing. But the judge and this court have the transcripts of the questions and answers and the evaluation of the questioning was for the judge to make. Did he get it wrong?'

Butler-Sloss LJ then quotes from the transcript, from which it appears that the technique adopted by Dr Jones was to put to the child that another child had told him things. This elicited the response: 'He shouldn't have said it' and that she 'didn't want him to, that's the problem'. The child was then clearly reluctant to give answers to any questions of importance and eventually the doctor asked if she would like to demonstrate on a doll. She said she did not want to answer. Dr Jones then said that he could only help her if she did answer. The child then indicated on the doll and in answer to what was then a series of open questions made allegations of abuse against her father. Butler-Sloss LJ continues:

> 'The judge relied on these answers, which, as I have already said, were clearly reluctantly given as one can see from the video-recording, as important and not in breach of any memorandum of good practice. I entirely agree with him. In my view, the doctor cannot be criticised for any of the style of questioning which he adopted. His objectives were not specifically to provide evidence for the court, but as he made clear, to make an assessment of the children. In the process of trying to ascertain what had happened he asked questions of P in an entirely appropriate fashion. Further, the way in which he elicited the answers was such as to entitle a judge to rely upon those answers for the purposes of family proceedings.

> It is important to draw distinctions between interviews with young children for the purposes of investigation, assessment or therapy. It would be rare, I would assume, that interviews for a specifically therapeutic purpose would be provided for use in court. Generally it is desirable that interviews with young children should be conducted as soon as possible after the allegations are first raised, should be few in number and should have investigation as their primary purpose. However, an expert interview of a child at a later stage, if conducted in such a way as to satisfy the court that the child has given information after acceptable questioning, may be a valuable part of the evidence for consideration as to whether abuse has occurred. No rigid rules can be laid down and it is for the court to decide whether such evidence is or is not of assistance. In this case, in my view, the judge was entitled to accept and rely upon the interviews with P as part of the evidence of abuse.'

Speaking for myself, and not just as a judge at first instance who is bound by decisions of the Court of Appeal, I respectfully agree with Butler-Sloss LJ's approach as set out in the extracts from which I have quoted, but I should be interested to learn if there is any dissent from it by any of the psychiatrists or psychologists participating in this conference.

CONCLUSION

I am conscious that the points which I have raised for discussion may appear somewhat eclectic, but they represent the issues which, in practice, I have found most difficult to resolve. If, as I suspect is the case, there is no real scientific certainty in this field, I look to see if there is at least a consensus of approach, or areas of practice which it is agreed are to be preferred. If neither of these is the case, then I, for one, shall be disappointed.

APPENDICES TO MR JUSTICE WALL'S PAPER

Appendix 1
Cases and materials on expert evidence

Appendix 2

Appendix 3

SECOND SESSION

APPENDIX 1

A SUMMARY OF RECENT JUDICIAL DECISIONS RELATING TO EXPERTS AND EXPERT EVIDENCE

A: OF GENERAL APPLICATION IN ALL FORMS OF CIVIL PROCEEDINGS

1 The duties of experts

There is uniformity of view across the various Divisions of the High Court in relation to the duties which an expert owes when writing an opinion for use in court and when giving evidence. Thus in *National Justice Compania Naviera SA v Prudential Assurance Co Ltd* [1993] 2 Lloyd's Rep 68, Cresswell J sitting in the Commercial Court said that the duties and responsibilities of expert witnesses included the following:

1) Expert evidence presented to the Court should be and should be seen to be the independent product of the expert uninfluenced as to form or content by the exigencies of litigation.

2) An expert witness should provide independent assistance to the court by way of objective unbiased opinion in relation to matters within his expertise ... An expert witness in the High Court should never assume the role of advocate.

3) An expert witness should state the facts or assumptions on which his opinion is based. He should not omit to consider material facts which detract from his concluded opinion.

4) An expert witness should make it clear when a particular question or issue falls outside his expertise.

5) If an expert's opinion is not properly researched because he considers that insufficient data is available then this must be stated with an indication that the opinion is no more than a provisional one.

6) If after exchange of reports, an expert witness changes his view on a material matter, such change of view should be communicated ... to the other side without delay and when appropriate to the Court.

7) Where expert evidence refers to photographs, plans, calculations ... survey reports or other similar documents they must be provided to the opposite party at the same time as the exchange of reports.

B: RECENT JUDICIAL MATERIAL RELATING SPECIFICALLY TO EXPERT EVIDENCE IN THE FAMILY DIVISION

2 The duties of experts

The most important statement of principle is undoubtedly the decision of Cazalet J in *Re J (A Minor) (Expert Evidence)* [1991] FCR 193 at 226–7, in which he said:

> 'Expert witnesses are in a privileged position; indeed, only experts are permitted to give an *opinion* in evidence. Outside the legal field the court itself has no expertise and for that reason frequently has to rely on the evidence of experts. Such experts must express only opinions which they genuinely hold and which are not biased in favour of one particular party. Opinions can, of course, differ and indeed quite frequently experts who have expressed their objective and honest opinion will differ, but such differences are usually within a legitimate area of disagreement. On occasions, and because they are acting on opposing sides, each may give his opinion from different basic facts. This of itself is likely to produce a divergence.

The expert should not mislead by omissions. He should consider all the material facts in reaching his conclusions and must not omit to consider the material facts which could detract from his concluded opinion.

If experts look for and report on factors which tend to support a particular proposition or case, their report should still:

    (a)   provide a straightforward, not a misleading opinion;

    (b)   be objective and not omit factors which do not support their opinion; and

    (c)   be properly researched.

If the expert's opinion is not properly researched because he considers that insufficient data is available, then he must say so and indicate that his opinion is no more than a provisional one.

In certain circumstances, an expert may find that he has to give an opinion adverse to his client. Alternatively, if, contrary to the appropriate practice an expert does provide a report which is other than wholly objective – that is one which seeks to 'promote' a particular case – the report must make this clear. However, such an approach should be avoided because it would:

    (a)   be an abuse of the position of the expert's proper function and privilege; and

    (b)   render the report an argument, not an opinion.

It should be borne in mind that a misleading opinion from an expert may well inhibit a proper assessment of a particular case by the non-medical professional advisers and may also lead parties, and in particular parents, to false views and hopes.

Furthermore, such misleading expert opinion is likely to increase costs by requiring competing evidence to be called at the hearing on issues which should in fact be non-contentious.

In wardship cases the duty to be objective and not to mislead is as vital as in any case, because the child's welfare which is a matter of extreme importance, is at stake, and his/her interests are paramount. An absence of objectivity may result in a child being wrongly placed and thereby unnecessarily at risk.'

3 The respective roles of expert and judge

It is of critical importance in discussing the role of the expert witness in children's cases to bear in mind throughout the respective functions of expert and judge. The expert forms an assessment and expresses his opinion within the particular area of his expertise. The judge decides particular issues in individual cases. It is therefore not for the judge to become involved in medical controversy except in the extremely rare case where such a controversy is itself an issue in the case and a judicial assessment of it becomes necessary for the proper resolution of the proceedings. The reason for this is obvious. Whilst the judge has knowledge and experience from practice and previous cases, he or she rarely has more medical knowledge than the intelligent lay person: the judge, almost by definition, is not an expert in the field about which the witness is giving evidence.

The judge brings to the inquiry forensic and analytical skills and has the unique advantage over the parties and the witnesses in the case, that he or she alone is in a position to weigh all its multifarious facets. This process, of course, involves an evaluation of the expert opinion in the context of a duty to make findings of fact and assessments of the credibility of witnesses. It follows that the dependence of the court on the skill, knowledge and above all the professional and intellectual integrity of the expert witness cannot, in my judgment, be over-emphasised. The judge's task is difficult enough as it is in sensitive child cases. To have, in addition, to resolve a subtle and complex medical disagreement or to make assessments of the reliability of expert witnesses not only adds immeasurably to the judge's task, but given his fallibility and lack of medical training, may help to lead him to a false conclusion.

It is partly for this reason that the current practice of the courts in children's cases is to require disclosure of all medical reports and to invite the experts to confer pre-trial. By these means the ambit of agreement and disagreement can be defined.

Re AB (Child Abuse: Expert Witnesses) [1995] 1 FLR 181.

4 The disapplication of the principle of legal professional privilege: *Oxfordshire County Council v M* [1994] Fam 151

This is a highly significant decision by a Court of Appeal presided over by Sir Stephen Brown, the President of the Family Division. Its effect is that a medical report obtained pursuant to the leave of the court to show the papers to an expert is not covered by the doctrine of legal professional privilege. That is to say, the party who commissioned it cannot refuse to make it available to the court and to the other parties: thus even if it is unfavourable to the party who commissioned it, it must still be disclosed.

The rationale of the decision is that children's proceedings are non adversarial. The objective is to produce a result which is in the best interests of the child. The consequence for experts is that they must give an honest and objective opinion even if it is hostile to the party who has instructed them. Whatever the expert writes will be placed before the court and will be scrutinised. The need for objectivity and absence of bias is thus re-emphasised.

The decision of the Court of Appeal in the *Oxfordshire* case has been approved by the majority of the House of Lords in *Re L (A Minor) (Police Investigation)* [1996] 2 WLR 395, HL. In that case, a mother, whose baby had ingested methadone, obtained in care proceedings, with the leave of the court, a report from a consultant chemical pathologist with the aim of showing that the methadone could have been ingested accidentally. The report discounted this possibility. The mother disclosed it in the care proceedings, as she was bound to do. The police, learning of its existence, sought its disclosure to them to assist them in their investigation of the injuries to the child. The mother claimed (inter alia) that the report was privileged from disclosure and that the *Oxfordshire* case was wrongly decided. By a majority of 3:2, the House of Lords rejected these propositions, holding that in proceedings in which a child's interests were the paramount consideration, litigation privilege did not apply.

5 The duty on the parties to disclose material relevant to the welfare of the child but contrary to their own interests

In *Essex County Council v R (Note)* [1994] Fam 167 at 168H, Thorpe J went further and said:

> 'For my part, I would wish to see the case law go yet further and to make it plain that the legal representatives in possession of such material relevant to determination but contrary to the interests of their client, not only are unable to resist disclosure by reliance on legal professional privilege, but have a positive duty to disclose to the other parties and to the court. To take this case as an instance: were it otherwise, a statement of great significance in judging the potential risk of the parents to their surviving child would have gone unsurveyed and its exclusion might therefore have resulted in a distorted assessment of that risk. Indeed, if parties initiate or are joined in proceedings, with or without leave, and within those proceedings seek to establish rights or to exercise responsibilities in relation to a child whose future is the issue for the court's determination, it should be understood that they too owe a duty to the court to make full and frank disclosure of any material in their possession relevant to that determination.'

In *Re L (A Minor) (Police Investigation)* [1996] 2 WLR 395, HL, the majority of the House of Lords left open the question whether such a duty existed. For the majority, Lord Jauncey of Tullichettle said that he did not find it necessary to come to a decision on the point. He added:

> 'It may well be that this further development of the practice in cases where the welfare of children is involved is to be welcomed. But I prefer to wait until the point arises directly for decision before determining whether such a duty exists and, if so, what is its scope.'

6 The admissibility of expert evidence in the assessment of credibility

In *Re S and B (Minors) (Child Abuse: Evidence)* [1990] 2 FLR 489, the allegation of sexual abuse depended critically on the credibility of a particular adult witness (A) who had made a statement alleging sexual abuse, depravity and perversion within the family naming amongst others her brother, who was the father of the children concerned in the case. A had attended therapeutic counselling sessions with a psychiatric social worker who gave evidence that from her experience of working with women who had abused their own children and who had been victimised as children themselves, there was little doubt that A's account was true. As to the admissibility of the psychiatric social worker's evidence, Glidewell LJ in the Court of Appeal said:

> 'I see no reason why the psychiatric social worker should not have been accepted as an expert witness. In that role, her opinion about A's psychiatric state and her propensity to fantasise or invent were properly admissible. To the extent that she was supporting these opinions by an expression of view that A's account of her previous history was apparently credible, this was also admissible. What, however, was not admissible was any direct expression of opinion that A was telling the truth and not telling malicious lies. The boundary between the two expressions of view is fine, but it does seem to me that the psychiatric social worker's evidence crossed that line, so that her expression of "little doubt that the accounts given to me by A are accurate" was a matter for the judge and not for her.'

Per Stocker LJ in the same case:

> 'It seems to me relevant to bear in mind that the psychiatric social worker was cross-examined to the effect that A was "loopy" or presenting the court with a pack of lies. Her opinion, properly accepted as being expert, was to the effect that she regarded the history as given to her by A as credible. I agree with Glidewell LJ that such evidence was properly admitted as representing the view of an expert, so far as her clinical assessment of A's description of events to her was concerned, particularly having regard to the nature of the criticism put forward with regard to A's mental state and veracity, but I agree that in giving as her opinion that A was telling the truth and not telling lies to the court she crossed the boundary – a fine one – between what was admissible and what was not ...
>
> The judge put specifically to the psychiatric social worker Mrs H's (another witness) version of (an) incident as described in her statement and contrasted it with A's version. He then asked the psychiatric social worker: "Either Mrs H is blocking out what must have been a very shocking recall, or alternatively A is building upon what was simply an inappropriate intrusion, a good deal of sexual detail. Do you have any views as to which is the plausible interpretation?" In posing the question, I feel the judge went too far and the question ought not to have been asked.'

Per Sir Roualeyn Cumming-Bruce in the same case:

> 'I accept the submissions of counsel as to the admissibility of (the experts' opinions) as to A's veracity for the purposes of their assessment of A's veracity when they were forming a view of A as a patient and had to decide whether she was so unbalanced that her account of her experiences as victim of her mother, her stepfather and brother ought to be rejected as the illusions of an unbalanced mind. As this was a prominent part of the defendants' attack on her credibility their opinions as to A's veracity were relevant and the judge was right to admit those opinions. The opinions ... were thus relevant in the context of their testimony, but irrelevant and inadmissible on the issue whether A's evidence should be rejected on the alternative ground propounded by the defendants to the effect that her accusations were not the illusions of a disordered mind but deliberate fabrications concocted out of malice and spite, motivated by an attempt to destroy the family relationships of other members of her extended family as a compensation for her sense of the loss of her own children.'

See also, however, *Re FS (Child Abuse: Evidence)* [1996] 2 FLR 158, in which experts expressed the view that a child had been sexually abused after having read the papers and watched a video interview of the child. In giving the leading judgment, Butler-Sloss LJ commented:

> 'Courts trying family cases are well aware of the great help they receive from the medical profession, child psychiatrists, paediatricians and psychologists among others. One particularly difficult area is the extent to which the statements of a child and particularly the video recorded interviews are to be acceptable or are to be criticised. There is a fine line between the advice an expert may give to the judge and the expert telling the judge what the decision ought to be. The latter is inadmissible and unacceptable.'

(Having cited the passages from the judgments of Glidewell LJ and Stocker LJ in *Re S and B (Minors)* which I have quoted above, she continued):

> 'In this case the judge was well aware of (the fine line between what is admissible and what is not) and indeed expressed the fact at the stage where he said, and I summarise: "I have to remind myself

that the question is whether I believe her not whether I believe those who believe her". The judge entirely correctly directed himself on this point, because both in their written and oral evidence, the child psychiatrists strayed over that line and into the latter and unacceptable evidence. At the end of the day the judge accepts or rejects the evidence at the recommendation of the experts who are there to help him, and the judge, and not the experts have to make that decision.'

Per Morritt LJ:

'The use of child psychiatrists is obviously of the greatest assistance to the court in many cases. In some instances that will extend to pointing out features of the child's evidence which tend either to support or undermine its credibility. But it is usurping the function of the judge to give an opinion directly on whether the man did that of which he is accused. In this case, three of the experts stated their respective beliefs that the father had sexually abused N in the way which she complained, not because of the results of medical examination, but because they believed what she said in the video interview. Not only was such evidence inadmissible, it was capable of being highly prejudicial . . .

My concern is not allayed by the fact that, although when faced with the point counsel did not seek to support it, in two of the skeleton arguments provided to the court it was submitted that the judge was wrong to reach a conclusion on the extent of the sexual abuse which was at variance with the evidence of N as the experts believed it. In my opinion, it is essential that greater care be exercised to ensure that in respect of accusations as damaging as these, inadmissible and prejudicial evidence is not put before the court.'

Per Hutchison LJ in the same case:

'I wish to emphasise my entire agreement with the observations that have been made as to the importance of ensuring that where such evidence is necessary, it is confined to what is properly admissible and does not extend to expressions of opinion as to the truth of the allegations made by the witnesses. Not only should such opinions not be given in evidence, but they should not in my view be voiced in the reports which such experts write, which often in one way or another become part of the evidence.'

Both *Re S and B* and *Re FS* must, however, now be read in the light of the decision of the Court of Appeal in *Re M and R (Child Abuse: Evidence)* [1996] 2 FLR 195 in which the judgment of the Court (Butler-Sloss, Henry and Saville LJJ) contained the following statements:

'Many if not all family law cases involving children feature expert opinion evidence. Recently the proper limits of such evidence have been the subject of a number of decisions. A conflict exists between obiter dicta of this court in *Re S and B (Minors)* [1990] 2 FLR 489 . . . and the Civil Evidence Act 1972, which was not cited to the Court . . . This conflict has been and is the source of much unnecessary forensic activity, and should be resolved . . .

In cases involving children, expert medical and psychiatric evidence from paediatricians and allied disciplines is often quite indispensable to the court. As Parker LCJ said in *DPP v A & B Chewing Gum Limited* [1968] 1 QB at 165A, when dealing with children, the court needs "all the help it can get". But that dependence in no way compromises the fact that the final decision in the case is the judge's and his alone.

In cases involving suspect child abuse, the expert evidence may relate to the presence and interpretation of physical signs. But it may also relate to the more problematic area of the presence and interpretation of mental, behavioural and emotional signs. That evidence often necessarily includes if not a conclusion, at least strong pointer as to the witness's view of the likely veracity of the child (ie credibility): indeed, his diagnosis and the action taken by the local authority may depend on the conclusion reached. The evidence also frequently includes a conclusion as to whether or not the child has been abused. At one time it was thought that an expert witness could not give evidence of his opinion on an issue in the case, especially when it was the ultimate issue, determinative of the case.'

After a discussion of the 'ultimate issue rule', The Law Commission Report (17th report 1970, Cmnd 4489), the consequent Civil Evidence Act 1972 and a general relaxation of the criminal law as to reception of expert evidence as to a defendant's mental state, the judgment continues:

'Against that background, it is not surprising that family law judges have received (without it would seem objection, demur, embarrassment or prejudice) expert opinion evidence, including evidence as to the accuracy or truthfulness of child complainants. Mr Justice Johnson in *Re B* [1995] 1 FLR 904 lists a few out of many possible examples where experienced family judges have admitted such evidence without question. While loyally following *Re S and B (Minors)*, he wryly quotes Professor

Spencer as commenting that the judgment of the Court in that case had been given "in a slightly conservative mood".'

After citations from *Re S and B* the judgment continues:

'The only legal reason given by the court for finding her opinions on A's veracity inadmissible for some (but not all) purposes are that this was ultimately a question for the court. But that objection would seem insufficient after the passing of the Civil Evidence Act 1972 which makes it clear . . . that the evidence cannot be held to be inadmissible *only* on that ground. It seems to us that the obiter remarks were made per incuriam.'

The court then goes on to consider *Re FS* and finds that the observations of Morritt and Hutchison LJJs were likewise made per incuriam. The Court then considers an unreported decision of mine in which I rejected the per incuriam argument and holds that I was wrong to do so. The judgment continues:

'But that is not the end of the story. The legal limitations imposed by the Section are that the expert's opinion must be on a matter on which he is qualified to give expert evidence. Thus a witness's evidence as to the right answer on the ultimate issue will often be inadmissible because he has no expertise on the final question – eg whether adult A's evidence should be preferred to adult B's. It would not (because of the Act) be inadmissible because it went to the ultimate issue or usurped the judge's function. But it would be inadmissible as not being relevant . . .

So the passing of the Act should not operate to force the court to . . . "waste its time in listening to superfluous and cumbersome testimony" provided that the judge never loses sight of the central truths: namely that the ultimate decision is for him, and that all questions of relevance and weight are for him. If the expert's opinion is clearly irrelevant, he will say so. But if arguably relevant but in his view ultimately unhelpful, he can generally prevent its reception by indicating that the expert's answer to the question would carry little weight with him. The modern view is to regulate such matters by way of weight, rather than admissibility.

But when the judge is of the opinion that the witness's expertise is still required to assist him to answer the ultimate question (including, where appropriate, credibility) then the judge can safely and gratefully rely on such evidence, while never losing sight of the fact that the final decision is for him . . .

The law of evidence should not be subtle and difficult to understand. And fine distinctions should be only tolerated if unavoidable and user-friendly – ie easy to make.'

7 The role of the court in ensuring the expert evidence is appropriately obtained and directed to the issues in the case

It must be recalled that due to the confidentiality of proceedings relating to children, the permission of the court has to be obtained before the case papers can be shown to an expert for the purpose of instructing the expert to give an opinion for the purposes of the litigation. There has recently been considerable discussion about the role of the court in this process. Is the court's role proactive, or is it a matter for the discretion of the parties whom they instruct and for what purpose? The courts have taken the former view. Thus in *Re G (Minors)* [1994] 2 FLR 291:

1   Generalised orders giving leave for the papers to be shown to 'an expert' or 'experts' should never be made. In each case the expert or area of expertise should be identified.

2   As part of the process of granting or refusing leave either for the child to be examined or for papers in the case to be shown to an expert the advocates have a positive duty to place all relevant information before the court and the court has a positive duty to enquire into that information and in particular into the following matters:

(a)   the category of expert evidence which the party in question seeks to adduce;

(b)   the relevance of the expert evidence sought to be adduced to the issues arising for decision in the case;

(c)   whether or not the expert evidence can properly be obtained by the joint instruction of one expert by two or more of the parties;

(d)   whether or not expert evidence in any given category may properly be adduced by only one party (for example by the guardian ad litem) or whether it is necessary for experts in the same discipline to be instructed by more than one party.

3   Where the court exercises its discretion to grant leave for the papers to be shown to a particular expert (whether identified by name or by category of expertise) the court should wherever possible go on to give directions as to:

(a)   the timescale in which the evidence in question should be produced;
(b)   the disclosure of any report written by an expert both to the parties and to the other experts in the case;
(c)   discussions between experts following mutual disclosure of reports;
(d)   the filing of further evidence by the experts or the parties stating the areas of agreement and disagreement between the experts.

4   Where it proves for some reason impractical to give directions under paragraph 3 above at the time leave to disclose the papers is granted, the court should set a date for a further directions appointment at which the directions set out in paragraph 3 can be given.

8 How experts should be instructed: what material should they be given?

See: *Re M (Minors) (Care Proceedings) (Child's Wishes)* [1994] 1 FLR 749, in which I said:

'(1) It is essential that medical experts asked to give reports or opinions in child cases are fully instructed. The letter of instruction should always set out the context in which the expert's opinion is sought and define carefully the specific questions the expert is being asked to address.

(2) Careful thought should be given to the selection of the papers to be sent to the expert with the letter of instruction. The letter of instruction should always list the documents which are sent. No doctor wishes to have to spend valuable time reading through papers which are irrelevant to the opinion which he or she is being asked to give. On the other hand, a doctor who ventures an opinion on inadequate material is taking a substantial risk that his or her opinion may be unsound.

(3) In my judgment, and following the decision of the Court of Appeal in *Oxfordshire County Council v M* [1994] Fam 151, where an expert's report is put in evidence the letter of instruction to the expert should always be disclosed to the other parties and included in the bundle of documents to be used in court.

(4) Doctors and other experts should not hesitate to request further information and ask for additional documentation.

(5) Doctors who have had clinical experience of the child or children outside the immediate ambit of the litigation (for example a paediatrician who has examined or treated a child prior to proceedings being taken) should carefully review their notes before writing a court report and ensure that *all* their clinical material is available for inspection by the court and by other experts called upon to advise in the case. This includes (not an exhaustive list) all medical notes, hospital records, photographs, correspondence, and X-rays.

(6) Experts who are going to be called to give evidence at the trial must be kept up to date with developments in the case relevant to their opinions. There is nothing more embarrassing for an expert (as well as time wasting in court) than to be confronted with a document or piece of evidence with which he or she has not previously been supplied, which he or she needs time to consider and which may vitiate the opinion previously expressed in writing.

(7) Experts should always be invited to confer with each other pre-trial in an attempt to reach agreement or limit the issues.

(8) Careful co-operative planning between the legal advisers to the different parties at an early stage in the preparation for trial should be undertaken to ensure the experts' availability and that they can be called to give evidence in a logical sequence. It must be repeated that child proceedings are non-adversarial. In difficult child abuse cases, it is often sensible to have what may be described, for example, as a "paediatrician's day" whereby the expert witnesses on a particular facet of the case can give evidence one after the other, listen to each others evidence and comment on it. This should occur irrespective of the fact that given witnesses may be called on behalf of the different parties and may thus be taken out of conventional order.

(9) Where an expert's opinion is uncontentious and he or she is not required for cross-examination that fact should be established as early as possible in the course of preparation for trial and the expert notified accordingly. The court appreciates that experts are busy people and that travelling to court and giving evidence in court are time consuming. The court will always try to accommodate an expert by interposing him or her at a given time: clearly, the greater the degree of planning the less the time wasted.'

9 Keeping the expert witness up to date

(1)   It is the duty of the solicitors who instruct an expert witness to ensure that the witness is kept up to date with developments in the case relevant to his or her opinion. Any such developments should not only be communicated to, but wherever possible discussed with the expert involved as far in advance of the trial as is possible;

(2)   It is the duty of the advocate calling an expert witness to satisfy him or herself:
(a)   that the witness has seen any relevant fresh material which has come into existence since the expert's report was written and is aware of any fresh developments in the case; and
(b)   that the expert's opinion either remains the same despite, or has changed as a consequence of, reading the additional material or learning of the new developments;

(3)   It is unacceptable for any expert witness in a child case whose evidence goes either to the disposal of the case or to issues canvassed by the guardian ad litem in his or her report to give evidence without having read the guardian ad litem's report.

Re T and E (Proceedings: Conflicting Interests) [1995] 1 FLR 581

10 The need for experts to confer and coordination of expert evidence

'It seems to me to be essential that each expert who is instructed should, as part of his instructions, be expressly required to hold discussions with other experts in the same field and then to set out in writing prior to the trial the areas of agreement and dispute. Also it may be that experts for different parties will be asked to advise on different sets of facts. For this reason it is important that each letter of instruction to an expert should be disclosed to the other parties, with any documents supplied also being identified. If this step is taken then if competing expert opinions are given it should immediately become apparent whether this has occurred because each expert has been advising upon a different set of facts. If there are issues between the parties as to certain factual matters which are relevant to the expert's opinion then each expert should normally be asked to give an opinion on each set of competing facts. Upon the Court determining the relevant facts it can then follow the appropriate expert view. Furthermore any later change of opinion by an expert, whether given orally or in writing, must of course be communicated to the other parties as soon as possible.

Although the circumstances of the present case were unusual it struck me that if one of the professionals concerned had been required to act as what one might call a general co-ordinator for the purpose of collating the expert reports and preparing a schedule for the court of the areas of agreement and dispute, a number of the problems would have been avoided. It is the solicitor's job to ensure that the expert concerned in his particular case has prepared the letter of agreement and dispute. The co-ordinator would then incorporate all these letters into one schedule. In the normal case the role of the co-ordinator would be carried out most suitably by the Guardian or the Local Authority although there is no reason why it should not be one of those advising other parties to the litigation. If such a co-ordinator is to be appointed his/her consent to that end should first be obtained.'

Cazalet J in *Re C (Expert Evidence: Disclosure: Practice)* [1995] 1 FLR 204

11 Consulting the professional convenience of expert witnesses: time-tabling their evidence

Extract from a paper given by Wall J to the Family Law Bar Association at Lewes on 11 March 1995:

'It is my experience that the profession often treats the convenience of expert witnesses with a casualness which is unconducive to any concept of mutual cooperation and which is likely to reinforce the reluctance which many expert witnesses have about giving evidence in court. The legal profession simply must realise that expert witnesses are busy people with many professional calls upon their time, and that giving evidence in court is both time consuming and takes the expert away from other important professional commitments.

Not only, therefore, should experts not be kept waiting when they come to court (judges usually ensure that this does not occur by interposing the expert witness where necessary) but more importantly, the time set aside for their evidence should be carefully calculated so that the expert witness is not required to return on another occasion to complete his or her evidence.

In *Vernon v Bosley* [1995] 2 FCR 78 Mr Justice Sedley held that the court had both the power and the duty in a proper case to achieve finality in its proceedings by placing a fair and realistic limit on the examination, cross-examination and re-examination of the expert witnesses to be called before it. He thus laid down a time-table for the duration of the evidence of a number of expert witnesses. He made it clear that the limits were not cast in bronze; they might not even be reached, and if they were reached in circumstances in which it was apparent that fairness required them to be extended, the court would retain the power to extend them. But such extensions, he said, would only be granted where something unforeseen made it necessary to do so. . . .

Speaking therefore for myself, I can see no reason why, in the future, the advocates who come before me on a directions appointment in a substantial case shortly before trial should not be able to tell me not only what practical and logistic arrangements have been made for the experts to give their evidence but also to tell me how long they have allotted for cross-examination and re-examination. I would then expect those estimates to be adhered to. If, at or before the outset of the trial there is reason to change them, I would expect the expert to have been given the maximum possible notice that his or her evidence may take longer than anticipated. I would furthermore expect the advocates to adhere to their self-imposed time limits.

I appreciate that the organisation and presentation of expert evidence is not easy. There are many complicating factors, not least the experts' availability and sudden changes in their plans due to other professional commitments. There are also the vagaries of listing. What I would look for is an assurance in each case that the profession has competently addressed its mind to the logistic problems thrown up by the case, and has consulted the experts' convenience in doing so.

Thus in the future, if insufficient time is allowed by the bar for the evidence of an expert witness the question will not be: "Dr A, when can you come back to complete your evidence?" The statement from the Bench to counsel will be: "Mr/Mrs/Ms B: you have x minutes in which to cross-examine the doctor." '

APPENDIX 2

(1) Extract from the judgment of Wall J in *Re A and B (Minors) (No 1)* [1995] 3 FCR 389 at 395–398

'This case provided a good example of a tension which has concerned me ever since, at the bar, I was instructed in my first case which involved an allegation of child sexual abuse. It is the tension between the process of investigation or assessment which results in positive clinical findings of sexual abuse, and the process of forensic investigation which results in judicial findings to the contrary. In the instant case, the tension is heightened rather than resolved by the disagreement between the psychiatrists on the methodology of the clinical investigation.

I can put the matter in stark terms. I am judicially satisfied, applying the criteria laid down by the Court of Appeal and culminating in the recent decision of that court in *In re W* that A has not been sexually abused by her father. Yet I have evidence from both Dr B, a well known and highly respected child psychiatrist and from a psychiatric social worker in his team, Ms T, that in their clinical opinion A has been sexually abused by her father. That opinion ranges from Ms T telling me that she would be "astonished" if A's behaviour at a group for children who had been sexually abused could be explained in any other terms than that she herself had been sexually abused, to the more cautious psychiatric opinion from Dr B that he remained "concerned" about A's statements relating to the abuse and that on the balance of probabilities it was likely that there had been some "inappropriate sexual contact" between A and her father: moreover that it had been contact which A "did not like" and "on a part of her body she did not like".

The fact that a judicial investigation produces a diametrically opposite conclusion to a clinical investigation carried out by experts is worrying. It is, however, by no means novel. In the series of seven cases reported at [1987] 1 FLR 269 at 346 (in two of which I appeared as counsel) there were categorical clinical findings of sexual abuse in six of the cases: those findings were rejected by the court in five of the six: only in one was there a judicial finding of abuse. There are a number of other cases in the reports where this has occurred; see for example *Re E (A Minor) (Child Abuse: Evidence)* [1991] 1 FLR 420.

It is in my view a matter of considerable concern six years after the publication of The Cleveland Report there should remain stark differences of approach and profound professional disagreements between distinguished psychiatrists on the subject of child sexual abuse: it is also in my view a matter of equal concern that elementary errors of investigation were being committed in this case by the police and the second local authority in 1992, some four years after the publication of the Cleveland guidelines.

The reason for the court's particular concern about a fundamental disagreement between experts on issues of child protection is the reliance which the court frequently needs to place on expert evidence in difficult child cases. That concern is heightened by the fact that it is not the judicial function to express opinions about the inherent value of clinical or assessment methodology. That is a matter for the doctors and needs to be debated in the medical literature and at conferences. At the same time, the judge has to decide the case, and what I do think a proper judicial function is the examination of a particular clinical investigation or assessment in the context of the case which the judge is called upon to try. Parliament has decreed that it is the judicial role to decide whether or not on the balance of probabilities a child has been abused. I therefore have to look critically at the clinical or assessment process and examine whether or not the opinions expressed are ones which, in the context of the case, I can accept. Inevitably, this involves looking critically at the approach adopted, and experts in the field would, I think, do well to bear in mind that their clinical methods will inevitably be subjected to such scrutiny in contested cases.

I stress that what follows is a forensic assessment of the issues. I repeat what I said in *Re AB (Child Abuse: Expert Witnesses)* [1995] 1 FLR 181:

> "It is not for the judge to become involved in medical controversy except in the extremely rare case where such a controversy is itself an issue in the case and a judicial assessment of it becomes necessary for the proper resolution of the proceedings. The reason for this is obvious. Whilst the judge has knowledge and experience from practice and previous cases, he or she rarely has more medical knowledge than the average lay person: the judge, almost by definition, is not an expert in the field about which the witness is giving evidence.

The judge brings to the enquiry forensic and analytic skills and has the unique advantage over the parties and the witnesses in the case, that he or she alone is in a position to weigh all its multifarious facets. This process, of course, involves an evaluation of the expert opinion in the context of a duty to make findings of fact and assessments of the credibility of witnesses. It follows that the dependence of the court on the skill, knowledge and above all the professional and intellectual integrity of the expert witness cannot, in my judgment, be over-emphasised. The judge's task is difficult enough as it is in sensitive child cases. To have, in addition, to resolve a subtle and complex medical disagreement or to make assessments of the reliability of expert witnesses not only adds immeasurably to the judge's task, but given his fallibility and lack of medical training, may help to lead him to a false conclusion."

I am also very conscious of the fact that when making the overall judicial assessment the judge not only has the advantage of material not available to individual witnesses, but is also able to make his assessment with the benefit of hindsight. I bear these factors very much in mind in reaching my conclusions in the instant case.

The disagreement between the experts in the instant case

In this case the matter was complicated because there was a difference of methodological approach demonstrated by Dr B and his team on the one hand and Dr W (instructed on behalf of the children by the Official Solicitor) and Dr D instructed on behalf of the father.

I hope I do not over simplify when I say that the essential difference between the two approaches seemed to me to be that the approach of Dr B and his team was, in essence, child led. As Dr B put it: "the basic information is the statement of the child". In another part of his evidence he said "the evidence of the child is likely to be the most helpful pointer". The approach of Dr W and Dr D was different. Dr W said that the first stage was to identify the problem. The child's statement was part of a complex picture, detailed information about which had to be assembled before treatment of the problem could be addressed. Dr D said the same. She told me that before expressing an opinion she would do her best to see all the parties and to try to understand the whole of the child's situation.

As I have already made clear, it is not for me to choose between the validity of these two approaches. The danger of the former, however, which in my judgment is graphically demonstrated by the instant case, is that if the information produced by the child is unreliable then a positive diagnosis of abuse stands a much greater chance of being false. This is all the more so if the statements of the child are initially reported through a witness (the mother in this case) who is herself unreliable. The dangers of reaching such a false positive are, moreover, increased in my view if, as here, the assessment either excludes the alleged perpetrator or only involves him after a clinical conclusion has been reached that abuse has occurred. This is a subject on which I shall have more to say in due course.

The forensic approach

It is my experience of cases involving allegations of child sexual abuse that the judicial investigation can only reach a satisfactory conclusion where there is a detailed examination of all the salient facts. This is a time consuming and expensive process, but one which, in my judgment, the gravity of the subject matter amply warrants. Child sexual abuse is a major social evil. The damage sexual abuse can cause to a child's emotional and psycho-sexual development is incalculable. It can and frequently does result in repetition of abusive behaviour in adulthood. By like token, however, there are few things more destructive of family life and relationships than a false allegation of sexual abuse. I have to say that in my experience some professionals in the field who make clinical findings of abuse seem to me insufficiently alive to the latter consideration.

I have no doubt whatever that viewed from the forensic perspective the detailed investigation which examines the underlying facts, which assesses the personalities of all the parties and which hears and weighs expert evidence is the most satisfactory way of resolving allegations of child sexual abuse. For the judge, therefore, the clinical investigation is part of the overall picture: it can never be viewed in isolation.'

(2) Extract from the Cleveland Report paras 12.18, 12.19 and 12.24

'The problem arises when there is reason to believe there may be abuse and the child may need help to tell, or where the assessment to that date is inconclusive and then a somewhat different type of interview may take place. This is a second or so-called facilitative stage which needs further consideration. The interviewer at this time may be trying a more indirect approach, with the use of hypothetical or leading questions, or taking cues from the child's play or drawings. According to Dr Bentovim, it should be used sparingly by experts, who may include suitably trained social workers.

He said: "it is worth waiting a couple of days for the people who are really going to have the best skills to interview children. I think a short period of days whilst doing that can save months and months of uncertainty and difficulty."

There is a great danger, which should be recognised and avoided from experience in Cleveland that this facilitative second stage may be seen as a routine part of the general interview, instead of a useful tool to be used sparingly by experts in special cases. In the first stage the child tells the interviewer. The second stage is a process whereby the professional attempts to encourage the child who may be reluctant to tell the story.'

At paragraph 12.24 Dr Bentovim is recorded as saying:

'We use a variety of open-ended questions to see whether children can speak of their experiences if there is a high index of suspicion of abuse, and we now reserve the use of clinical techniques of interviewing, eg use of alternative possibilities, hypothetical questions until the later part of the interview when it is clear that a child is unable to respond to open questions and when there is a high index of suspicion from the behaviour or manifestations or context in which the child is living.'

Dr Bentovim also said:

'It is extremely important that interviews are carried out in a very open way and that is the attitude which the interviewer conveys to the child, which is open-minded and that is the way in which he should conduct the interview.'

The report continues:

'This is equally essential when a child unexpectedly speaks of abuse during therapy.'

(3) Extract from a statement made in care proceedings by a consultant paediatrician relative to her interview with a child (C) now aged 13, who had made allegations of sexual abuse against her mother's cohabitee (P). C had been 9½ when first seen but she had made further allegations when she was 14. The paediatrician first deals with the interview when the child was 9½

'She (C) made a number of allegations, in a piecemeal minimalist fashion, with manifest reluctance, and obvious distress. She found it difficult to talk to me and presented as sad, confused and fearful.

She never used skilled rhetoric, at no time did she appear rehearsed and at no time did she appear to be maliciously over-embellishing or attention seeking. She told me that she was scared, and she appeared just so. Her mother was strikingly immobile and emotionless and I well recall her saying "He will find us wherever we go, another town, another place – it doesn't matter."

Both C and her mother described P as big and powerful and able to "put any door in – what's the point of an alarm, he would not care".

All these statements of intimidation of fear were made during our first meeting and were reiterated in later contacts. I do not accept that the 9½ year old C would have made any allegation which had the obvious potential for increasing physical risk, if she was not moved by the misery of the abuse she was describing. Even at that time, however, there was a strong sense of C's feelings of protectiveness towards and bonding with her mother, and subsequently she has never been able to sustain any safe placement away from her mother.

More recently, when C described further abuse, she had changed in affect. She did not seem to have a clear expectation of any outcome and was an angry, suspicious young girl. While I found her believable again, there was some loss of the spontaneity noted on the first occasion. Despite the apparent move to a more "streetwise" position, however, she still presented as embarrassed and could not readily use sexually explicit language on this second occasion.

I am not a child psychiatrist or psychologist and these observations and interpretations must be viewed with appropriate regard to my routine role in child abuse assessments. Every year I listen to at least 400 children giving some sort of account of painful unpleasant experiences and naming an assailant. It is rare that I utterly disbelieve an account (perhaps once a month or less). A lot more often, I feel that something is distorted or amiss or an account is incomplete. This does not usually cause me urgent concern. I recognise that many children will release only so much information as is bearable and as is sufficient to "test the waters" or provide for their safety.

With this background experience, I can report that I experienced no unusual misgivings when I interviewed C. Her account seemed incomplete but the pattern of her disclosures was in keeping with that of many other children whose accounts have led to guilty pleas by or convictions of assailants.'

APPENDIX 3

OUTLINE OF THREE PROPOSED CASE HISTORIES FOR DISCUSSION

CASE 1: *In re A and B (Minors)* [1995] 1 FCR 289: Ann born 9 July 1987 and Betty born on 13 December 1990

In the context of marital breakdown, the mother alleged that prior to her separation from the father, the latter had digitally interfered with Ann then aged 4. This was the second time she had made this allegation: the first time, two years previous, a brief investigation by the local social services department had concluded that the allegations did not warrant further investigation since the parents had at that stage separated. They were, however, reconciled and the second allegation followed the second separation.

When interviewed twice (on each occasion inexpertly and inappropriately) by an inexperienced social worker and equally inexperienced police officer Ann gave no indications of abuse: she was only interviewed a third time when the mother told the social worker that Ann had made a further allegation. This time the child did appear to make an allegation of digital interference, although what she was saying was by no means clear and in any event masked by inappropriate interviewing technique.

A was then referred to a specialist hospital as a sexually abused child. The assessment at the hospital did not involve the father at all, but took all its information from the mother. The hospital concluded that the child had been sexually abused and advised that she should attend a group for sexually abused children. That course was objected to by the father but ordered by a circuit judge. The father was then 'assessed' by the hospital which reconfirmed its diagnosis of abuse. When the matter subsequently came to trial it transpired that the mother suffered from a personality disorder during the course of which at times of stress she became paranoid and disordered in her thought processes, and was incapable of distinguishing between fact and fantasy. For example, she insisted that she was pregnant and that her psychiatrist had impregnated her. The judge found that the allegations of abuse were a product of the mother's fantasy which she had imposed onto the child.

A second psychiatrist instructed by the Official Solicitor was highly critical of the hospital investigation and insisted that before a diagnosis could be made the allegation had to be seen as part of an overall picture. The judge summarised the difference between the two approaches in this way:

> 'I hope I do not over simplify when I say that the essential difference between the two approaches seemed to me to be that the approach of the hospital and its team was, in essence, child led. As Dr X put it: "the basic information is the statement of the child". In another part of his evidence he said "the evidence of the child is likely to be the most helpful pointer". The approach of Dr W and Dr D was different. Dr W said that the first stage was to identify the problem. The child's statement was part of a complex picture, detailed information about which had to be assembled before treatment of the problem could be addressed. Dr D said the same. She told me that before expressing an opinion she would do her best to see all the parties and to try to understand the whole of the child's situation.'

Questions

1 Is there an acceptable and uncontroversial methodology for the investigation of child sexual abuse? If not, is there any psychiatric guidance as to what is clinically acceptable and what not?

2 Where a child is subject to proceedings, is it ever acceptable for that child to be treated in a group for sexually abused children before there is a judicial finding of abuse?

3 To what extent is it appropriate for judges to intervene in the clinical debate about the investigation of child sexual abuse and to dissect clinical findings?

CASE 2: LEN, aged 6 years

(This case is ongoing, and it is therefore included only as an example of the divergent psychiatric opinions expressed as to the interrelationship between placement and psychotherapy)

Len's mother was 17 when he was born. His father never played any part in his life. Len's mother (Kate) initially found it very difficult to relate to him and much of her early care devolved on his maternal grandmother (Queenie). When attempts were made to return Len fully to his mother's care after he was one, they ran into difficulty and there was evidence that Kate had lost her temper with Len and struck him. This led to him being accommodated with the local authority and to a series of foster placements.

Eventually, when his latest and longest lasting foster parents said that they could not keep him any longer (he was by then aged 4/5) a botched attempt was made to restore him to his mother's care which never got off the ground: and as a matter of emergency, an interim order had to be made that he live with Queenie. The question then became not *whether* but *how* he should be rehabilitated to his mother.

The court was faced with a stark divergence of psychiatric view. On the one side it was said by Dr X:

> 'Len has had a very difficult early life with considerable disruptions and he is left in an emotionally damaged and vulnerable state. He needs to remain within his extended family and the aim would be for him to return to the care of his mother when he and his mother are emotionally able to undertake what will be a difficult, painful and demanding adjustment ...
>
> Len needs intensive help several times a week to assist his emotional and psychological recovery. Len is outwardly functioning as a pleasant child but this is learnt cooperative compliant behaviour, a false self. Internally he is a very confused child whose emotions are in a chaotic state. These feelings can lead him to be provocative, manipulative, aggressive and destructive.'

This view, accordingly, was that before Len could return to his mother's care work needed to be undertaken simultaneously on two fronts. On the one hand, Kate and Queenie needed in therapy to address their relationship with each other: at the same time, Len needed help to build up his self-esteem and to make sense of his life and his place within the family. Dr X saw both pieces of work as necessary prerequisites of a successful rehabilitation of Len to his mother's care. Crucial to her view, as I understood it, was the need for Len to achieve a cognitive state in which he could make sense of the world around him, understand his true place in the family and thus accept a move to his mother's permanent care. Without work to this end, Dr X took the view that Len's current sense of internal chaos and bewilderment would cause him to react adversely to the move: he would in all probability manifest the characteristics Dr X listed in the final sentence of the extract from her report set out above: there was, on this analysis, a real risk of breakdown in the placement. This was a consequence which could only be damaging to Len, and might, at worst, result in his placement outside the family.

Dr X was of the opinion that a decision on the timing of Len's return to his mother should be taken as the clinical work evolved and that a review in six months would seem appropriate. When pressed in oral evidence to give a time scale for Len's return to his mother, she thought a period of about a year would be appropriate, although she said it could be longer.

On the other side was Dr Y. Dr Y did not quarrel with Dr X's assessment of Len. The point of difference between herself and Dr X was the way in which she perceived the family's needs should be approached. She says that Dr X saw individual treatment for Len as the primary need. She commented in her letter of 22 October:

> 'Where we disagree is that in my view it was more important to address the issues between the adults FIRST, as they are the basis of the problem, rather than to make the child the problem. Until Len can feel safe with a long term caretaker with a reasonable expectation that he will not be again moved, it is unlikely that he will be able to tolerate the anxiety of looking at his internal problems. In my view it is unlikely that even the three times weekly input proposed could be helpful whilst Len's basic situation remains uncertain. Once he is settled, both Len and his carer would benefit from further help.'

Dr Y's advice, therefore, was that there should be:

'Joint work between Queenie and Kate to work out areas of agreement and responsibility for Len probably 6–8 meetings at weekly intervals, with increasing contact between Len and Kate.'

Len should then transfer to his mother's care following which there should be:

'family meetings with Len, Tim (Len's half brother) and Kate together to enable some of the anxieties between them, probably over a further period of three months; Len to visit his grandmother once fortnightly, staying overnight, with other contact to take place when Kate and Tim visit Queenie or other family members.'

Dr Y also felt that there should also be individual work with Len and Kate as later felt necessary. The pre-transfer work could take place at a local family clinic: equally, the post-transfer work would either be at an intensive treatment programme run by the family clinic (a letter about which was produced, addressed to Dr Y and dated 13 October 1994) or by means of another programme which would be worked out with the clinic during the pre-transfer sessions.

Discussion

This case raised a stark divergence of psychiatric viewpoint. I am sure the judges would welcome further analysis of the scientific/philosophical method underlying each approach and the relative merits and demerits of each.

CASE 3: HARRIET, born 2 January 1987 – see [1995] 3 FCR 611

Harriet was the middle child of three siblings. Her elder brother Edgar was born on 10 January 1985: the younger child Mark was born on 24 December 1991. Harriet's parents were married but serious doubts arose at an early stage about her mother's parenting capacity and her ability to form relationships with any of the children. The parents married because the mother was pregnant with H and their relationship was never happy. After the birth of Mark the father effectively opted out for a substantial period: he drank to excess and gambled, thereby seriously affecting the family's standard of living.

On 14 May 1993 bruising was observed on Harriet's leg and arm which the mother admitted causing. By agreement she was accommodated with the local authority with foster parents with whom she was still living when the case came to trial.

A clinical assessment of Harriet carried out in June 1993 found that she was in an extreme state of trauma. She was described as frozen, watchful, withdrawn, frightened and wary. The report continued:

'Harriet presents as a very troubled and frightened little girl who shows all the signs of having been subjected to trauma. It is extremely worrying that she also shows signs which may be related to abuse. Classic signs such as frozen watchfulness, wetting and soiling are frequently associated with children who have been sexually abused and while this may not be the case for Harriet I would strongly recommend that this matter be further investigated ...

Harriet, in my opinion, has suffered psychological abuse and presents as traumatised by her experiences. I am of the view that H has experienced rejecting, degrading/devaluing, terrorising, isolating, exploiting, denied essential stimulation emotional responsiveness or availability, has experienced unreliable and inconsistent parenting. ... I have already suggested that further investigation be carried out into the meaning of her descriptions during play with the rag dolls.'

Finally, in the section of her report headed 'opinion', the psychologist repeated her concern about H's frozen watchful behaviour and commented:

'this, together with her wetting and soiling presents a very disturbing picture. It is well documented that children who have been sexually, physically or emotionally abused present in a similar manner to that shown by Harriet. Harriet is so worried and frightened that she is quite unable to talk about anything that has happened to her either in terms of any abusive experiences or in terms of anything else that has happened. It is impossible that a child can present so psychologically disturbed a picture as Harriet does without having had extremely disturbing experiences in their family.'

The local authority sought care orders in relation to all three children. By the time the matter came to trial in January 1994 the parents had separated: Edgar was living with his father who had ceased to drink and gamble and was coping well with him; Mark was living with his mother. The local authority's care plan was for Harriet to be adopted and for there to be an assessment of the father's capacity to care for both Edgar and Mark.

Views are sought about the proper treatment of Harriet. The judge found that she was 'a very needy little girl who has been greatly disturbed in the past' but made no specific finding about the nature of the abuse she had suffered. After the judgment the local authority instituted 'play therapy' for Harriet with a play therapist, the rationale for it being as follows:

> 'Harriet is happy and has settled extremely well with her foster parents. She has become a happy and relaxed child responding well to the excellent care she receives. But she wets and sometimes soils. She is still unable to share any of the feelings she had, she remains frozen in this respect. The plan is for Harriet to be adopted, so it is essential work begins with her before she could be placed; without therapy any future placement may fail.'

In September 1994, Harriet whilst in a temporary foster placement during her regular foster parents' absence on holiday was overheard inviting another child in the house aged three to look inside her genitalia and show Harriet her 'private parts'. Inappropriate questioning by the temporary foster mother led another psychologist and the child's play therapist to advise the local authority that Harriet had definitely been sexually abused and that her mother was the perpetrator. The social worker in the case suggested that play therapy was the way forward for Harriet to describe anything else that may have happened to her. In the reactivated care proceedings relating to Mark, heard in February 1995, the local authority initially sought his removal from the family for adoption and asked for a finding that Harriet had been sexually abused. However, the allegation of sexual abuse was abandoned at trial as untenable after the psychologist in question had been cross-examined.

In the meantime, prospective adoptive parents had been found for Harriet and she was about to be introduced to them. She was still doubly incontinent, and suffered periodic 'freezing' episodes described by the play therapist as a form of catatonia. There had been no investigation of any physical cause for Harriet's condition.

Questions:

1   Once the local authority had a care order – or even before – how should Harriet have been treated given the findings by the clinical psychologist in June 1993?
2   Should she have been treated with psychotherapy and if so at what stage? Was 'play therapy' an appropriate course of action? What could thereby be achieved?
3   Is it common ground that 'play therapy' should never be used as an investigative clinical tool?
4   What is the psychiatric advice about the manner in which Harriet should be prepared for her move to prospective adopters? Should she be treated by psychotherapy before or after the move or both?
5   At what stage should there have been an investigation designed to eliminate any medical cause for the soiling and freezing episodes?

SECOND PLENARY SESSION

DISCUSSION

The role of the judge

It was agreed that the office of judge demanded a degree of remoteness because the public looked to the judiciary to embody the impartiality of 'the Law'. Most judges who decided family cases were 'user friendly' (given the accepted need to maintain the necessary distance) and were 'friendly' to expert witnesses (although the same could not be said for advocates – given the adversarial nature of much cross-examination and the issues involved). It was agreed that judges and psychodynamic practitioners should be 'more open' with each other in Court so that experts appreciated what was expected of them.

Should family cases be heard in open court?

It was agreed that it was necessary to maintain confidentiality and therefore the court hearings should not be open to the public. However, it was felt that judgments should be in the public domain so that the public had access to decisions and the reasoning behind them.

The expert's role in the assessment of a child's credibility

There was general criticism of the recent decision of *Re FS (Minors)* which, it was concluded, sought to propound an artificial test. The judges present considered that they could only assess expert evidence if they were appraised of the unabridged basis upon which the conclusions had been reached. This, of necessity, included the expert's view of the credibility of the child or other witnesses who had been interviewed. The expert's view of the child was important because, in normal circumstances, that child was not seen by the judge in the course of the trial. Moreover, the expert's view of an adult witness was important because it provided an insight into that expert's ability to assess the people involved. Thus, whilst it was generally accepted that there was a fine line between an expert saying that 'X was capable of being believed' and 'I actually believe X', the essence of an expert's report was that he/she should give good and sound reasons for their conclusions. Accordingly, it was essential that the expert be allowed to comment upon anything that he/she felt was appropriate and that the same should be admissible as evidence.

The role of the child psychiatrist

It was important for a psychiatrist to listen to the child and assess from the facts related/statements made (which might not reveal the whole truth) the message which the child was trying to convey. Often, reality would only be gleaned after several interviews – as snippets of information were given as to the true underlying position. It was the role of the psychiatrist to seek to understand the child's concerns in the context of his/her overall circumstances and to interpret them for the Court.

Freudian theory

Whilst many of the separate groups had discussed Dr Trowell's paper in detail, there was little general discussion in the plenary session concerning the important points which it raised. Dr Trowell explained that the findings in her paper were based on knowledge and experience gained over a number of years with 'normal' as well as disturbed children. The paper was an attempt to explain the developmental processes which children undergo in their formative years and to explain, in a simple way, how that development could be affected by abuse. She wanted to provide a conceptual framework which would enable judges to understand the theoretical basis for some of the work which she undertook. Some of the concepts may be outside 'normal' experience, but they had to be understood against the background of tumultuous change which occurred in the first five years of life. This period of 'conflict' is cut off from our recollection and therefore it is difficult to contemplate the mental processes which each individual has undergone. However, research shows that early experiences are not lost but are transferred to the unconscious mind. Although a child's earliest emotions, feelings and experiences are not easily accessible, they do remain important and will affect behaviour throughout life.

EXPERT WITNESSES – RESPONSES TO MR JUSTICE WALL'S QUESTIONS

The experts responsible for the responses are:

Dr Roger Kennedy
Dr Tristan Fundudis
Dr Judith Freedman
Dr Carol Caplan
Professor I Kolvin
Dr Brian Jacobs
Dr Robert Jezzard
Dr Hamish Cameron
Dr Jill Hodges
Dr Judith Trowell
Dr Danya Glaser

Case 1: *Re A and B (Minors)*

1   Is there an acceptable and uncontroversial methodology for the investigation of child sexual abuse? If not, is there any psychiatric guidance as to what is clinically acceptable and what is not?

There is no universally acceptable and entirely uncontroversial methodology for the investigation of cases of child sexual abuse. Child psychiatric guidance as to what is clinically acceptable is as follows:

There are four questions which require clarification as far as possible:

   (i)   Has the child been sexually abused?
   (ii)   By whom has a child been abused?
   (iii) Is the child safe from reabuse?
   (iv)   What are the child's and family's therapeutic needs?

The task of answering the first three of the above questions lies primarily with Social Service and Police Child Protection Teams according to formal guidelines. These include the need for all parties to be seen. In order for this process to be carried out appropriately, there is a need for adequate resourcing and training for professionals involved. The process of assessment needs to pay particular attention to the early evolution of concerns. The child's account of the alleged abuse is of foremost importance. It is particularly important to ascertain the context in which the child had first described the abuse and the content of the early descriptions.

As part of the investigative process, it is important to hear the response of the alleged abuser. However, denial of the allegations is frequently the response, and it is extremely difficult to distinguish clinically between a true and false denial. Furthermore, there is no definitive clinical profile of a person who sexually abuses children.

It is not clinically useful or desirable for the child to be seen and questioned repeatedly. This places an onus on those who have heard the early accounts given by the child, to record as fully as possible what they have been told by the child, as well as their own statements and questions. This should be done at the time or immediately after the conversation so that it is fresh in the mind. Information obtained in informal settings such as conversations with adults including a foster parent or a teacher may be much more useful than what the child says or declines to say in a formal interview. Research has shown that children who have not previously described abuse, are unlikely to do so for the first time in a formal interview.

In order to determine the child's and family's therapeutic needs, a child psychiatrist or another member of a specialist child mental health team requires answers to questions (i) – (iii) above. It is inappropriate for a child mental health service to duplicate an investigation, but it is important that details of the process of the investigation and the answer to the specific questions are available. It may be deemed necessary to interview the child again as part of a second opinion about the likelihood of abuse. From an evidential point of view, a later interview is less likely to be useful.

In planning appropriate treatment, it is important for all parties to be seen on at least one occasion. A child psychiatric assessment seeking to delineate psychiatric disorder and a diagnostic formulation addressing issues not directly related to the abuse, may additionally be required as part of the overall assessment of treatment needs.

From a clinical point of view, the child's treatment needs to take precedence over all other considerations. It is important that a clinician has the freedom to determine how best to meet the child's therapeutic needs, in consultation with the child's primary carer. The first goal of therapy is to alleviate the child's distress and in the course of this, considerations of the cause for the distress are relevant. In the course of early therapeutic work with a distressed child, it is however possible that the question of sexual abuse may arise and it must be left to the judgment of the clinician to what extent and how the subject matter relating to sexual abuse is to be handled. It is essential that the therapist make a written record of the process of the conversation relating to any new information about abuse. The way such subject matter is handled may be the focus of cross examination in any subsequent legal proceedings.

2   Where a child is subject to proceedings, is it ever acceptable for that child to be treated in a group for sexually abused children before there is a judicial finding of abuse?

For a child who has been sexually abused, it is unlikely that therapy in a group for children who have been sexually abused will be the only and first therapeutic intervention, and is, therefore, unlikely to be regarded as necessary at an early stage. However, group therapy which does not specifically address sexual abuse may be indicated and useful.

If the clinician is aware of the possibility that legal proceedings in the case are likely to ensue in the foreseeable future, it is not appropriate for the child to be offered treatment in a group specifically designed to help children who have been sexually abused. However, situations do not infrequently arise in which a child is referred for treatment following investigation of child sexual abuse at a time when later legal proceedings are not envisaged. When a clinical team has been satisfied that on clinical grounds, child sexual abuse is likely to have occurred, it is not appropriate to delay offering a comprehensive treatment approach which might well include group work given that, currently unforeseen, legal proceedings in the case are not expected.

3   To what extent is it appropriate for judges to intervene in the clinical debate about the investigation of child sexual abuse and to dissect clinical findings?

From a clinicians' point of view, the judge's role is to seek clarification about the reasons for clinical decisions which include explanations of the process by which a decision to offer any particular treatment is reached and the relative advantages and disadvantages of not offering the treatment. Such a process of clarification is helpful in enabling experts to explain the conceptual framework which governs their thinking, the process underlying their clinical judgment, their experience, the treatment resources available to them and their awareness of available empirical findings. The judge will want to evaluate the completeness of the clinical assessment undertaken, whether it is multi-faceted and the extent to which it has taken account of alternative views.

It is important to draw a distinction between the process of clinical treatment and legal decision making. The former is continuously evaluated and modified during the process as is necessary in the light of feedback and responses by a child and family. This is in contrast to legal decisions which, being made at one point are, therefore, not easily amenable to modification in the light of change. Legal decisions can, therefore, only legislate for treatment in general terms. The judge's role in making a finding is crucial to the treating clinician who has to consider the implication of the judge's finding for further treatment of the child and family.

Case 2: Len, aged 6 years

Comment on the divergence of clinical opinion

Where psychiatrist have divergent or opposing views, it is very important to try and clarify the contentious issues. Each psychiatrist needs to explain how and why they have arrived at the opinion they hold. They need to clarify what is fact and what is opinion.

The opinions will vary with:

(a) The conceptual framework
(b) Their experience
(c) Their awareness of current research
(d) Their clinical judgment

Relative awareness or lack of awareness of resources may also influence recommendations. The ascertainable wishes and feelings of the child will need to be carefully considered and depending on the age of the child, different psychiatrists are more likely to give greater or lesser weight to this information.

Some psychiatrists have particular views or positions that are well known, eg supporting open adoption at all times, supporting involvement of fathers extensively in spite of strong reasons against it, or supporting the blood tie against the tie to the 'psychological' parent. Other psychiatrists try and assess each case on its merits without too many preconceptions. Some psychiatrists are very convinced that one form of treatment intervention is superior in most cases, others consider a range of interventions and try and select the appropriate one for the case.

Case 3: Harriet

1   Once the local authority had a care order – or even before – how should Harriet have been treated given the findings by the clinical psychologist in June 1993?

Before an Order was obtained, Harriet's needs were first and foremost to be kept informed about the process of decision making in relation to her future care, the possible options and the timing of the decisions. Following removal from her family to the first foster home, it was clearly necessary to explain to Harriet very carefully why she had been removed. In the course of these conversations, the concern about her emotional state would have been alluded to and possible explanations by Harriet for her very disturbed state could have been sought. This would have been in the nature of a therapeutic investigation, not amounting to a formal investigation. She should also have been given the opportunity to talk about her feelings and wishes.

In addition, her carers needed skilled and supportive help in Harriet's management, and Harriet and her foster parents would have needed help with her soiling, wetting and her sexualised behaviour.

2   Should Harriet have been treated with psychotherapy and if so, at what stage? Was 'play therapy' an appropriate course of action? What could thereby be achieved?

Harriet needed a specialist placement, either a foster placement or a residential therapeutic community. Harriet needed stability and commitment and there must be questions about the appropriateness of this foster family who went on holiday, leaving Harriet behind. Certainly, given the extent of her disturbance, care needed to be exercised about placing her in a household with younger children where there could not be constant supervision.

Psychotherapy/play therapy

Individual work with children is very important to help them make sense of their experiences and to help them with any distortions or disturbances in their developmental process.

Individual work can be:

- Cognitive behavioural therapy
- Play therapy
- Creative arts therapy
- Psychodynamic psychotherapy

(*See Individual and Group Psychotherapy*, Trowell J, *Child and Adolescent Psychiatry* (3rd edn) (Eds – Rutter, M, Taylor, E, & Hersov, I, 1996).)

Psychodynamic psychotherapy attempts to address conflict, distress and turmoil in the inner world of the child. Children may be troubled and need help because they may have experienced trauma, adverse life events or physical illness. Learning difficulties do not preclude the need or appropriateness of psychodynamic psychotherapy.

However, training in psychodynamic psychotherapy is very limited. There are four approved training schools in London. Most qualified therapists live in the South East of England. The possibility of child and adolescent psychotherapy being available across the UK is not likely in the near future, although the profession has now been included for the first time in properly funded training arrangements under EL (95) 27.

Outside London, there are approved training schools in Edinburgh/Glasgow and in Birmingham and small nuclei elsewhere. Even in the South East resources are very limited. One way forward is play therapy. This can be undertaken by:

- Occupational Therapists
- Specialist Nurses
- Psychologists
- Social Workers
- Teachers

If they have specialised in the work with children, they are eligible to undertake play therapy. They cannot work at such a deep level to restore and repair the damage but they can provide very considerable relief from distress and help to clarify the situation for the children.

Play therapy with supervision provided by a child and adolescent psychotherapist may be the most useful way of providing help for younger children. Adolescents are more appropriately treated using verbal or creative therapies.

In the case of Harriet, it may well have been that play therapy could have been a useful intervention if provided by a person trained to work with children with good supervision. Other parallel interventions would also have been needed. (Virginia Axline *Play Therapy* (Revised edn) (New York Ballantine, 1989), Kate Wilson et al *Play Therapy: a non directive approach for children and adolescents* (London Ballere Tindall, 1992), Sue Jennings *Play Therapy with Children. A practitioners guide* (Blackwells, 1993).

3 Is it common ground that 'play therapy' should never be used as an investigative clinical tool?

If there are still questions that require investigation, then investigative interviews are needed.

Individual play therapy should be for the child's use to assist and help the child. This is the usual form of play therapy – a place for the child to talk or play about any worries or concerns they have, with a neutral, empathetic adult not involved in their care. The child is informed that the time with the therapist is theirs to use and that anything talked about will be confidential, with the exception of matters which may affect the child's safety.

Unstructured, or open ended, or unfocussed or child-led therapy cannot be used as an investigative tool. If during the course of this therapy further information emerges that might be of use for an investigation, then the therapist needs to discuss this with statutory agencies and a decision will then be made whether to re-interview the child or not. This interview might possibly be done by the play therapist with police/social worker present but is more usually carried out jointly by the police child protection team and social services, in a different setting.

There are specific interventions involving some play therapy techniques that are used to help prepare children for particular events, eg going to Court.

4   What is the psychiatric view about the manner in which Harriet should be prepared for her move to prospective adopters? Should she be treated by psychotherapy before or after the move or both?

Psychodynamic psychotherapy is a specialist skill which is acquired as a result of a long and rigorous training. The training equips the therapists to help children to work through very distressing and difficult feelings and then enables them to rebuild relationships and recover their capacities to function more adaptively.

It is likely that a child like Harriet would have unresolved feelings which would include fears, confusions and feelings of sadness and loss in relation to the separation from her family, any abuse which she would have experienced, and possible associated feelings of guilt. Any therapeutic work would need to be undertaken by a professional skilled in psychodynamic psychotherapy in whom the child can trust and who will see the child at predictable intervals. Some aspects of the therapeutic work are of a factual nature. However, the child's responses invariably include unconscious feelings. It is work concerning more unconscious processes and unresolved feelings which requires more intensive psychotherapy over a longer period of time and which, due to the intensity of the feelings evoked, requires a secure caring environment to which the child can return from therapy.

Unless the child can continue therapy with the same therapist following the move from short term foster parents to a long term, permanent home, it is usually advisable to postpone psychotherapy until the child is settled. However, many children need and benefit from skilled short term work focussed on preparation for moving on.

In Harriet's case, her needs were primarily for permanency which should not have been postponed pending completion of psychotherapy. Linking a move from a foster family to a permanent family with termination of therapy faces the child with two simultaneous seperations and this is not desirable. Preparation for a move is part of good social work as well as of psychotherapy. (The child is bound to have feelings in relation to the move which, if the child is already receiving therapy, will be brought up in therapy.)

5   At what stage should there have been an investigation designed to eliminate any medical cause for the soiling and 'freezing' episodes?

Any child who presents with physical symptoms ought to be investigated for a physical cause for the symptoms, although the investigation need not be invasive. Furthermore even when physical symptoms such as soiling have a psychological basis, there are sometimes medical means of dealing with the symptoms alongside psychological treatments other than play or psychotherapy, for instance behaviour therapy, which may help to alleviate specific symptoms, alongside more insight orientated psychotherapeutic work. There are good reasons for alleviating symptoms since these can lead to secondary difficulties.

There is no mention of Harriet having been seen by a child psychiatrist and any child who presents with very worrying behaviour such as 'freezing' requires a full assessment of their psychological state before commencing any therapy.

CONCLUSION

The issues raised for the children in these cases illustrate the multifaceted nature of the world of the child and the wide range of skills required in meeting their needs which include good assessment, decision-making and treatment.

RESPONSE TO MR JUSTICE WALL'S PAPER: ISSUES ARISING FROM THE INVOLVEMENT OF AND EXPERT EVIDENCE GIVEN BY PSYCHIATRISTS AND PSYCHOLOGISTS IN PROCEEDINGS INVOLVING CHILDREN

Anne Zachary[1]

This paper raises many stimulating and important professional issues at the interface between the legal and the medical professions. Mr Justice Wall both informs the medical profession and acknowledges how he needs to be informed, highlighting the difficulty in what he stresses is a multi-disciplinary setting (family law), of communicating with each other accurately when our professional structures and languages are not the same.

The child psychiatrists at the conference were affected enough by his challenge to add a working meeting to the conference time-table in which they met to discuss the points he raised and questions he asked in order to respond collectively. As a psychiatrist, I was pleased to be invited to this meeting and learned a lot myself about how child psychiatrists work. But as a psychiatrist trained to see adults and used to working with the perpetrator rather than the victim in abuse cases I found that I had a different perspective on the discussion and wanted to respond to the paper raising different issues.

Starting from an elementary level perhaps we take for granted that other professions understand our own professional developmental paths and hierarchies. Within the Royal College of Psychiatrists there are various sections overseeing separate trainings. The major division is into general (adult) and child but there are also sections specialising in old age, forensic, learning difficulties and psychotherapy. It is possible to train within a section, subsequently being eligible to apply for certain specialist posts, but it is also possible to belong to a section out of interest. Members who train in the psychotherapy section usually supplement their NHS training with a private training. This gives rise to some overlap in that, for instance, many child psychiatrists are also trained as psychoanalysts. On the other hand many psychoanalysts and child psychotherapists are 'non-medical' ie, they were originally trained as psychologists, social workers, teachers, etc. I am explaining this briefly to illustrate the professional diversity of what might have seemed like a uniform group of people at the conference.

There are two main areas which I would like to focus upon, arising from the paper. The first concerns the practice of psychaonalytic psychotherapy and responds indirectly to Mr Justice Wall's questions about the timing of treatment at the end of the case summary of Harriet, but more directly to his opening plea on page 36 for some light to be shed on the underlying philosophy of the psychodynamic approach. The second concerns professional boundaries and the important guidelines suggested in Appendix 1, particularly 1 and 2 (the duties of experts); 3 (the respective roles of experts and judges); and 6 (the admissibility of expert evidence in the assessment of credibility).

The first area I would like to focus upon relates most directly to Mr Justice Wall's questions on page 42:

    (a)   on what criteria do you assess the need for treatment?
    (b)   when do you treat?
    (c)   how do you treat?

The specific issue discussed is about the problem of offering a child treatment for having been sexually abused before it has been determined by the court that there was in fact sexual abuse.

To outline the philosophy behind the psychodynamic approach to treatment provides a solution to this dilemma. Freud gave us the fundamental rule in psychoanalysis, which is, that all

---

[1] MB, MRCPsych, Psychoanalyst and Consultant Psychotherapist, Portman Clinic.

the patient has to say in treatment is whatever comes into their mind at the time. This is the rule which underpins the concept of free association. The therapist will always allow the patient to begin the session (unless there are any practical announcements). The child in question, as any patient, will thus choose what to talk about and this may be sexual abuse or not. If sexual abuse is suspected the therapist may make interpretations later which then enable the child to disclose details. The therapist may observe sexually explicit behaviour which points to the possibility of sexual abuse. But there is no starting point for the psychoanalytic psychotherapy of a child who has been abused, with treatment specific to that or to any other problem. Psychotherapy is not like an antibiotic, used directly to treat an infection. It approaches whatever the problem is indirectly and non-specifically but by its nature, no less effectively.

There are the practical difficulties then raised by Mr Justice Wall, ie, whether treatment can begin before the court proceedings are complete. This always presents the problem not so much of diagnosis but the practical problem of stability. Will geographical changes take place? Will the treatment have to be interrupted?

For these reasons rather than any risk of wrong diagnosis we prefer when treating the perpetrators, to wait until a decision is made by the court, to prevent the trauma of interrupting the treatment abruptly, for instance because of a sentence of imprisonment. But where there is a long delay or the possibility of a hopeful outcome, sometimes treatment can begin whilst the uncertainty is acknowledged.

The above description of technique I hope addresses Mr Justice Wall's question on page 42 about the need for a diagnosis. Psychotherapy is not medically based in the way he outlines and a patient/child who has emotional needs of whatever kind, including finding themselves in the upsetting situation of alleged trauma or false allegations, can benefit from treatment. I would agree with Len (Appendix 3, p 60) needing to be in a secure and permanent placement before beginning treatment for the same reasons. Psychotherapy does not only help people feel better (whilst it is in progress). On the contrary, if it helps them feel worse in certain areas this is a good prognostic sign that it is reaching the emotional trauma. Of course, to place a child in a group which is specifically for the treatment of child abuse before it has been established whether or not there has been any abuse, one of the questions raised at the end of the first case, would be unnecessarily exposing and inappropriate. Any prospect of treatment at this stage, practically insecure as it would be, needs to be individual.

I find this question of whether treatment can begin before the court proceedings are complete stimulating in terms of our own specialised practice at the Portman where we usually only see perpetrators. But this illustrates another of the principles of psychodynamic practice. People have to come for treatment personally motivated, it cannot be prescribed. (Of course this does not apply to young children but for them parental or guardian responsibility is the essential substitute.) But adults come to the Portman often independently of the law asking for help with a specific problem. If the law is involved they are usually pleading guilty or already convicted. Where there is a denial of abuse but a wish for treatment this can focus on the reality and so be useful in helping someone face up to a problem.

Perhaps for other reasons than those cited from Dr Jones in the Cleveland enquiry (page 43) I would agree with the comment about not attempting to gather information in an assessment in the context of treatment. I have discussed this further in my second main point later. As Mr Justice Wall says, assessment is not therapy. In my professional view, assessment allows direct communication with the court. Therapy does not. However, where some measure of communication is necessary regarding confirmation of attendance or progress, a second professional can act most effectively in the role of clinical manager.

The second area I am concerned with, has to be with professional boundaries. In view of the diversity of training I briefly outlined at the beginning, within our own very specialised field, views about these may vary considerably. There are psychoanalysts who work solely with patients on a full-time basis who feel that we should have absolute privilege regarding confidentiality. A case which upheld the privilege of confidentiality, involving Dr Anne Hayman, which offers some security, was written up in the Lancet in 1965 'Psychoanalyst sub-poenaed'. However, medical privilege, though fundamental to the clinical relationship, according to law is not absolute and practitioners, beholden firstly to their clinical judgment, will expect to inform in certain situations. Much depends on the specific role in which professionals find themselves in any particular situation. When a forensic psychiatrist reports to the court it is within a contract of confidentiality (Eastman), ie the patient and the psychiatrist have agreed that the assessment is for the purposes of the court. A forensic psychiatrist or a psychotherapist, who is also a psychoanalyst, who would expect to respond as Dr Hayman did in the test case in relation to their patients in treatment, would in different circumstances, when asked to see a patient in order to report to the court, report within these same contractual boundaries. The particular role of the practitioner in relation to each individual patient must always be remembered.

A recent book *The New Informants* written by an American trained as a psychoanalyst in Britain, Christopher Bollas, and an American lawyer, David Sundelson, raises the alarm about what has happened to clinical confidentiality within the psychoanalytic profession in America. The title refers to the development of a body of psychotherapists who have been trained in order to investigate child sexual abuse within the treatment relationship and to report their findings. This conjures up a disturbing image of 'the psychotherapy police' and indicates that in terms of their professional identity they have lost their way. We are concerned in Britain that the same unboundaried situation does not arise. Psychoanalysts have the skills needed to create space and thinking-time rather than as can happen all too often, allowing guidelines and procedures to be implemented in a mindless way in order to relieve anxiety within the professionals.

In his notes on experts and expert evidence in Appendix 1, Mr Justice Wall draws attention to our own professional dilemmas in a way which can help us to protect our own boundaries. Indeed it is sad that this is necessary and that it has not always been possible for mental health professionals to keep to the right side of the line although it is acknowledged in the quotations that it is indeed a fine line. For example, Glidewell LJ in the Court of Appeal, re an adult witness (A):

> 'I see no reason why the psychiatric social worker should not have been accepted as an expert witness. In that role her opinion about A's state and her propensity to fantasize or invent were properly admissible. To the extent that she was supporting these opinions by an expression of view that A's account of her previous history was apparently credible, this was also admissible. What however was not admissible was any direct expression of opinion that A was telling the truth and not telling malicious lies. The boundary between the two expressions of view is fine, but it does seem to me that the psychiatric social worker's evidence crossed that line, so that her expression of "little doubt that the accounts given to one by A are accurate", was a matter for the judge, not for her.'

and eg, (page 49) Butler-Sloss LJ, in another Court of Appeal case:

> 'there is a fine line between the advice an expert may give to the judge and the expert telling the judge what the decision ought to be. The latter is inadmissible and unacceptable.'

My view is that if we have agreed to do an assessment in order to report to the court and the patient knows that, then whatever comes up at interview informs that report. But as the excerpts from recent judgments, particularly in the Court of Appeal quoted by Mr Justice Wall, illustrate, it will be for the judge to decide what determines truth.

This has a profound bearing on the situation regarding treatment. Since the contract between the patient and the therapist, led by the patient in a free associative manner, does not address issues of true or false or right or wrong but instead focuses on the meaning of the material in the patient's internal world, is it appropriate for this possibly 'mad', possibly chaotic, disjointed, out-of-context material, ever to be of access to the court?

Once a psychotherapist has made a regular treatment arrangement with a patient, I would argue that absolute privilege regarding confidentiality should apply. Within the psychoanalytic treatment model, the therapist is not in a position to distinguish fact from fantasy and therefore cannot inform the court in a straightforward and facilitatory manner. Since the court considers it is solely the judge's task to decide upon the truth then there is already agreement here and sadly as can happen, sometimes a need for the judge to step in and protect the therapy from too much exposure. To safeguard against this, the therapeutic relationship needs to be separate from any ongoing court proceedings and the multi-disciplinary team can be useful in making interim assessments for reporting if necessary.

To conclude, whilst ultimately it is the judge's decision, there is a parallel between the perspective of the psychoanalyst and that of the judge in that as Mr Justice Wall describes, there is a need for the judge to keep an open mind as to whether abuse has occurred or not occurred. It is within the circumscribed clinical structure of assessment that information which can inform the court can be collected but in my view this is a very different setting from a treatment arrangement. I have argued that treatment should be confidential. If the judge's views questioning the validity of certain expert witnesses' statements are taken seriously, I understand this to have some support from within the judiciary. There remains an area of controversy between the psychodynamic professionals regarding child psychotherapists reporting to the court. Trudy Klauber addressed this in her paper to the conference when she acknowledged that the assessment of a child who has possibly suffered child abuse will be a lengthy process. The idea of an extended assessment is an expedient compromise.

REFERENCES

Bollas C and Sundelson D, *The New Informants* (1995) Karnac Books.

Eastman N, 'Clinical confidentiality, a contractual basis'. (1987) In: Gudjonsson G and Drinkwater J (eds), *Psychological Evidence in Court, Issues in Criminological and Legal Psychology*, No 11, Leicester, British Psychological Society.

Freud S, *On beginning the treatment* S.E XII (1911) Hogarth Press.

Hayman A, 'Psychoanalyst sub-poenaed' (1965) *The Lancet*, (16.10.65) pp 785–6.

THIRD

THIRD SESSION

Dr Roger Kennedy

INTRODUCTION TO HIS PAPER

Dr Kennedy explained that he had begun his professional life as a psychoanalyst and was now working in the field of applied psychoanalysis. The work which he undertook was not capable of 'clear' definition because it involved people in difficult circumstances. He saw his role as assessing parents and their ability/capacity to change whatever the horrors and/or deprivations which may have occurred in the past. His form of psychoanalysis was particularly in point because it confronted the parent's destructive behaviour. In essence, he saw his task as being to assist with 'bearing the unbearable'. A 'good enough' parent had to recognise the shift in development as a child moved from absolute dependency, through partial dependency to independence.

Working with families that had broken down meant that a psychodynamic practitioner had to become involved in the 'family pathology' with the result that there was a danger that this involvement would affect the expert's own attitude to and analysis of the situation. Consequently, Dr Kennedy stressed that it was important for a judge to have a dynamic view so that he/she could develop an insight into what might be occurring. Issues could then be clarified and decisions would be made from a neutral standpoint.

ASSESSMENT OF PARENTING

Roger Kennedy[1]

Assessing and treating families in which there has been severe child abuse is anxiety provoking and stressful for professional workers. There is a need to keep the children safe, to establish where possible a working relationship with the parents and at the same time to confront the often severe family pathology, especially where there is the possibility of change within the family. Each one of these aims can provide enormous difficulties for the professional, where all three have to be maintained simultaneously, the task can feel overwhelming. Making judgments about what should happen to a family, whether or not children should remain with their parents or be separated from them permanently or temporarily, and trying to assess the potential for rehabilitation are very complex and difficult tasks.

What I have to say is based on nearly 13 years of working with problem families at the Family Unit of the Cassel Hospital, which uniquely provides in-patient treatment for the whole family. We have built up extensive experience of undertaking the arduous and occasionally nerve-racking task of rehabilitating families for which other forms of treatment have either failed or have been insufficient.

My approach is from a psychoanalytical viewpoint, which views human beings as having complex and often unconscious motives underlying their manifest behaviour. Psychoanalysis consists of a body of theoretical and clinical knowledge concerned with looking at people's conflicts, feelings, anxieties and reasons for actions, which includes an understanding of their unconscious processes. A psychoanalytic approach seems at first sight to be antagonistic to the legal framework which underpins much contemporary child care work, for legal theory is heavily weighted towards the notion of the 'reasonable man', whose unconscious ideas and emotions are only significant if they lead to an intention to act illegally and the carrying out of an illegal act. As yet the law does not punish us for our mere fantasies.

However, from my experience, I would suggest that the day to day practice of family law can be enriched by a more rigorous attempt to understand human emotions, which are only too often very 'unreasonable', confusing, painful, and frustrating, and involve unconscious motivations.

My 'applied' psychoanalytical approach, which I should say is fairly eclectic, may provoke a certain amount of scepticism; indeed, I would be surprised, and even a little disappointed, if it did not. I hope to show, through detailed argument and the use of clinical illustrations, that such an approach can both address the difficult inner worlds of disturbed children and their parents, while also being in touch with the complex issues of child care and child protection. I do not rule out the use of family therapy, behaviour therapy, the occasional use of psychotropic drugs, and anything else that may work with difficult families. The advantage of the Cassel environment is that we can do both sophisticated therapeutic work and confront everyday living issues with families, particularly through the nursing work. I also think that the advantage of an analytic approach is that it is particularly useful in the treatment of intractable problems, because it is a form of therapy that by its very nature aims to tackle directly destructive and negative behaviour.

I have to say that quite often when I have had to appear in court over difficult cases, I have come up against naïve and over optimistic treatment reports given by untrained or inexperienced counsellors, who are so caught up with a wish to see the best in their clients that they have missed their clients' destructive side, which they may have directed at their vulnerable children. Not that I am advocating only looking at the negative side; obviously a balanced approach is wisest. However, it is often difficult for workers in the field, especially when they have put in a lot of work with a family, to maintain their objectivity, so that they may find themselves

---

[1] Consultant psychotherapist, Family Unit, the Cassel Hospital.

swinging either too much against or too much in favour of parents, while forgetting the needs of the children.

If I had to summarise what we do in a phrase, it would be to 'bear the unbearable'. What I mean by this is that in the treatment of abused and abusing families, time and again the staff and the families are called upon to bear unbearable experiences, traumatically painful experiences of abuse which the immature child cannot and could not deal with. By helping the children and their parents to bear these difficult experiences, to find words to express their distress, we hope to enable them to take charge of their lives rather than continue to be victims of their past. Our aim is to help the children recover as much as they can from the damage inflicted on them, and to help the parents to stop inflicting this damage.

When dealing with problem families, child mental health workers are constantly being asked directly or indirectly to assess parenting capacities. Courts and social service agencies often wish to have an opinion about the ability of parents to look after their children, keep them safe and to attend to their physical and emotional needs. With the troubled family, one can see how parents may wish to give up their responsibilities to professionals and ask for parenting for themselves. They may give up their children, or be tempted to do so, even when offered treatment. They may fight off attempts to help them, or may feel that they cannot face the responsibility of being a parent for the whole day. The responsibility of parenthood may provoke a breakdown in the parents' functioning, making them unsafe to be with their children. Some parents may be very confused about how much responsibility they can take for their own emotions, how much should be kept between adults and how much may spill over into the children's lives. Such confusion may result of course in physical, sexual or emotional abuse of the children, in which the children's needs and interests come second to those of the adults' needs.

Though there is much we still do not understand in this field and though the practical task of making judgments about the future behaviour of families is complex, difficult and often confusing, there would seem to be three essential questions that are raised time and again when family assessments of such problem families take place.

1. What do we mean by good enough parenting, and how do we assess parental capacity?

2. When are children safe to be with their parents and when is it best to remove them?

3. When should a problem family be given the chance to stay together, despite major problems, and when should treatment be abandoned?

A thorough assessment of parental capacities, or, to use the terminology of the Children Act, of parental responsibility, is the basis for providing answers about questions of children's safety and the chances of successful treatment outcome. My account of parental assessment is based on extensive experience of working with multi-problem families at the Family Unit of the Cassel Hospital. We have a severely disordered population of families for assessment and treatment; yet I think that issues raised by tackling such families highlight, admittedly perhaps rather starkly, issues relevant in other assessment and treatment settings. Before tackling the clinical issues directly, I shall raise a few general points about parental responsibility, and then outline some main criteria for assessing parental responsibility.

PARENTAL RESPONSIBILITY

The Children Act defines parental responsibility as 'all the rights, duties, powers, responsibilities and authority which by law a parent of a child has in relation to the child and his property,' (s 3(1)). However, the Act does not define in any detail the nature of these rights, etc, as the list, it is argued, would be constantly changing to meet different social situations. The issue about the relationship between social attitudes and the practice of family law is complicated. The courts cannot isolate themselves from society, nor on the other hand do they wish to be seen too often to be in advance of social attitudes. Thus, to take one example from the family field, that of marriage, in the nineteen-fifties, it was considered relatively abnormal for a couple to live together without being married; but by the sixties and early seventies, judges recognised that this situation had significantly changed and that cohabitation was an acceptable way of life for families. Similarly attitudes, at least in the courts, to one-parent families have also dramatically changed. There is a much more tolerant, flexible and pluralistic attitude to the nature of family life. Family lawyers are increasingly beginning to realise that there is a need for them to be more informed about child care issues, and for them to keep abreast of research as well as different practices in other countries. However, there is still usually an assumption that the ideal family for a child involves having a loving mother and a father, and that this view is maintained by the majority of the population. It is, indeed, difficult to avoid promoting values of one sort or another in this field. I have to admit that I also believe that it is better for a child to have an actively involved father and mother; but it is obvious that their mere presence does not guarantee adequate and effective parenting. For this reason, and because we need to answer specific questions about problem families, I think there is a need to be specific about the nature of parental responsibility, even if definitions have to change as society changes. But because of the difficulty, if not impossibility, of avoiding value judgments, it is probably important to attempt to find criteria for looking at parenting issues which can be applied to a variety of different family constellations.

What seems to be common, and perhaps not too controversial, to most theories of human development, is their stress on how the relationship between parents and children changes as the child grows. It appears to move from one in which there is absolute dependence on the child's parent to relative dependency; or from close, primary ties to the parents to a situation in which these ties are loosened over time. As the responsibility for their children changes, so does the children's responsibility for themselves change. There is a constant and shifting relationship between the parents' and the child's responsibilities. A good enough parent probably needs to recognise these shifts, as indeed do we all, including the media. It is noteworthy how often events involving children, such as those involving acts of violence perpetrated by children, are either seen as all the children's fault, or all the fault of the parents, rather than something which has involved a difficulty in the relationship between parents and children. It is worth noting that the House of Lords ruling on the *Gillick* case concerned the right of a young person under 16 to have contraception against her parents' wishes, provided that she was capable of taking some responsibility for herself and could understand what this involved. Thus the law at that point found common ground both with the findings of child development and with the changes in contemporary society, which had been leading to increasing recognition that parents no longer had total control over their children. The landmark nature of the ruling was that the law recognised and made specific children's rights and the limitations of parental rights, introducing the notion of developing responsibility. Though the judges were right to emphasise that young people can take responsibility for themselves, it is perhaps worth emphasising that very young children also have a right to be dependent on their parents and not have to be responsible prematurely.

Theories of human development also have their own stated or implied theory of human agency, concerning reasons for actions and the nature of human freedom. For example, each theory tries to address how much freedom children have, or should have, in relation to their parent. Most theories seem to state that as the child grows up, there is a need for the caretaker to allow the child increasing freedom to explore and to discover himself, within a reasonably secure environment. But there are also some very difficult issues involved, for example how much freedom to act children may be allowed, how parents may foster children's freedom to think while at the same time offering limitations on their freedom to act, and the issue of how parents can allow children a life of their own, by offering some kind of model with which they can identify, yet which can allow them to find their own way to conduct themselves. There is probably a need for parents and children to be actively negotiating such issues as the children develop. It is certainly my experience with problem families that very often the children are seen as mere extensions of the parents, with little life of their own. Much of the therapeutic work is aimed at changing the parents' perceptions of their children, so that they are no longer seen as mere objects to be used or abused, but as separate and living beings whose identity should be respected and fostered.

In general, I would suggest that parental responsibility consists of the following conditions.

The parents, or parent, needs to provide a reasonably secure physical environment, given limitations on income and social conditions. They need to have the child's needs and interests to the forefront of their thoughts and actions, to allow the young child to be dependent on them, and to allow the developing child increasing freedom and autonomy. They need to appreciate the child's world, with its need for good enough physical and emotional security, reasonable flexibility, appropriate disciplining which does not lead to physical abuse, and warmth and understanding on a daily basis. Parental responsibility involves taking responsibility for one's own emotions as an adult, not exposing the child to adult sexuality, which may lead to sexual abuse. It implies accepting the reality of the child as a separate life developing in his or her own way, but needing guidance and some structure. Parental responsibility also involves recognition of the need for the child gradually to take on more responsibility, and that there is a shifting relationship between child and parental responsibility.

MAIN CRITERIA FOR ASSESSING PARENTAL RESPONSIBILITY

Perhaps the main overall criterion for assessing parental responsibility is the willingness and capacity of parents to take appropriate responsibility for their actions. If parents constantly blame others for their own failings, or if they blame the courts and the social services for all that has gone wrong in their family, then the chances are that the prognosis for change in the family is poor. It may be difficult to be precise about degrees of responsibility, but the capacity of parents to own up their negative thoughts and actual negative and destructive actions sets the tone for any detailed assessment of their parenting.

Particularly difficult judgments about degrees of responsibility arise when assessing a parent who has not actively carried out abuse of a child, but has been indirectly implicated. Of course, parents may be relatively blameless in such circumstances, particularly if they have acted swiftly and effectively and taken appropriate action to make sure their children are safe. Sometimes the 'passive' partner in abuse has been so physically intimidated by the 'active' abuser that she/he has been unable to seek help. Assessing these situations is fairly easy. But, it is the more subtle circumstances that make for difficult assessment judgments. There may be, for example, a mother who has turned a blind eye to what has been going on in the home, and has not been able to notice severe bruising of her child. Clearly, by any ordinary criterion, this is evidence of parental neglect. The prognosis for treatment of such a mother will depend critically on her admitting that she was at fault and to be willing to accept help. Parents who repeatedly blame their abusing partner for all the abuse and cannot see that their own blindness was part of the abusing situation are very difficult, if not impossible, to treat. Sometimes, the complicit partner has only a limited memory of what has taken place in the home, either because of alcohol or drug intoxication during the incidents, or because the memory has been repressed as too painful to bear. A series of interviews in the context of a therapeutic relationship may be necessary to get to the truth of the matter, and before the parent can have access to the memories, particularly when they have been repressed for emotional reasons. Though, it may be important to reconstruct the events which led to the abuse, it may not be possible to know all the details at once. Sometimes it takes months to find out what really happened. It would seem to me usually enough that one has a basic understanding of the events, with a certain amount of detail, particularly when the parent is willing to admit fault and to seek help.

Other aspects of the assessment of parental responsibility include the following major areas of concern.

1   Adequate provision of physical care, including being physically present for the child

This is usually the easiest capacity to assess, as it can be seen by a home visit and by pooling of evidence from outside observers, including nursery and school staff. But the presence of physical care alone is of course no guarantee of good enough parenting. A child may have a comfortable bed, but an adult may be sexually abusing the child in it.

2   Consistency of behaviour and functioning in regard to the child

This includes providing appropriate and safe boundaries for the child, respecting the child's own world, perceiving the child as different from the adult and with different needs, and providing appropriate restraint of adult needs and impulses. It entails the parent keeping the children in mind, particularly, when they are vulnerable and in need of a parent. It probably also involves some capacity to function as an adult, to be able to socialise with adults and not expect a child to take the place of adults for the parent, so that the children do not become little adults. One would expect the parent to have reasonable impulse control, not to expose the child to criminal, delinquent and destructive behaviour. If a parent cannot keep a child safe, then parental responsibility has broken down. Under this heading one could include states of mind which may impair parental responsibility to a greater or lesser extent, such as acute psychosis. Some parents may lose the capacity to parent temporarily due to illness, but may recover it once they are better.

Where there are two parents, it is of course essential to assess the quality of their relationship. Particularly areas to focus on include how much they can communicate between themselves, and how much they use their children as vehicles for communication; their capacity to talk to each other about difficulties; and their capacity to both support one another and yet retain independence. Collusive partnerships, where an abusing parent is backed up by the other partner, despite clear evidence of abuse are of course particularly worrying. One needs to assess the degree to which the collusion is maintained when challenged.

Grey areas include circumstances when children have come to harm when not in an adult's care, for example, if they had been left to play with other children in the road or at a playground. The media repeatedly draw attention to tragic circumstances when a child had been abducted and/or murdered while away from their parents. One may ask at what age a child can be left to play unsupervised. While not willing to provide rigid answers to this question, perhaps one could say that in this day and age, most children of primary school age should have clear guidelines about what is or is not acceptable about where they should play, with whom and for how long they should be absent from their home. Merely allowing a young child to go out to play without clear expectations about what is acceptable may be very risky in contemporary society.

3   Capacity to empathise with the child

One would expect the parent to be able to understand the child's needs and wishes, though the parent may need help in this area, particularly with adolescent children who tax most parents' patience. Empathising implies not expecting the young child to take responsibility for the adult, though it is unfortunately not uncommon for children to feel they are responsible for what goes wrong in a family. Emotional liability or flatness in parents may interfere with their empathy for the children. Empathy includes a capacity to put oneself in the child's shoes, to try to feel what the child feels. This is different from imposing what the parent feels on the child, or not allowing the child to have any sense of being separate from the parents.

In the assessment of empathy, one would look at how parents respond to a child's emotional and physical pain, whether or not they express love and concern, or rejection and hate, and the degree of ambivalence. With mothers and babies, one is particularly looking at the quality of the bond between parent and child, the capacity to keep the baby in mind for the whole day, and to provide adequate intense physical and emotional care.

4   Capacity for trust

A major indicator of parental responsibility is the parent's quality of relating, both as observed in the family relationships and in the relationships between the family and the professionals. It is my experience that often successful work with problem families depends on a process of trust developing between the families and the network of professionals. These are families who have been enormously threatened by the possibility of experiencing feelings of vulnerability or dependency, with the result that their vulnerable and dependent children have been subjected to neglect or abuse. A useful indicator of parental responsibility is the degree to which the professionals feel that they have to take on responsibility for the child. If many professionals are working endlessly around a family in the hope that the family will benefit, and if the professionals are pouring in emotional and financial resources, it is often the case that the family are not engaged in significant work with the professionals, who are in fact really taking over from the parents. Workers close to a family may need supervision in order to extricate themselves from being caught up in the family pathology. This is true when the workers are over involved and over identified with the family, as much as when the workers have an over negative view of the family.

A capacity for play may be an important indicator of a reasonable parent-child relationship, even when other indicators are negative. Such a capacity indicates sufficient trust and intimacy between the child and parent. Woodenness in play, or totally confused play, may be indicative of poor parenting, especially when combined with one or more of the other criteria of parental responsibility.

5   Capacity for change

This would seem to be a crucial area of assessment, involving all the various aspects of parenting. In the end, if parents can change their attitude and behaviour, despite major difficulties, then obviously there is more hope that they can become more effective parents. But judgments about change are difficult to make, and may require observation over a period of time. I have already suggested that a developing capacity for trust is an important prognostic factor. I would add here some developing capacity for insight, and a shift in the quality of their relationships, particularly in the relationship with the children.

6   Historical factors

Many parents who have difficulty taking on parental responsibility have had deprived childhoods, and a number of them have been sexually and/or physically abused as children. Never having being truly allowed to be children themselves, some of these abused adults are compelled to harm their own children. But historical factors in themselves may only indicate risk factors. Not all abusing parents were abused as children, though the great majority have had an emotionally deprived upbringing. In particular, a number of problem parents have been major adolescent problems. Instead of having had an opportunity to grow gradually into adulthood through the transition period of adolescence, they have resorted to premature sexual behaviour, or may have left home early to escape from family difficulties, or have become parents very early and before they were emotionally ready for parenthood.

7   Behavioural criteria

Using each of the above categories, it may be important to focus on specific behavioural criteria of parental responsibility for each family undergoing assessment. For example, it would be important to assess how a family coped with everyday tasks such as eating, sleeping and playing with the children, and then correlate their behaviour with emotional factors. One may look at how consistent and safe their behaviour was in these situations. Observations in an out-patient clinic alone may not really show up the family's day-to-day functioning. It may be important to make observations in the home, or the foster home were appropriate.

8   Pooling information

It is often necessary to pool information about problem families from a variety of sources, including from social services, mental health workers, general practitioners, health visitors, paediatric facilities, schools, nurseries, play groups, relatives, friends, neighbours, the police, the probation services and the courts. Sometimes it is necessary to meet the relevant workers before making an assessment, in order to clarify essential details and to get a feel for the professional relationships. One has to weigh up the usefulness of such a prior meeting against the possibility of prejudging the issues before actually seeing the family. I personally prefer where possible to see the family first for myself. I like to focus on the quality of the relationships between the parents and the children, because in the end that is what will determine what happens to the family. It is surprising how often I am expected to do an assessment of a family without the children. I virtually never agree to doing an assessment without seeing the children

THIRD SESSION

with the parents. Without observations of what actually takes place between them, one may be foiled into being too optimistic or pessimistic about the parents' capacities. Subsequently, one may have to see the workers, including foster parents, in order to match up one's own observations with those of other professionals.

CLINICAL EXAMPLES

Making judgments about parenting capacities is in the end a complicated matter, involving fitting together a number of different elements, including direct observation of the family and information from other workers. I have tried to indicate the main areas on which to focus, but in the end it is the total picture that has to be kept in mind, and that is often a very difficult task, given the often extreme anxieties aroused by problem families, and the many detailed about their current and past lives that have to be examined. I think one has to avoid trying to explain everything about a family's current life by means of their past, because one may avoid the current issues of safety to the children. Yet at the same time, it is obviously important to have some understanding of what went on in the past, in order to assess what might happen in the future. I have chosen to present details from three difficult assessments, in order to highlight the complexity of this work, as well as to give some guidance in an often confused and anxiety provoking field. I shall also tackle some treatment issues as it is often difficult and indeed unrealistic to sharply distinguish assessment from treatment, as the assessment process involves looking at the capacity to change and to respond to treatment. In addition, treatment often involves continuing assessment of parental responsibility, based on several or all of the elements I have outlined.

Example One: Mr and Mrs A and daughter B

These parents, in their mid twenties, had mild learning problems. Their 9-month-old daughter had been removed from them following non-accidental injury at the age of 6 months, when the parents presented at casualty. Mother was apparently the perpetrator. The child was placed in a foster home, and care proceedings were begun. When assessed by a specialist unit, there was great worry expressed about the parents' capacity to look after their child. Mother in particular seemed quite inept in her handling of the baby. Father, who was better with the physical care, was very angry with his wife. The couple hardly communicated, and there was not much hope that they could have their child back. On the other hand, Mother was full of guilt and remorse about what had happened, and the couple were desperate to have their child back. They co-operated with the social service plans, including keeping up regular access visits.

When I saw the family, I was also struck by the quality of the remorse, which seemed genuine enough. But there was a certain amount of ambiguity about the injuries. Mother insisted, when pressed, that the trouble had been that she had let the baby's head hit the pram. She denied that she had thrown the baby across the room onto the wall, as had been suspected from the nature of the injuries. Although I had considerable doubts about the couple's capacities, we thought it worthwhile admitting them for a 6-week assessment, in order to test out their capacity to change and to find out more about the abuse. We arranged that they would be admitted first of all without the baby, in order to settle in. The baby, who went home for most weekends to the foster home during the admission, was then admitted after about one week. At once, the couple showed how dependent they were; they made themselves homeless on the day of admission, and we had to insist that they find accommodation, in this case a bed and breakfast hotel. Although both parents were immature and needy, there was some benefit in the fact that they moved out of a difficult family environment, the home of the paternal grandmother. Indeed, as came out, the abuse took place in the context of a difficult relationship between Mrs A and her mother-in-law. Mr A's loyalties were very divided, and he came across as very unsupportive to his wife.

At first, Mr A, took over the care of baby B, while mother was very clumsy with her. But soon this situation changed in that she became more confident, and indeed the baby started to flourish and look well, despite the fact that the fostering arrangements broke down and another foster family had to be found at short notice. The severe pathology in the couple's relationship soon became evident. Mr A revealed a history of violence, going back to his rather delinquent adolescence. He showed a great lack of trust in his wife. On the other hand, he doted on his daughter. Mother felt from early on in the pregnancy that the husband was only interested in her being pregnant in order to have his child not for any other reason. She had become the receptacle for a number of his projections, eg that she would be unable to keep the foetus safe. His daughter represented for him the ideal baby that could overcome all his own childhood damage.

In our assessment, it was clear how difficult it was to come to a clear decision about the possibility of rehabilitation, as we were still not clear about the parents' own capacity to change enough to be able to be effective parents for their daughter. We felt that it would not damage the baby to extend the assessment for a further period, particularly in view of the fact that the fostering had been interrupted. I was particularly surprised that the baby had flourished. This could not be accounted for simply by being in a supportive environment. In my experience, it does require the mother in particular to be providing something good for this kind of phenomenon to occur. But we were not happy to go ahead with treatment. Instead, we proposed to reassess the family and to have clearer answers to the following points. We needed to know more about the abuse. We kept almost hearing what was probably the truth, but the mother kept backing off from fully admitting to her violent impulses, which clearly took place in the context of both a difficult marriage and family environment. We were also quite suspicious about the father's role. He came across as a man seething with rage, but who could hardly dare admit this openly, except when it concerned his wife. The couple needed to be more engaged with others in the hospital and be less dependent on them.

The next period of assessment in fact quite soon gave a much clearer answer. After an initial period of unrealistic euphoria from the mother, who believed we were recommending treatment, when we were still in fact not certain about what was best, the true picture became clearer. In a sense, nothing new was learned, in that the couple did not shift. Mother maintained that the injuries were essentially accidental, and the couple were unwilling to budge in the story. In addition, and crucially, the baby rapidly lost weight. We acted quickly and removed the baby back into the foster home during the week. Our next assessment meeting was difficult, particularly as we routinely have the parents in during the meeting; but it was clear that rehabilitation was not possible, and that the baby needed to have a permanent placement, preferably adoption. Due to its young age, it was likely that there would be no access to the parents after the adoption.

One might ask why we bothered with the assessment in the first place, given the obvious parental difficulties. After all, there were problems in most of the areas I have outlined. The mother had difficulty providing basic physical care of the baby; she could not play with the baby; there was a basic unwillingness to own up to the injuries, given the medical and forensic evidence; the marital relationship was very difficult, with intense mutual projective processes; and the couple did not readily trust professionals. I would agree that there were always great doubts about the couple's capacity for change. But the workers felt it important to test this out. Indeed, at first it did seem that this was a wise decision, in that the baby began to flourish. But clearly our caution was correct. The change was not sustainable. I suspect that the main reason for this was when it came to it, the mother did not want the baby. In fact, it was quite noticeable that once her daughter was removed from the hospital, she herself began to brighten up. We did offer some treatment for the couple, for which funding became available, but the father in particular did not wish it. The couple left the hospital together and apparently united, but angry with us having made our decision.

Example Two: Mrs D and daughter E aged 3

This single mother, in her twenties and diagnosed as having Munchausen Syndrome by Proxy, administered a household substance to her eldest daughter until she nearly died. The child was removed permanently, but the mother, who was on a probation order, was admitted to the Cassel with the younger daughter for assessment. At first, mother was aloof and showed little capacity for empathy with her child, whom she treated like an object; and she showed little remorse for what she had done. She soon became enraged when challenged, and we felt that there was little chance for rehabilitation. At the out-patient assessment there had been some signs of empathy with the child and some willingness to seek help, but that had apparently changed on admission. Mother used the child for comfort, often sleeping with her at night. On most of the criteria I have outlined, this mother seemed to fail to show the necessary degree of parental responsibility. However, just before the formal assessment meeting was due, we made it clear to her that we were unlikely to be offering help. This produced both panic, and then the sudden revelation that she herself had been subjected to repeated sexual abuse as a child by a family member. Though sceptical at first, we took the allegation seriously, and it turned out to appear to be genuine. The revelation coincided with her suddenly showing a more vulnerable and less aloof side to her character, which in time made her more amenable to treatment.

However, treatment was difficult and stormy at times. We had to constantly focus on the essential parenting issues. Mother showed a supersensitivity to separations from her daughter, who continued to live at a foster home until we felt more able to trust the mother's capacities to empathise with the child. Mother seemed at times to be near to disintegration when near to expressing feelings of dependency. At other times she would go into omnipotent and bullying states, when she believed that she had the right to do what she liked to herself and her daughter.

Assessment of her mothering capacities was a constant and ongoing process, and very much part of the treatment process itself. Slowly in treatment she began to develop a capacity to feel for her daughter's state of mind as well as her own, that is a capacity for empathy. She also began to tolerate and express her aggression towards staff, other patients and particularly her male therapist. What seemed to become clearer in the therapy was that she had little inner maternal representation; the image of herself as a mother was very damaged and fragmented. It seems a crucial piece of work when she was more able to acknowledge her critical, poisonous side. She was then more able to present a more integrated sense of identity. She seemed less fragmented as a person and coincidentally less dangerous to her child. Her daughter, meanwhile, appeared to become more robust and less caught up with her mother. There are still concerns some two years after discharge, but mother is more trusting of professional help.

Example Three: Mrs E and son, A aged 10

Mother, in her late thirties, was diagnosed as schizophrenic. She and her son were referred in order to clarify whether or not she could look after her son permanently, or whether he would remain in his long-term foster home. The boy, who had been removed from her care a couple of years previously because of her mental state and mothering difficulties, was placed in a foster home where he was subjected to sexual abuse. He was then placed in a safe foster family; but obviously there was major concern about what had happened; and the local authority, who were being sued by the mother, felt that they had to make every attempt to look into the family situation and to fully assess the mother's capacities to care for her son in the long term.

Mother had a long psychiatric history. As a child she was severely sexually abused. Her mother was a prostitute and the patient was involved as a child in pornography. She spent much of her childhood in care, and was also sexually abused in foster care. She began to cut herself around puberty, and as a result she was placed in a variety of residential placements which could not contain her. She finally ended up in a secure unit. She had a history of alcohol and hard drug abuse, and was eventually diagnosed a schizophrenic. She suffers from auditory hallucinations and delusions, and has periods of acute breakdown requiring acute admission. She also had lost several children because of her problems.

On admission, she was on depot injections of major tranquillizers. In the 6-week assessment period, mother was co-operative. In individual therapy sessions, she came across as mechanical, emotionally cut off and fragmented at times. However, as the admission proceeded, she was able to express more of her anger about the abuse of her son, yet she also maintained an unrealistic view of her capacity to look after him. In small group sessions, she was, in contrast, surprisingly able to relate to the others and the situation, becoming at times the most insightful member of the group. But in general she was only just able to hold herself together by means of nursing and patient support. She was out of touch with her child's needs. She described how she needed him in order to 'keep her boundaries'.

Her son was able to use the therapeutic setting well. He expressed in moving terms, in his individual sessions, a deep sadness and a wish for stability. Memories of the sexual abuse kept breaking through. He was happy in his foster home, but also fond of his mother, and wished to continue to see her.

Because of the mother's great difficulties in being in touch with her son in a realistic way, it was clear to us at the assessment meeting that we could not possibly offer rehabilitation. But we offered instead to do focal work with both of them to help them to say goodbye. But we also aimed to help the mother to be able to maintain some limited access to the foster home. Until then, access had been unrealistic as she had been angry with, and suspicious of, the foster parents.

A further 4-month period of treatment with the mother was begun, while the son returned to the foster home. There were a few meetings with the son and the mother and son together. We also facilitated meetings between mother and foster parents. This was a very difficult time for the mother. She felt drawn to her world of violent destructiveness, with drink, drugs and sexual promiscuity. She began to hear voices and to break down. However, we increased her major tranquillizers for the while, and were able to keep her going through this period. She found a 'voice' for herself with the other mothers, and also established a good relationship with her nurse. She became able to talk more realistically in therapy sessions about her own abuse, her wish to destroy men, and her ability to get into abusing relationships with the world, including social services. By discharge, she had a friendly relationship with the foster carers, and arrangements were made for regular access visits. Her son was also able to see how unrealistic it was for him to live permanently with his mother, and further therapy was arranged for him.

I think that the treatment was successful because we kept to a focal task as a result of our assessment. We were not aiming to cure the mother, but to help her deal with the specific issue of letting her son go. The process of allowing separation in this instance required in-patient treatment because of her constant pull towards psychotic breakdown. In her own words, she needed her son to keep her sane. Without the hope of him being there for her, she began to go mad again and thus needed in-patient holding.

DISCUSSION

The three clinical examples I have presented involved particularly difficult assessments. However, the three questions I raised earlier informed the decision-making process. In each case, we had to answer the question of whether or not the children were safe with their parents and whether or not to recommend treatment, once we had established as far as possible the quality of the parents' relationships with their children. In the first example, though there were signs that the parents might change enough to become safe, in the end they were unable to do so. They continued to deny their responsibility for the abuse to their daughter, and the mother could not in the end bear to be close to her child. The mother in the second case was able to reveal a more human and vulnerable side, once the reality of her own childhood abuse was revealed. While in the third case, we were able to both recommend continued removal of a child yet at the same time offer a therapeutic opportunity for both mother and child, despite the mother's severe pathology.

Each assessment we do opens up complex and difficult clinical and, indeed, social issues. In making these assessments, we hope to be acting in the interests of the child; but we also come up against society's problems, expectations and dilemmas concerning the nature of the family. I have tried to convey an approach that can be applied both rigorously and humanely across different social and ethnic conditions.

I should say that there have been times when our recommendations have been diametrically opposed to the opinion of social services. Sometimes we have been proved right, sometimes they have been proved right. The rehabilitation of one case at the Cassel was held up for nearly two years because of the opinion of a social service department, and needed the intervention of an independent expert and a High Court case before our own opinion carried the day. However, these situations are happily fairly rare. Though there may be differences of opinion, most situations can be resolved provided professionals are willing to make time to get together to share information. Just meeting in a room can almost of itself be therapeutic to a case.

So often misperceptions and negative fantasies about other workers dominate the workers around families. For example, not infrequently workers, particularly lawyers, think that our Unit is rather harsh to patients because we expect so much of them. They are so used to hearing complaints about the hospital that they are often taken aback when they actually visit and rather like being on the Unit, and even find it friendly.

Our own research findings in general match the experience of Great Ormond Street (Elton, 1988) who have divided assessment of outcome into hopeful, doubtful and hopeless, depending on the degree to which the parents take responsibility for what has happened in the family, whether they can recognise their children's needs and the quality of family attachments.

Our own formal research (Fonagy, Kennedy et al, 1996) has so far shown that parents who have experienced abuse as children but who show a capacity for self-reflection during assessment and treatment are able to deal more effectively both with their abuse and show evidence of change in their parenting capacities.

Other research on our treatment programme (Healey and Kennedy, 1993) had indicated that families benefit from treatment when their parent or parents can remember at least one good childhood relationship; when they own up to any abuse; and when they can engage in a reasonable treatment process, when the child and the parent–child relationship can be attended to.

Making effective assessments is obviously a vital part of work in the child care field, for it is on this basis that decisions as to the future of a child are made. I have tried to indicate specific areas of parenting that need to be looked at in any assessment. But there are other factors often at work in these cases that may interfere with the assessment process. One common finding in dealing with the problem family is that workers may be so caught up in the confusion and uncertainty of the family that they forget the basic principles of the work, that of keeping the best interests of the child to the forefront. Instead of making a thorough assessment of need, workers may take unhelpful attitudes that merely reflect the family's pathology. In a sense, these attitudes are a part of the assessment but only if there is the possibility of looking at what is going on through, for example, peer support of supervision from seniors or outside consultants.

A main issue in any assessment and treatment of the problem family is how to encourage parents to take on parental responsibility once they have partly or totally given it up, while not taking over from them. It is particularly difficult for the professional to stand by while a parent is actively rejecting a child or is not relating well to a child. The professional usually wants to intervene and prevent the child from suffering. While this attitude is understandable and may be essential, there are also times when it is just as important to stand back and allow the parents to discover, or recover, responsibility rather than take it away. In treating problem families, there is a constant tension between the need to intervene and the need to foster responsibility by not taking over. In order to have an effective assessment of the degree to which a parent can change, it is necessary for the worker to be able to see when they can stand back and when they simply have to intervene. This is not an easy task, especially these days, when anxieties about being negligent abound, and when time for the assessment and basic facilities are in short supply.

THIRD PLENARY SESSION

DISCUSSION

This took the form of a question and answer session.

(a) How did the 'time scale of the child' dovetail with the assessment of parents' capacity for change?

Dr Kennedy said that a delicate balance had to be drawn between giving the parents another chance and affecting the child's ability to make attachments at any given age. Thus, a baby's needs were the most urgent, because research had shown that adoptions had a much better chance of success when the adoptee is a baby capable of making early, long-lasting attachments.

However, if the child had reached the age of eight or nine years, it was probable that there was pre-existing damage from a lack of proper attachment and so there may not be undue harm if additional time was given to an assessment.

The time to be allowed was a matter of professional experience – for example, if a baby was nine months old (see example Baby B) an assessment totalling three months may well be reasonable in all the circumstances.

(b) What were the criteria upon which an assessment was made?

Dr Kennedy said that an assessment was based upon all the evidence which had been allocated up to that point – including interviews with the family and Dr Kennedy's 'hunch'.

He stressed that the criteria set out in his written paper reinforced and informed his thinking, but his assessment was primarily based upon the experience of working with numerous deprived families. It was essential for the family to acknowledge that they 'had problems' and to be willing 'to change'. If a family made these two 'admissions' then, provided that there was not a significant level of violence or drug abuse, he was willing to work with any family.

(c) At what point should an assessment be made?

A referral to the Cassel Hospital was appropriate when all local agencies had failed and yet, it was still felt that an attempt should be made to keep the family together.

(d) Was there a model which could be applied at the outset of an assessment?

It was not possible to apply a simple model because assessments were based on 'life experiences' and a 'mish mash' of other factors. Thus, each family has its own particular needs which were not susceptible of resolution by formula. Indeed, each hospital unit had its own particular method of assessment. For example, the Tavistock Clinic operated a day clinic which carried out similar assessments over six separate days with very basic criteria – such as: (1) did the parents attend the initial meeting?; and (2) did they acknowledge, even for a short period, that there was a problem in the family and that their children had a right to be considered?

(e) What sort of families attend the Cassel Hospital?

Dr Kennedy explained that a family would be appropriately referred to the Cassel Hospital, if all other methods of keeping the family together had been tried and failed – but the judge still felt that there was some 'hope' for a good relationship in the longer term. However, in order for there to be a successful outcome, there had to be a genuine acknowledgment that something had gone wrong and the parents had to accept that they had played a part in the difficulties.

The ability of parents to accept that they had been responsible for failures within the family differed in each case. Moreover, many parents considered that admissions of failure were 'dangerous' in the context of outstanding legal proceedings because such admissions might be used against them. This dilemma for parents was acknowledged although most practitioners felt that abusive parents were surprisingly open in the context of a clinical interview and were often prepared to acknowledge fault on their own behalf.

To have a successful outcome parents had to acknowledge that: (1) there were problems within their family; (2) those problems were their fault and not the fault of some external agency; and (3) they needed help. As parents might find it easier to accept that certain forms of abuse had taken place, the acceptance of responsibility could not be seen as a unitary phenomenon. Parents should not be expected to 'own up to everything' but had to accept a level of responsibility for their actions. In order to work with parents it was necessary to build up a relationship based on trust with the result that it was often counter productive to approach matters by concentrating on particular incidents (which focused on the negative aspects of parents' behaviour). It was important to seek aspects to good parenting because families in this situation often felt 'powerless and on the spot'.

(f) How was it possible to work with the fact that parents feel helpless and trapped?

Dr Kennedy stressed that a good outcome would only be achieved if the parents felt safe enough to tell the doctor of their fears and needs. The work of the Cassel Hospital could only be accomplished in combination with the network of other professionals who had been involved in the case. Whilst this might be difficult to organise and, to an extent depended on resources, it offered the best solution. Dr Kennedy stressed that for a family 'on the edge', a good social worker would often make the difference between the assessment succeeding or failing. Moreover, whilst the Government had sought to ensure a co-ordinated approach to the recognition and assessment of child abuse within the framework of *Working Together*, it had provided less guidance in relation to the proper management of a family after such a finding had been made. Indeed, there was no integrated planning at that stage with the result that, in reality, long term success or failure was often a matter of resources rather than proper planning.

FOURTH SESSION

Trudy Klauber

INTRODUCTION TO HER PAPER

Trudy Klauber introduced her paper (which was additional to the papers originally circulated) by explaining that, in her work as a child psychotherapist, she was concerned with a child's internal world. As children are often unable to explain their problems coherently, observation is all important. The work of a child psychotherapist involves absorbing and thinking about the intense emotional impact – as with all such experts. A child often communicates through play, assigning a role or set of characteristics to the therapist. This 'transference' often affects the expert's own emotions (countertransference). Trudy Klauber acknowledged that these sessions and her own reactions to them and thinking about them were not objective evidence, but they give her insight into children's experiences and their real feelings, and are deserving of much more consideration in important decision-making processes.

Most child psychotherapists still work in London or the South East, but there are now some 35 to 40 child psychotherapists practising outside London and it was important that details of these practitioners be made more widely available. A list of addresses of organisations was attached to her paper. Child psychotherapists are not play therapists, but psycho-analytic psychotherapists with a lengthy training and a long, intensive personal analysis – partly to safeguard the vulnerable children who are offered psychotherapy or assessments of their needs.

CHILD PSYCHOTHERAPY: WHAT IS IT? WHO DOES IT? HOW CAN IT BE USEFUL?

Trudy Klauber, Consultant Child Psychotherapist, Donald Winnicott Centre, Queen Elizabeth Hospital for Children, London

INTRODUCTION

Training in child psychotherapy is lengthy, lasting at least 4 years, more often up to 6, at post-graduate level, and after a minimum of 2 years' work in an associated field (teaching, social work, psychology, medicine, with experience of direct work with children of all ages, and with their families).

THE SIGNIFICANCE OF LEARNING TO OBSERVE

The underpinning of the training lies in *observation*. The task is given to all trainees of finding a family where a baby is about to be born, and to arrange, with the parents' permission, to visit once a week, for an hour, for a period of 2 years, in order to observe a baby growing in her family. We are expected to be observers but not blocks of stone, to be friendly but not to make overtures in terms of talk or comment on what we see, nor to talk about ourselves. We are trained *not* to jump to conclusions. We are truly there to learn what it is for a baby to grow up in a 'normal' family. After each visit, we write a description of all that we can remember of that hour in as much detail and with as much accuracy as we can manage. Some teachers encourage students to include a description of what they were feeling and thinking, if it seems to be noteworthy. We attend seminars where we take turns to present our observations, with an experienced teacher leading the group. Most often, many of us develop more skill at observing in great detail as the weeks pass, although initially we are reliant on the seminar and its leader to assist in offering any understanding of the meaning of what is happening for the baby and her family during any of the observations we bring for discussion.

We discover what a painful and fascinating task we are undertaking, learning that alone, without support and the benefit of the group's thoughts and capacity to 'hold' the experience for us, we may 'know' very little, and understand rather less. The seminar group functions as a safe place to share the events, feelings and difficulties of being an observer with others who are sharing the same task. The group offers to the observer something akin to one of the most important, and least tangible, aspects of good parenting; holding things together, remaining intact under the onslaught of the raw, non-verbal communications of very early infantile experience.

LINKS BETWEEN OBSERVATION AND THE GROWTH OF SOUND, NON-JUDGMENTAL, CLINICAL OBSERVATION

The group uses its collective mind to gather together raw data until ideas and meaning begin to emerge. Again and again it becomes evident in infant observation, that being open to the experience of the baby is intense, nerve-wracking and awe-inspiring. The impact of the baby's point of view is normally *so* much diluted, by other activities, by distance from it, and by the usual adult defences. Even mothers (if they are the 'significant caregivers') seem, over time, to lose some of the exposed openness and emotional availability which is so apparent, and sometimes so upsetting to observe in the early weeks. We endeavour, within the seminar, to develop ways of thinking about events and sequences of observation which may then begin to make sense. We also see how development is extraordinarily unpredictable, week by week, so we have to live with uncertainty about how the child will develop. Anxiety can be great at times, and we need to keep all these tidal waves of feelings, impressions and thoughts inside us, when we are with the families. Notes are not taken during the observations, just as they are not taken during psychotherapy sessions with children and young people. The ability to memorise, and the capacity to hold events and details in mind and to depend on that capacity, increases with time.

Some of us are also given the opportunity to undertake the same task with nursery age children, either at home or in nursery, playgroup or school, and to see and experience, at first hand, the rich and dramatic lives of little children in their pre-school years. Through these first experiences in training, we learn an enormous amount about a sample of four or five infants and four or five toddlers, who are not chosen to be observed because of their pathology, but, we hope, because there is likely to be an absence of it.

THE PROFESSIONALS' DEFENCES AGAINST SEEING WHAT IS TO BE SEEN, INDIVIDUALLY AND COLLECTIVELY

My emphasis on learning about observation, *at the beginning of our training*, is based on the belief that *observation could and should become a much greater part of all professional life, particularly where children are involved*. It is often extremely difficult to see what we see, and to feel what we feel. Professional roles can shield us very effectively so that we cannot and do not process our observations and allow them to have an impact upon us. The roles encourage a divorce between the private and the public in us, and between the adult point of view and that more intuitive and spontaneous perspective which links with our own childhood experience, which may include painful experiences of loss, fear and high anxiety.

While the shielding has its undoubted importance (in accomplishing certain tasks with the necessary calm and minimum interference), it also carries with it the potential to 'forget' or to lose touch with certain aspects of ourselves, especially the difficult bits. When we do get out of touch with 'forgotten' parts of ourselves, we may be hindered in using what some psychological professionals call 'the capacity to identify', and more simply, what poets and writers have called 'sympathetic understanding' based on taking in with the senses, and with the emotions, what seems to be going on. John Steiner (unpublished paper, 1995), the psychoanalyst, has recently suggested that the striving for sympathetic understanding through close observation of the patient and himself, in the consulting room, leads to the possibilities of restoring some sense of balance in interactions where he has found himself becoming judgmental and distant, to the detriment of the patient's real (and child-like) need for tolerance and concern.

Our psychological defences are many and varied. We seek to avoid the difficulties, the discomfort and the upset which may feel like catastrophic incursions into our own mental balance. In the family courts, and written about in the Conference papers, are stories of the lives of children, which *are* almost unbearable to hear. Yet decisions must be taken about evidence which is given, about 'expert' opinion offered, in the best interests of the child. In the court room, as everywhere, the impact on all present, including judges and expert witnesses, of unconscious and powerful forces can temporarily create imbalance in individual minds and on the mind of the group (or the court). Within any group of people gathered together for a particular purpose, task-oriented work can be accomplished very effectively, with many points of view taken into account. There is, none the less, a grave danger of going off task and into states of mind where attempts to maintain the status quo and to avoid internal upset become unconsciously dominant and overwhelmingly powerful, especially in the face of the need to make difficult decisions. Examples of fights between experts, or between witness and judge, might indicate such mentality within a courtroom, where the real task could be lost in the heat of some quite irrational alternative activity which can be difficult to halt.

PERSONAL PSYCHOANALYSIS: 'KNOW THYSELF' AND LEARNING TO TRUST SUBJECTIVE DATA

The child psychotherapist, who, like all psychodynamically trained practitioners, has had a personal analysis, from three to five times weekly, for anything from 5 to 10 or more years, comes to know those parts of herself which are likely to resonate with certain children, events or histories. While the analysis is seen as a safeguard against inflicting our own pathology on our patients, it is more than that. It is what underpins our training. We learn slowly and painstakingly, not only to observe minutely the details of the psychotherapeutic session itself, but also how we ourselves react, feel and think in the presence of our patients, children, adolescents and their parents. We take this information, or 'evidence' seriously and use it as part of the framework through which we begin to get some kind of grasp on the reality the patient is trying to convey to us. Personal supervision during training, and afterwards, for most of us, provides another perspective to combine with our own in an attempt to verify and clarify the nature and meaning of patients' communications.

TRANSFERENCE AND COUNTER-TRANSFERENCE

Within any psychoanalytic session, much time is devoted, in the psychotherapist's mind, to trying to work out the nature of the 'transference'. Within the quiet, neutral setting of the consulting room, we find ourselves in a position to observe that patients, of all kinds and all ages, treat us as if we were someone other than the person we feel ourselves to be. So, to give a simple illustration, we might greet the patient in a fairly friendly way and enter the room. only to find ourselves being accused of being cold, stern or hostile. If we are not behaving in that way, and do not find that we feel such feelings towards the patient, then, where does this attitude originate, and why are we being treated in this way? It is an extraordinary fact of all human interaction that people *transfer* on to other people a role or part in a personal drama. In the consulting room, we are experienced in a way which is not of our making, but of theirs; we are treated as if we were, in reality, a character originating in their internal world. Thus, we take for granted, that we will be treated on different occasions, or within the same session as if we were variously, benign, and perhaps supportive, extremely hostile or beatifically perfect. We may find, as we observe more closely, that we are being seen as a child, not the adult we believe ourselves to be, and that the child in question is one who is acutely disliked, feared or despised by the patient. We may also be cast in the role of a warm but corrupting or cold abuser, to be mistrusted or placated by the child. We may be seen as an adult who is extremely cut off and out of touch with children, or one who actively hates them. These dramas, with children, in particular, are often enacted through play, and while we are, as adults, aware that this *is* play there is a counterpart to the drama. The emotional experiences which accompany the dramatic events described or enacted and played out in therapy sessions very often evoke acutely strong emotional responses within us. This 'counter-transference', as Freud originally named it, is the strongest evidence we get within the therapeutic setting, of the reality of the patient's experience, and the nature of the character and drama which is enacted on his internal, mental stage. The way in which children are treated within this internal world, the kinds of parents which are present there, are the blueprints by which all of us, children and adults alike, live our lives. This *internal* reality is the one we believe and the one we live by. External reality and external events clearly have an impact upon the internal, and may modify it one way or another. Internal reality is, in fact, so powerful, although unconscious, that it can dominate in such a way as to act against an individual's best interests, and may lead to self-destructive and even suicidal, homicidal or violent acts.

A final comment on counter-transference. The psychotherapist's emotional response to what is being communicated by the patient provides a sense of veracity when some things are told to us, or allows us to doubt a story, when we feel our response to be out of line with what might be expected. It allows us to feel confident that when our senses and our internal experiences do not coincide, we need to try to understand what the meaning might be. We begin to trust a feeling of warmth and sympathy towards one patient, while another, telling the same story, evinces suspicion, or dislike or absence of much feeling at all. Clearly, learning to believe in such feeling is one thing. It must be supported by other evidence within sessions. There is also a danger that the therapist's own emotions are being mistaken for the patient's. Personal analysis continues to play its part in distinguishing the one from the other, until the therapist has developed sufficient self-understanding to be able to think fairly clearly about what happens between herself and a patient. In addition, most of us continue to have supervision (the personally-sought equivalent of using the group to 'hold' the experiences of infant observation) to allow us to describe and to think in detail about what has gone on between us and a patient.

ASSESSMENT AND THERAPEUTIC JUDGMENT

We are building a picture on observation and, of course, on theories of 'attachment' or 'object relations' which can allow the description of a detailed and testable notion of what the child's and parents' internal situation could be like. The internal images, or 'mental representations' of adult figures, which children, and all of us, carry around with us, are felt by child psychotherapists, and other psychodynamic psychotherapists, to be the blueprint mentioned above. This blueprint will determine, to a large extent, how actual, real adults will be experienced or treated by the child. It will determine repeated patterns of behaviour, so that earlier patterns may be seen again and again, despite marked differences in the actual circumstances of the child's current life. It most certainly shows, for example, when good, well-planned placements for children break down, despite the best efforts of social workers and foster carers. It indicates how external reality can be terribly distorted by what some children have made of their experiences.

It is often the case that child psychotherapy assessments take a long time, precisely because the gathering of the pieces to build the picture from the child's point of view can take a number of meetings with the child, and can take further time to form coherently in the mind of the therapist. Within the picture, we develop a sense of what the adult figures (sometimes called internal mental representations, or objects, or significant attachment figures) are like within the child's mind. Are they trustworthy or perfidious, supportive or unfriendly, encouraging and lively or flat and unresponsive. This exploration of these figures also allows us to see the child's own response to them. One may, to use a simple example, see that a boy most often identifies with the aggressor rather than the victim within an internal scene in which there is often conflict between the strong and the weak. We are looking too at the strengths of children and young people, how they communicate, and whether they have the capacity to feel and to think (perhaps only a little, in assessment) about painful reality.

There is now a growing body of evidence, about adult attachments, as well as those of children, which suggests that those who can describe or put into some words, painful experiences like loss, are more likely to be able to make reasonable attachments, to work on the repair of internal damage, and to be helped in developing their capacity to think about themselves and others with concern. Child psychotherapy assessment is always a combination of creating a picture of the internal, unconscious world of the patient, and of putting some aspects of it to him, to see whether he can share an interest in it and whether or not he has any desire to take help if it is offered.

Very often assessments from child psychotherapists are done within the context of a team's work. We are accustomed to working with psychiatrist and social work colleagues in particular, and in bringing together a variety of points of view in an attempt to gather a more coherent view. Our powerful tools are primarily directed to creating a picture of the internal situation, in families, between parent and child or within the child himself. We need the wider external context as it is understood and explored by colleagues. There is, perhaps, too little emphasis these days on the opinion of the child mental health *team*, which is also a model of the teaching seminar in child psychotherapy training itself, allowing points of view which can be in conflict to co-exist in a space where balanced conclusions may be reached.

It is often difficult, within the context of child psychotherapy alone, to offer 'hard' evidence for court proceedings. None the less, our conclusions about what might really have happened to children, as distinct from what might be seen as likely to be phantasy, can be taken seriously. We can offer observations and descriptions of our own experience with children, as patients, or in assessment, which stand up to scrutiny. We are able to say what evidence our conclusions are based on, and then to allow the courts and the judges to assess the sense of accuracy in what we report. For this reason, our reports and assessments are likely to be quite lengthy, with good reason. Arriving at conclusions about children's lives and experiences does and should take time. It should also be noted that the child psychotherapist's opinion and the basis on which it is formed should stand up to questioning. There is a foundation to it, based on observation, theoretical framework and therapeutic experience which should lend it veracity under criticism. There is a distinction betweeen healthy questioning and out and out attack on psychoanalysis. The former will be welcomed by psychotherapists who have the child's best interests at heart.

CHILD PSYCHOTHERAPY AND ASPECTS OF SEXUALITY

The language used by child psychotherapists, and other psychoanalytic psychotherapists is often believed to be sexually explicit. An accusation may then follow; ideas of a sexual nature, or about sexual activity are put into the minds of child patients by child psychotherapists. Such ideas taint evidence and 'lead' the child. Then the understanding of what is meant by infantile sexuality becomes confused with adult knowledge of the sexual act. Children, as Freud (1905) described at the beginning of the twentieth century, have always had theories about sexual activity. They can become sexually aroused, and can link their own, sometimes, excited states of mind, with feelings which Freud linked with the Oedipus complex. The widely held opinion about oedipal feelings is that all children have adult sexual desires towards the parent of the opposite sex and hostile wishes towards the other parent. In fact, infantile sexual theories and phantasies are based on feelings of excitement, jealousy, anxiety and hostility mixed with muddled ideas about feeding, evacuating, genital arousal and other bodily sensations which creates for each child a unique picture of what they believe adults actually do when the child is not present.

Part of the child psychotherapist's role is to try to build a picture of the child patient's ideas and to help to put them into words which can be consciously considered. Within this framework we are extremely unlikely to use words which the child has not used, and we do not provide education as part of our work. Where children have actually been physically or sexually abused, we are often placed in the difficult position of being given a role, in the transference, of abuser or victim, just as with severely deprived or neglected children we are likely to be made into dupes or victims again. It is now well known that with such children we need to be extremely careful about using particular kinds of language, especially when children are so disturbed or confused by their life experiences that they cannot distinguish between symbolic and concrete. It also becomes essential to follow the child's ideas and language closely so as not to introduce something new, which may be felt as an actual intrusion or assault, or a threat to the beginnings of a precarious experience for the child, of beginning to feel a little understood, or recognising that the therapist is not the character she was perceived to be. This does not always protect the child psychotherapist, particularly the man, from being accused of abuse by children. The truly infantile needs of children, as distinct from their wishes, are actually what preoccupies us most frequently, so that we are more likely to be considering the kind of parent the child has in mind, rather than concentrating on the sexual excitement and talk which is so often used as a distraction against the pain of neglect, cruelty or indifference from the adult to the child in need.

I do not intend to dismiss the difficulty of working within a framework where questions about actual physical cruelty and sexual assault are so important, not least to their distorting impact on any child's view of the adult world and its values. However, child psychotherapy, as I understand it, is more concerned with the overall needs of the child for containment, understanding, predictability and support, and sadly, with the frequent absence of what Donald Winnicott (1972) called the 'good-enough' parent all children ought to have.

REFERENCES

Freud, S (1905) *Three Essays on the Theory of Sexuality – Chapter II: Infantile Sexuality* Standard Edition VII London: Hogarth Press
Winnicott, D (1972) *The Matrimonial Process and the Facilitating Environment* London: Hogarth Press

USEFUL ADDRESSES

Association of Child Psychotherapists
120 West Heath Road
London NW3 7TU
Tel: 0171 794 8111 (call will be transferred to new number)
Fax: 0181 458 1482

The Child Psychotherapy Trust
120 West Heath Road
London NW3 7TU
Tel: 0181 458 1411
Fax: 0181 458 1482

The Anna Freud Centre[1]
21 Maresfield Gardens,
London NW3 5SH
Tel: 0171 794 2313

The Birmingham Trust for Psychoanalytic Psychotherapy[1]
96 Park Hill, Moseley,
Birmingham B13 8DS
Tel: 0121 449 9552

The British Association of Child Psychotherapists[1]
37 Mapesbury Road
London NW2
Tel: 0181 452 9823

The Scottish Institute of Human Relations[1]
56 Albany Street,
Edinburgh EH1 3QR
Tel: 0131 556 0924

The Society of Analytical Psychology[1]
1 Daleham Gardens,
London NW3 5BY
Tel: 0171 435 7696

The Tavistock Clinic[1]
120 Belsize Lane,
London NW3 5BA
Tel: 0171 435 7111

FOURTH SESSION

[1] Denotes recognised Training Schools in Child Psychotherapy, leading to eligibility for membership of the Association of Child Psychotherapists, and eligibility to take posts in Child Psychotherapy within the NHS.

ASSESSMENT OF RISK IN THE FAMILY JUSTICE SYSTEM

Donald Campbell

INTRODUCTION TO HIS PAPER

Donald Campbell explained that he had a particular interest in the boundaries between Family and Criminal Court proceedings. Consequently, he sought feedback from the assembled company as to whether a distinct line should be drawn between the two systems of justice or whether it might be more appropriate to have a cross-over between them. For example, could minor delinquent behaviour within the family and acting out of current family conflicts outside the immediate family be dealt with by the Family Courts?

He reiterated that aggression was caused by a perceived need for self-preservation (the most primitive level of psychic functioning) or by sadism (involving the organisation or control of the victim). It was important to assess which type of aggression was being used by a given perpetrator. He considered that the first type of aggression was more dangerous because the perpetrator was unconcerned about the victim's fate, whereas, a sadistic aggressor needed the victim to 'survive' in order that he/she could be used/controlled during the sadistic act.

Donald Campbell confirmed that it was important to consider the circumstances of a given offence so as to assess the potential of later offending. He also drew attention to offenders who possess a chamelon-like capacity to identify with the values and expectations of authority figures. Mr Campbell identified particular problems in assessing risk with offenders who are adept at deception.

ASSESSMENT OF RISK IN THE FAMILY JUSTICE SYSTEM

Donald Campbell, Consultant psychotherapist, Portman Clinic

INTRODUCTION

Any decision regarding the best interest of the child, whether he is the victim or the perpetrator, should take into account the element of risk. The child and his family would need to be assessed in order to make a judgment about the likelihood of the child being victimised again or of perpetrating further offences. I will propose a model for the assessment of risk which is based on an assessment of the child or adolescent within the family. Furthermore, I think it is worth considering referring alleged perpetrators of minor delinquent acts, especially those which occur *within* the family, or are clearly seen as *enactments of current family conflicts*, to a family court.

It may be argued that my focus on adolescent delinquents would be more appropriately discussed in the context of the Criminal Justice System. However, The Law Commission (1988) noted that most important decisions made within the Family Justice System involve not merely establishing relevant facts and adjudicating upon past actions, but also working collaboratively with several professional disciplines to arrive at decisions regarding the management of a family's future (Murch, 1994). Furthermore, it is often not feasible to establish guilt in cases involving alleged offences within a family. Even if feasibility was not an issue, a preoccupation with establishing guilt can lead to denial, entrenched defensiveness, stigmatisation and polarisation within families.

My contribution to the discussion of the highly problematic subject of risk assessment will be based on observations I have made in the course of my psychotherapeutic work with offenders at the Portman Clinic[1]. I want to introduce a model for understanding the young offender which is based on the premise that his or her delinquent behaviour functions as a solution to mental conflict. This will lead me to consider two types of aggression and the impact of offending behaviour on the participants in the legal process.

SELF-PRESERVATION AND SADISTIC AGGRESSION

Psychoanalysts have long postulated a self-preservative instinct, that is an instinctual response we all possess to stay on the tightrope, to fight to survive as a physically, mentally and emotionally coherent human being. Anything which threatens our physical or psychological survival constitutes a danger. The danger may come from the external world (the demands and limitations of reality) and/or our internal world (our sexual and aggressive wishes, our guilty conscience, depressive feelings, etc).

Anxiety is a feeling state that alerts us to a present or future danger. We respond to anxiety with defensive manoeuvres I will call solutions. The 'best' solution is that which creates and maintains a feeling of safety and well being. A neurotic or psychotic state, a symptom, a character trait, a defensive mechanism, or a criminal act, however maladaptive in the outside world, may be the 'best' solution that an individual can negotiate given the external circumstances and his/her internal resources (Sandler and Sandler, 1992).

When these solutions or defensive manoeuvres are effective they are invisible to us and to others. In fact, all of us employ a variety of invisible defensive solutions to problems which we encounter every minute of every day. However, when aggression is employed as a solution everyone is aware of its impact.

---

[1] The Portman Clinic is an outpatient National Health Service Trust facility which offers psychoanalytically oriented assessment, treatment and management to patients of any age and both sexes who are delinquent or suffer from a sexual deviation.

Self-preservative aggression is, I believe, the earliest defensive solution to threats to our survival and, hopefully, we never lose the capacity for fight or flight when we feel that our survival is at risk. However, the exercise of self-preservative aggression is not without its liabilities.

I will provide a model for understanding offending behaviour by briefly introducing a conflict faced by that earliest exponent of self-preservative aggression – the baby. When a baby's well being is disturbed by hunger, cold, physical pain, frustration, etc, he resorts to physical solutions or what I call *primary defences*, that is a large and diverse repertoire of physical responses which include motor reactions, such as muscular tension, clenched fists, waving arms, violent kicking and screaming, which temporarily alter the infant's physiological state by affecting blood pressure, temperature, etc. When this occurs the child associates these motor responses with getting rid of painful or frightening feelings. As the infant develops it is not unusual for him to perceive his mother as the person who is responsible for the pain he feels. When this occurs the child directs a physical reaction towards the mother. This is a precursor of self-preservative aggression which aims to get rid of an object which is perceived as threatening the survival of the self.

However, in this situation, intimately linked to the original threat to physical survival (say, hunger due to mother's failure to feed), the child now becomes aware of a second anxiety aroused by the threat of eliminating the very person upon whom he is dependent for his survival – mother. The threat of losing the mother due to the child's aggressive attack and/or abandonment by her in retaliation motivates the child to transform its destructive aim of aggression (the getting rid of mother) into an aim to control her via sadism. The fear of loss of mother is changed into pleasure derived by making her suffer and witnessing that suffering.

During an act of self-preservative violence at any age the fate of the object is irrelevant once the threat to physical or psychological survival posed by the object has been removed. During a sadistic attack the aim is not to destroy the object but to preserve it in order to control it. The process of assessing the risk of an offender committing further offences can benefit from considering the nature of the offence and the antecedents of the offence in the light of those two types of aggression. A delinquent act which has been mobilised solely by self-preservative aggression aims only to negate a threat to physical or psychological survival. The perpetrator has, in carrying out a physical or sexually aggressive act, no relation to the victim other than to eliminate the threat which the victim poses: the feelings and fate of the victim in this context are a matter of irrelevance. For this reason the victim's survival is in jeopardy.

When sadism is added to aggression the aim of preservation of the self remains, but the relationship to the victim changes dramatically. The additional aim towards the object is to cause the victim physical or mental suffering and is essential to this form of aggression. In order to fulfil a sadistic aim the object must survive in order to be controlled. The relationship between aggressor and victim must be maintained rather than eliminated. Unfortunately, serious crimes often occur when the sadistic relationship to the victim breaks down and the perpetrator resorts to his or her last line of defence – a self-preservative attack.

ADOLESCENCE

Usually, during the phase of development which precedes puberty, which we refer to as latency, oedipal wishes to have a sexual relationship with the parent of the opposite sex and get rid of the parent of the same sex are repressed. However, the physiological and hormonal changes, which take place during puberty and which initiate the adolescent process, thrust the sexual and physical body into the forefront of the adolescent's mental life. With the emerging appearance of a man or woman, the adolescent can, for the first time, enact when he or she could only wish for previously. After puberty the adolescent has the capacity to impregnate or bear children and the potential strength to convert into reality any wish to kill the rival parent. This newly developed sexual maturity heightens wishes and anxieties about sexuality and puts pressure on the adolescent's defenses aimed at maintaining the incest barrier. *In this developmental context the boy and girl face the fundamental tasks of adolescence: assuming ownership of a sexually potent body, that is separate from their parents, in the context of heterosexual relationships with non-incestuous objects.*

The pain associated with the awareness of the failure to integrate genital sexuality with heterosexual relationships outside the family motivates many adolescents to search for excitement in delinquency. The physical excitement experienced by the delinquent before, during and after an offence is linked to their emerging sexuality. In my view, the adolescent's delinquent act, whether it be motivated by self-preservative or sadistic aims, is the fulfilment of a sexual fantasy and, as such, it generates sexual excitement which momentarily blocks out internal distress.

When viewed from this perspective, delinquent behaviour can be seen as an enactment of an internal conflict which becomes intolerable and can no longer be dealt with internally. Whatever has precipitated the current emotional crisis for the delinquent, it is likely to be linked to traumatic, perhaps now unconscious, events of childhood over which the child had no control. These earlier childhood traumas are revived by puberty and must be dealt with again during adolescence. For this reason I believe that minor delinquent acts, especially those which occur *within* the family, or are clearly seen as *enactments of current family conflicts* would benefit by referral to a family court. Helen and Roger are two examples of such cases.

Helen: Stealing as a hopeful response to early deprivation

Helen was referred to the Portman Clinic after her mother discovered she had stolen jewellery from the mother of two children she had been working for as an au pair. Helen had been stealing from her own mother and shops for as long as she could remember.

Helen's father was away on business so much that he felt like a stranger to her. While she was extremely possessive and protective of Helen's older sister, Mother handed over the care of Helen to a succession of nannies, some good and some bad, who were all, in the end, found to be inadequate by Mother and abruptly sacked. Mother also kept the family isolated from the rest of the village behind the walls of the grandest house in the area. Helen put on a cheery face, and denied the deprivation she had experienced. Her 'solution' was to identify with her mother's possessiveness and, in this way, she managed to feel close to her mother without being smothered by her as she felt her older sister had been. Helen's stealing from other mothers, or taking objects associated with her own mother, appeared to serve at least two functions: it was the means by which Helen displaced her enormous rage toward her mother onto mother substitutes who were, like Helen herself, forced to suffer the loss of something valued; it also enabled her to reverse the experience of deprivation and loss which she couldn't control by actively taking from another mother figure what she could not get from her own mother.

Donald Winnicott (1956) held the view that where an anti-social tendency exists there has been what he called 'a true deprivation'; that is to say, there has been something good and positive in the child's experience up to a certain date that was then withdrawn. The withdrawal extended over a period of time which was really too long for the child to keep alive a memory of the good experience. Winnicott always believed that lack of hope was the basic feature of the deprived child. However, it is during the anti-social time that the child is actually expressing hope because it believes that the environment is there to be contacted and will respond, albeit in a punitive way.

Helen's stealing represented, at one level, her search for something that was good and had been lost. She was trying to take back a mother upon whom she still believed she had a child-like claim. However, Helen's attempt to master the deprivation of her childhood by stealing also served to defend against properly mourning the loss of the good experience that Winnicott referred to. Helen invited her mother to discover her delinquency by leaving the stolen jewellery on top of her chest of drawers in order to provoke containment and restraint. Helen, like other delinquents, unconsciously wished that her mother (or those authorities who represent Mother) would respond to her stealing by taking care of her. In this way Helen tried to master the relationship that originally she could not control to her satisfaction.

Roger: Exhibitionism as oedipal triumph, revenge and punishment

While Helen illustrates the influence of early deprivation on later delinquent behaviour, Roger is an example of a delinquent 'solution' to later, oedipal conflicts as they are revived during adolescence.

Roger, a diffident, passive sixteen year old, had been exposing his genitals to women for six months but had only recently been apprehended by the police for the first time. He said that the excitement and fear associated with risk was the strongest feeling. A smile crept across his face when Roger described the 'surprised' look on the woman's face. Roger did not know why he did it. Exhibiting himself did not, in any way, fit the image he had of himself. But, then, he was not sure who he was anyway. He admitted that he would rather not think about exposing himself and thought he would never do it again now that he had been caught. When he exposed himself Roger explained that he was in a state of mental confusion, at war within himself and cut off from everything around him which was outside a three yard cube. The war inside was described as one part of himself trying to stop another part from exposing himself. He seemed disassociated from both. Only the fear of being caught ever restrained him. However, when his 'defences were down' or when he was 'a little drunk' he felt out of control and unable to stop himself. At no time did Roger convey any concern for the women he had exposed himself to.

Roger started 'flashing' shortly after his eighteen year old brother's girlfriend Caroline moved in to live with the family and shared a bed with his brother. Roger told me that the occasion that resulted in his being arrested was unlike all the others because he exposed himself from a window in his parent's bedroom (while his mother was away) to women passing by on the pavement.

His father, a high-ranking police officer, had little time for Roger and appeared to have been dominated by his ambitious and unpredictable mother. There were rows and a chronic state of tension between his parents. Mother returned to pursue a high powered career in advertising when Roger was six months old and left him in the care of au pairs. Roger gave me the impression that he grew up with a narcissistic mother who was withdrawn and preoccupied at times and close and intimate at other times. Roger said that she related to the whole family via 'emotional blackmail'. He would wait for her to come home from work and study her face to see what sort of mood she was in so that he could determine whether she was approachable or not. If he got it wrong or tried to confront her, she would verbally attack him for his insensitivity towards her and then become sullen and withdrawn.

Mother's reaction to Roger telling her about his offence illustrates the intrusive, seductive dimension to their relationship. Mother was lying in bed with the curtains drawn. Roger sat on the bed, told her what he had done, and they 'cuddled'. She then reported that she told Roger that perhaps he had his father's physiology. His father wakes up every morning with an erection. If Roger had the same physiology, his mother said, it must be difficult for him to cope with his erections. After all, his father had herself right there every morning, but Roger had no one.

Recently, Roger had become more concerned about his inability 'to get beyond friendships with girls'. Roger confirmed my view that his relationship with his mother and the tension between his parents may well have contributed to his difficulties in developing sexual relationships with girls. He agreed that he felt more despairing when he compared himself with his brother who was sleeping with his girlfriend, Caroline, and was particularly upset when she moved in. He felt crowded out of his own house. All this left him feeling depressed and sorry for himself. After all he went through growing up in his family, after all the hassles from stupid and insensitive teachers at school, why should he have to contend with the police and court? All he could think of was, 'Why me?'

As early as 1916 Freud (1916) remarked upon children who were naughty on purpose to provoke punishment and were then contented after being punished. He believed that these misdeeds were motivated by an unconscious sense of guilt arising from repressed oedipal wishes to kill father and have sex with mother. Both the guilt and its source were unconscious. The adolescent who is overwhelmed by guilt arising from the revival of oedipal fantasies may commit delinquent acts in order to attach the guilt to something conscious and find some temporary relief when he is caught.

Freud's theory is useful in understanding why Roger moved into his parents' bedroom in order to exhibit himself after months of exposing himself on the streets without being apprehended. It would appear that the incestuous excitement aroused by being sexually active in his parents' bedroom also increased his guilt and anxiety about being able to control himself as he moved closer to his parents. Roger's revenge and triumph over his oedipal rival are evident in his violating the parental bedroom, exposing his father's ineffectual defence of the incest barrier to his police colleagues and the court, and shaming his law enforcement father who raised a son who committed a crime. The sadistic gratification derived from his encounters with women is also evident in Roger's pleasure in the 'surprise' the woman registers in response to the sudden exposure of his penis. Roger unconsciously behaved in such a way as to ensure that law and order would be brought into the parental bedroom and that his oedipal guilt would be punished.

Roger also brings to mind Freud's (1916) paper about those characters who feel they are justified in no longer submitting to any disagreeable reality. They feel they are *exceptions* because they have already suffered enough, unjustly so, during their childhoods. I believe Roger sees himself as an exception. The process of taking responsibility for his exhibitionism, acknowledging that he committed an offence and facing up to the reality of that image of himself, and then thinking through, albeit with a professional's help, why he did it, represents a disagreeable reality for which he would like to claim an exemption because he has already suffered enough.

DIFFERENTIAL DIAGNOSIS

No two victims or offenders are identical and a differential diagnosis is required if we are to understand the individual child or adolescent. A differential diagnosis should include: (1) the study of the offence itself, (2) a psychosexual developmental history of the child or adolescent, including, (3) family history (for sources of identifications and signs of collusions as well as the onset of delinquent or pre-delinquent behaviour), gender influences, racial and cultural backgrounds, and (4) the nature of his or her childhood or adolescence. The aim is to develop a picture of the internal world of the child or adolescent victim or offender. It is likely that an in-depth study of a perpetrator will discover an early history of victimisation.

Details of frequency and persistence of delinquent behaviour over time contain important clues to understanding the nature and function of the offence or the role played by the victim. The setting and the relationship with the victim are also important: was he or she a relative, a friend or a stranger? How old was the victim? The victim's account and details of the act may also give us clues about the severity of the offence and the adolescent's disturbance.

I want to illustrate the value of a differential diagnosis by considering a specific group of offenders, namely adolescent child sexual abusers. In light of the fact that approximately half of the adult sexual offenders coming before the courts began their sexual deviancy in adolescence (Davis, 1987), one can see the enormous prophylactic potential in work with adolescent abusers. Care should be given to any consideration of transferring an adolescent child sexual abuser to a criminal court since there is a need to consider their offences in a family context in order to identify patterns of collusion with the adolescent's individual psychopathology.

Adolescence is such a turbulent and complex phase of development that it is difficult to categorise adolescent abusers by their behaviour, but it is helpful to try to locate them along a continuum from less to more severe disturbance.

At the less severe end of the continuum are the adolescent abusers whose sexual identity is heterosexual. In their masturbation fantasies and sexual daydreams these adolescents are involved with adult or contemporary female partners. Their sexual abuse of children is infrequent, not persistent, and done in reaction to rejection by or anxiety about approaching female peers. There is no overt violence. Although they relate to the child on the basis of their own needs, they recognise that he or she is an independent person and they respond with shame and guilt to their abusive behaviour.

FOURTH SESSION

Sixteen year old Sidney was babysitting an eight year old girl he had known for several years when he fondled her genitals and climbed on top of her. Two weeks earlier his first girlfriend had broken up with him to go out with an older bloke. Sidney's father who worked a night shift was denigrated by Sidney's mother who worked a day shift. Sidney felt estranged from his father. Sidney felt uncomfortable when his parents tried to minimise the incident and sought help so he could have 'a proper girlfriend'.

This was Sidney's first offence. He represents the kind of offender who could benefit from referral to the Family Justice System where his case is more likely to be quickly expedited and where he is less likely to be stigmatised as a criminal.

At the more severe end of the continuum is the adolescent whose sexual fantasies are exclusively about children. Their abusive fantasies and behaviour are frequent, persistent, often accompanied by violence, and function to defend against a psychotic breakdown. They show no concern for their victim. In contrast to the less severely disturbed abuser, this adolescent sees the child as existing only to gratify his needs. These adolescents are usually lonely, isolated from their peers and uninterested in adult homosexual or heterosexual relationships.

Harry is 17, unhappy, friendless, unemployed and living in a hostel after his third offence of indecent assault on 10 year old boys. On the last occasion Harry forced a boy to go on to the roof of a high rise block of flats. Harry began truanting from school at 12 and spent his days riding buses around London in order to look at young boys and daydream about buggering them. During my interview with Harry for a Court Report, I discovered that he had nurtured a suicide fantasy and had made a suicide plan. Although I alerted the hostel staff to the risk of suicide, Harry's determination was such that he eluded the staff supervision at the bail hostel and tried to hang himself while awaiting trial.

Harry's abusive behaviour was chronic, severe and clearly outside his home. Not surprisingly Harry's single parent mother had abdicated her parenting role when Harry began truanting. Harry's dangerousness merits his being seen within the criminal justice system.

ASSESSING RISK

Decisions regarding the treatment, management and placement of child offenders and their victims should take into account the risk of the offender repeating delinquent behaviour as well as the risk of the victim finding themselves or putting themselves in dangerous situations. If William Kvaraceus (1954) was right when he said 'nothing predicts behaviour like behaviour', a study of an offender's behaviour over the course of his life should give clues about the potential for dangerous behaviour in the future. Three categories in Nigel Walker's (1991) *Typology of Dangerousness* provide a useful framework for considering an offender's behaviour as well as the behaviour of the victim. The first category is the conditionally dangerous individual represented by (a) those who are brought into situations of provocation by inclination. There are two categories among the unconditionally dangerous: (b) the opportunity seeker, ie someone who searches for opportunities to be delinquent, and (c) the opportunity maker.

Although these conclusions are tentative, my impression from studying patients at The Portman Clinic is that those whose delinquent behaviour was primarily self-preservative tend to be more seriously disturbed and suffering from primative anxieties with paranoid orientations to others. Those patients who resolved conflicts primarily through sadistic behaviour, either sexual or physical, tend to be less disturbed and more object oriented. Perversions (of which sadism is always a component) function as solutions to neurotic or psychotic anxiety by encapsulating the mental disturbance in the perverse activity. Therefore, one should be cautious about an assessment of the severity of mental illness when dealing with perverse patients. The 'successful' perversion often enables the perpetrator to function more or less normally in society often exercising authority, as we know, in public life, which contributes to genuine shock when offending or perverse behaviour is discovered. Consequently the offending behaviour appears 'out of the blue', is considered irrational or without psychological explanation.

Roger and Harry were unconditionally dangerous. They were opportunity seekers. There was a driven quality about their offending. Helen was a borderline case. She was inclined to steal from mothers but she did not look for victims. However, she took advantage of opportunities to steal when she was babysitting just as she had done from her mother. Sidney, on the other hand, was conditionally dangerous. He did not search for girls to molest, but was not able to resist the temptation to abuse the girl he was babysitting.

THE IMPACT OF CHILD ABUSE UPON DEVELOPMENT

An act of child abuse bisects the line of normal development and disrupts the natural timing of the biological clock, turns the oedipus complex upside down, and undermines the 'bedrock of reality' by challenging the view that children are not the same as adults and males and females are different. Incestuous wishes are gratified with parents, siblings, or adolescents or adults who are perceived as sibling or parental substitutes. The sexually abusive act over-stimulates the mouth, anus, or genitals. These traumatised erotogenic zones must be incorporated into the child's sexual body image.

Likewise, the experience of being overwhelmed by a genitally mature person will reinforce passive submissiveness and undermine the normal progress toward heterosexual relations in adolescence. For instance, a boy who is buggered may feel he has been feminised, used like a woman, and find it difficult as an adolescent to think of using his penis in relation to a woman. As a consequence, the abused child can be expected to think of himself or experience himself in pregenital and pre-oedipal terms.

Whatever the relationship between a child and his abuser, the child will directly or indirectly feel that the parents are responsible, if only for failing to protect his body. Behind the child's feeling that the parents have failed to play the role that is needed and expected of the adult generation is a sense that if the parents had been tuned in to what he or she felt about his or her body they would have protected their child. The parents who fail to respond appropriately to their child's abuse confirm the child's feeling of abandonment. When the abuse is unshareable, it is unacceptable, and the rage, fear and sexual excitement cannot be psychically digested. Most children need the help of a parent, close friend, relative, or professional to help them work through the helplessness, betrayal of trust, anger and sexual confusion generated by their abuse. If left alone, the child is likely to repress, deny or disavow the traumatic experience. Shame, guilt (conscious and unconscious) and fear of retaliation haunt the victim. All this is rekindled and intensified when the child victim enters puberty.

The adolescent who was abused as a child will be confused about his sexual identity, feel guilty about and ashamed of his pre-genital fantasies and be ill-equipped for the tasks of adolescence. He feels a failure and is unable to identify with his peers. When separation from his parents becomes too frightening and the prospect of genital contact with peers is too dangerous, the abused adolescent looks for a sexual partner among children.

The case of George

George was referred to the Portman Clinic for a Court Report after he was accused of buggering four neighbour boys between the ages of 7 and 10 while he was babysitting. At the time he was apprehended, George confessed for the first time to being sexually abused himself by a family friend who was a father himself, whom I will call Mr Chambers, when he was seven years old. Mr Chambers was currently in prison for numerous sexual offences against children.

The first time I met George in the waiting room he impressed me as an appealing lad who looked younger than his 14 years. He had a broad smile, a mop of dark hair, a bouncy step, and was wearing an Arsenal jersey. George was eager to come with me but waited for cues from his mother. Mrs Russell was a small, tough, wiry, Cockney lady with a few teeth missing and the gregarious air of a woman experienced in dealing with social workers and other professionals. Mr Russell was a large man with a weak handshake, a pleasant smile and lazy eyelids, who said nothing through the family interviews unless actively drawn in by someone, like a child waiting for permission.

Mrs Russell did not differentiate between George and her husband. The boundaries between the generations were easily blurred. For instance, mother viewed George as being powerful while she herself was helpless in the face of his demands. 'He won't take no for an answer,' she explained. George's mother presented him as responsible for everything that went wrong in the family, including the power to generate rows between Mr Russell and herself.

Mrs Russell also relied on projection and introjection to avoid taking responsibility for herself and her son. She gave the impression that she, like her son George, was trapped at home, but blamed this on him. She said she would like to go out and work but doesn't dare because she would 'get it from George when she got in.' Then she suddenly said, 'So much hurt. I am frightened to be on my own.' George's stepfather interrupted to say how often he is sent out to look for George. Mother became quite emotional and burst out, 'I don't know what George is doing. That's what buggers me up.' Buggery is an apt metaphor for mother and son's mutual intrusiveness and the absence of protective boundaries.

When George was a toddler, Mother was unable to help her son control himself or protect him from himself. She recounted incidences of his making sandcastles out of flour, sugar and water on the kitchen floor, as well as innumerable accidents including the time when he was two and fell on the heater and 'burned his private parts. It just missed his little penis and he still has a scar.' It is not surprising that George wet his bed at night until he was nine.

Mrs Russell painted a picture of generational roles turned upside down with George tyrannising his mother. 'I am a miserable woman. As soon as I put a smile on my face George puts me down again.'

After blaming George for her miscarriages the last two years, Mrs Russell haltingly and vaguely shared the secret that she had been sexually abused by her father. 'No wonder I was hated by my mother. I was my father's favourite but no one understood why. As a child I kept saying to myself, the next time he did it I would cut it off.'

The first thing George told me when we were alone was about the family's card game of Fish which they played on the train on the way to the session as well as other times during the week. The pattern is always the same because, as George said, he is smarter than his parents and usually wins.

On the one hand, his parents seemed unable to function as parental authorities, while on the other hand, George clearly saw himself in a rather omnipotent position, that is, as a child who is equal to his parents and, as far as the game of Fish is concerned, superior to them. George agreed with my observation that he had to compete for almost everything in the family but there was no one around, no adult, to ensure that he got his share. He always had to do that for himself.

I wondered aloud if he felt he had to compete with and defeat me and then doubted that I could help him. It was then that George admitted that he was worried about the violence between his mother and stepfather when he hears them quarrelling at night. He couldn't go to sleep at night because he was wondering about what was going on between them. I commented that adults seemed more like easily overpowered children during the day, but violent and frightening when they went to bed at night.

In our fourth session, George was able to talk about his assaults on the younger boys. However, at first he projected his failure to stay in tune with these boys, his failure to protect their bodies, by blaming his own parents for leaving him with those youngsters. Then he blamed the parents of the boys who shouldn't have left them in the first place. The incident occurred when the parents had left George to babysit, or rather to play with the younger children, while the parents went out. He then changed his defence saying that it was the boys' fault because they were playing in their underpants. As he said, 'If you lock up a man and a woman, not a girl, something is going to happen'.

George's association to heterosexual activity provided a clue about what he imagined the violence between mother and stepfather to be about, and the heterosexual fantasy that underlies his homosexual activity with the young boys. It is not uncommon for homosexual activity between boys in early adolescence, that is, from puberty to fifteen, to be motivated by heterosexual fantasies. What is worrying in George's case is the absence of peer relationships and his use of boys from a younger generation.

George denied any pleasure when having sexual contact with the boys because they were 'too small'. There was excitement and challenge in misleading the boys into thinking they could beat him up, because he knew that they really couldn't hurt him. The pleasure was in seeing the shock and confusion in the boys when he turned the tables on them. I took up his sexual play, getting on top of the boys with his penis in their bottoms, as something which makes the boys feel small and enables him to feel big by dominating them with sex. George said triumphantly, 'Yeah, they thought of me as the grown-up'. He reversed what he had set up in the play fights and betrayed the boys just as he felt betrayed and confused at home over who is the grown-up and who is the child. In this way George clearly identified with the aggressor.

Mrs Russell called just before his next session to say that she had just found out that George was due to see me, but she couldn't bring him because she had no money and had not known ahead of time. We arranged to meet again next week.

George walked into his fifth session with a bald head, hid his face in his shoulder and looked embarrassed. He told me that he had shaved all his hair off because he was impatient with his mum who had delayed giving him a hair cut herself. He was also able to acknowledge some anger at her for delaying his session a week. George went on to tell me about a game he had invented called 'Booby' which he destroyed when his parents wouldn't continue playing. George apparently felt that the most effective way of attacking his parents was to turn his aggression against himself. I took up George's shaving his hair off as aimed at hurting his mother by presenting himself as someone she didn't protect – in this instance from himself. George's defiance gave way to shame about his shaved head. I was reminded of the Nazis shaving the heads of new concentration camp prisoners to shame and depersonalise them. This is what George had done to himself, I said, to show me he felt shame about his own abuse. I added that his abuse of the boys may also have been a way of getting rid of his feelings of shame and being unprotected by making the youngsters feel them.

George then put into words, for the first time, his own experience of being buggered when he was seven (the same age as two of the boys he buggered). 'Everyone had gone out except the kid's dad, Mr Chambers. I was lying on my tummy watching telly. He pulled my pants down. I didn't know what Mr Chambers was doing, but I felt it. Felt his penis . . . cold inside . . . then wet. He left 20p and told me it was just between us. I never turned around. I never said anything because no one would believe me. And there might have been a fight.'

In my report to the Court, I maintained that George was at risk of re-offending due to his parents' inability to maintain sexual and generational boundaries. In my recommendation, I gave priority to separating George from his parents and I recommended that George be referred to an adolescent residential centre where he could receive psychodynamic treatment. I also stated that the Portman Clinic would welcome a referral for assessment with a view to offering out-patient psychotherapy upon George's discharge.

THE IMPACT OF OFFENDING BEHAVIOUR ON PROFESSIONALS

Bearing in mind that offending behaviour is a solution to conflict, one would expect that the offender will rely upon similar behaviour in his legal defence, particularly as anxieties will be increased in the offender because of his fear of the consequences of the loss of a solution. Consequently, for the offender the bind is something like this: how to get help without having his aggressive solution (the capacity to commit offences) taken away leaving him more vulnerable and helpless. Although it may not be apparent to the lay observer or indeed other professionals who have not had an opportunity to treat offenders over a long period of time, my experience is that most offenders have cruelly persecuting consciences which continually burden them with bad feelings about themselves. These offenders often feel that the legal process reinforces their self-denigration. There is a particular defence against the persecuting conscience which I find in adult and adolescent child sexual abusers, paedophiles and perpetrators of incest, which I would like to bring as an example of offending behaviour which may be repeated in the legal process and mislead attempts to assess risk.

FOURTH SESSION

I refer to this defence as the *chameleon defence*. In order to escape from severe self criticism, the perpetrator unconsciously splits off and disavows the abusive part of himself and employs a chameleon-like facility to identify with external representations of one's conscience, such as idealised parents or authorities with statutory responsibilities, or even the judge himself. This is not a self-conscious pretence. The abuser actually believes that he or she is an ideal parent, caring childcare worker, or wise administrator, and is their child victim's best friend, sensitive babysitter, or helpful tutor.

These chameleon identifications are so believable for the professional because the perpetrator is a believer himself. Consequently, the abuser's internal world and motivation for change is difficult to assess, as is any sign of behavioural change. The abuser may all too readily identify with the attitudes and behaviour promoted by the caretakers, including acknowledgement of his own abusive behaviour, in order to believe he is a good client and win external approval. Issues of what is good and what is bad are preferable to facing more painful anxieties associated with fear of mental breakdown or looking again at an original overwhelming trauma, such as their own experience of being abused as children.

Any assessment or treatment approach that adopts an authoritarian role or focuses exclusively on behavioural change without understanding the paedophile's internal conflicts and anxieties is in danger of being sabotaged by the abuser's capacity to adopt language, concepts and whatever is suggested as normative behaviour, in the same way as the chameleon takes on the colour of its environment as a protection against attack. Momentarily, one will see changes in the abuser's behaviour as the result of this kind of identification with the therapist, probation officer, or forensic psychiatrist. However, since underlying anxieties are not affected, the abuser is at risk of returning to abusive behaviour as a solution once the external supports have been taken away and old anxieties re-emerge. Put into the language of child abuse, any assessment, treatment or management programme that does not take the abuser's internal world into account is very likely to be victimised in the same way as the child victims are, that is by being deceived by the outwardly positive but inwardly fraudulent behaviour of these offenders. This is, in fact, a repetition of the act of child abuse which arouses hope and trust in order to destroy both in the soul of the child.

PUTTING PROFESSIONAL COLLABORATION AT RISK

We would expect the anxieties and rage aroused within the victim and projected through the delinquent act by the offender to affect those professionals who are collaborating on the case.

> 'This incessant projective redistribution of unmanageable anxiety between agencies can only serve to rigidify the structures and practices through which (agency) members attempt to ward it off. In the relevant service network constellated by a given case, the practitioners involved may be impelled to use institutional defences (such as fight and flight) not only internally against their own, but externally against each other to the detriment of collaboration.' (Woodhouse & Pengelly, 1991).

The risk to the professional is that he or she will use their 'agency or work group as a defence which protects the practitioner's professional identity and status and which sustains professional self-esteem when competence is challenged both by the client/family's situation and/or by practitioners in other settings with different professional perspectives'. (Murch, 1994 p 16). This results in a 'ghetto' mentality which blinds professionals to their own defensiveness and their projection of their own anxiety into colleagues in other disciplines. When pathological identifications with the victims or perpetrators go unnoticed, mirror splits develop within families, and the assessment of risk in the family justice system is, itself, at risk.

REFERENCES

Davis, G E (1987) 'Adolescent sex offenders', *Psychol Bulletin*, 101, pp 417–427.

Freud, S (1916) *Some character types met within psychoanalytic work* Standard Edition IV London: Hogarth Press.

Kvaraceus, W (1954) *The Community and the Delinquent* New York: World Book Co.

Murch, M (1994) 'The cross-disciplinary approach to family law: are we trying to mix oil with water'. A paper based on a seminar given at the Centre for Family Law and Family Policy at the University of East Anglia on 2 March 1994.

Sandler, J and Sandler A-M (1992), 'Psychoanalytic technique and theory of psychic change' *Bulletin Anna Freud Centre* XV, pp 35–51.

Walker, N (1991) 'Dangerous Mistakes' *British Journal of Psychiatry*, 158, pp 752–757.

Winnicott, D (1956) 'The anti-social tendency' In: *Collected Papers* (1958) London: Tavistock Publications, pp 306–315.

Woodhouse, D and Pengelly, P (1991) *Anxiety and the Dynamics of Collaboration*, Aberdeen: Aberdeen University Press.

FOURTH SESSION

FOURTH PLENARY SESSION

DISCUSSION

ASSESSMENT OF RISK VERSUS PROTECTION OF THE CHILD

Although the concept of 'assessment of risk' was important, it was concluded that a practical judge was bound to make decisions based on the need to protect of the child rather than based primarily on an assessment of the risk of future harm. Judges were inclined to adopt the 'worst case scenario', so as to avoid potential abuse – albeit that a judge's primary target was to ensure that a child remained within the family if he/she could be sufficiently protected from the perpetrator. Donald Campbell explained that by studying the nature of the offence and the circumstances in which it occurred, it was sometimes possible to evaluate whether the perpetrator would repeat the offence. In order to assess that risk it was necessary to look at the perpetrator's actions in the context of the whole family – for example, the level of the mother's collusion and/or whether the father was prepared to remove himself from the home. There was some debate as to whether any experts had sufficient expertise to avoid being 'conned' by a perpetrator and the general consensus was that it was extremely difficult to decide whether an alleged abuser was telling the truth simply on interview. Consequently, it was agreed that the Court proceedings were the best method of providing a neutral overview and an evaluation of all the evidence.

THE RELATIONSHIP BETWEEN AN ADOLESCENT YOUNG ABUSER AND THE FAMILY COURT

Donald Campbell considered that (in the interest of the victim and possible future victims) certain perpetrators should be dealt with by the Family Court rather than the Criminal Court, because the former is able to look at the offence within a broader context. It was suggested that a new remedy, to be called – say – a 'Treatment order', should be created (because a care/supervision order would not be applicable). A Treatment Order would provide the mechanism whereby the young perpetrator received treatment in circumstances where he/his family were otherwise not prepared to enter into therapy. It was suggested that it might be simpler for the Criminal Courts to deal with these cases because a structure – via probation orders – was already in place. However, concern was expressed, about (a) the standard of proof in criminal proceedings (by which a perpetrator might avoid conviction) and (b) the willingness of a perpetrator to confess his crime (if, as a result, he risked prosecution). It was therefore concluded that it would be necessary to amend the Children Act and this was a matter for Parliament. Concern was expressed that there might be political outcry, if this was seen as a 'soft' option for criminals. The Scottish system of Children Panels was discussed – where, once a conviction has been obtained or the child has admitted the offence, the case is removed from the criminal jurisdiction to the Panel. In that context, the sole criterion is the best interests of the child and 'punishment' is meted out accordingly. Some doubt was expressed as to the success of the system, but the general consensus was that an alternative method of dealing with some perpetrators was necessary.

FIFTH SESSION

Dr Clifford Yorke

INTRODUCTION TO HIS PAPER

Dr Yorke introduced his paper by giving details of the establishment of the Anna Freud Centre. Three of the presentations at the conference, including his own, had been written by past or present members of its staff. He explained that Anna Freud had set up wartime residential nurseries for children who had lost, or were separated from, their parents as a result of the Second World War, and she and her staff had studied in detail the ways in which separation affected the child's development and long term well being. The Centre was the post-war successor to the nurseries, founded for the (non-residential) psychological study and treatment of children with a wide range of difficulties and disabilities.

Dr Yorke recommended two publications of Anna Freud's, written in collaboration with Professor A J Solnit of the Yale University Child Study Centre and Professor J Goldstein of the Yale University Law School. These were *Beyond the Interests of the Child* (which concentrated on family breakup and its effect upon the children) and *Before the Best Interests of the Child* (which concentrated upon issues such as when the Law should intervene). These have now been revised and updated in the light of judgments made in the intervening years, and together with a third *In the Best Interests of the Child* will shortly be re-issued in a new, single volume.

On the question of child abuse, Dr Yorke confirmed that most cases which pass before the Courts involve some violation of the child, but pointed out that there are other cases in which the abuse amounted to a 'seduction' of the child (whereby the child became in part a willing if guilty participant). In this type of case, the abusive behaviour might never come to the knowledge of the Court or other agencies but would still have long term sequelae.

CHILDHOOD AND SOCIAL ORDER

Clifford Yorke[1]

I want to say at once that I'm not a forensic psychiatrist. I can't even claim any special knowledge of the law, the courts or court procedure. Like any other psychiatrist, I have, from time to time, written reports or given evidence, and, on rare but unhappy occasions, done so to coroner's courts. So I thought it might be helpful to speak on matters about which I'm rather better informed, and to look briefly at some of those stages in the development of a child that may have a bearing on behaviour that, later on, may get people into trouble or help to keep them out. That means saying something about *conflict* in relation to childhood, and conflict that lies *within the self* and not simply between the child and the earliest society – the family or its substitute – in which he grows up. In particular, it may be useful to try to understand a little about the way conscience develops, and how an *internal* law giver may stand in relation to an *external* one. Whether that is of any practical use or not, it may I suggest, be something that neither the lawyer nor the professionals who advise him should altogether neglect[2].

Freud did not invent the notion of conflict within the self, nor was he the first to speak of it. Montaigne was hardly breaking new ground when he wrote:

> 'We are, I know not how, somewhat double in ourselves, so that what we believe we disbelieve, and cannot rid ourselves of what we condemn.'

Every rediscoverer of conscience knows, on the basis of simple introspection, something about discord within the mind. Most people are easily, or perhaps uneasily, aware of guilt and the conflict within themselves when they want to carry out some particular action but feel at one and the same time that they ought not to do it. But this easy familiarity with an internal arbiter may not be a decisive influence on our behaviour. For although, as Shakespeare pointed out, conscience *can* make cowards of us all, and 'enterprises of great pith and moment lose the name of action', it can also vary greatly in its effectiveness. Indeed, it is perfectly possible to feel guilty about something one is in the act of doing while still continuing to carry it out. So Shakespeare's statement is certainly no rule, though it's sometimes strikingly true of those who suffer from a conscience of such severity that it borders on, and sometimes even amounts to, the pathological. It's not too difficult to think of people whose sense of right and wrong effectively interferes with their everyday lives and makes the most trivial of decisions a matter of earnest and unending internal debate.

For all that we regard conscience, however imperfect, as a major guide to human behaviour. But it is important to understand how its role as internal watchdog stands in relation to the external forces of social expectation and censure. An issue of this complexity is easily shirked, or sidestepped altogether, by excessively simple formulations. Of these, the doctrine of total conditioning had, for long, a clamorous appeal. From this standpoint, human development is quite uncomplicated: our views, opinions, and sense of right and wrong are simply the results of *social* forces. People are purely the products of their upbringing. Changes in society will radically alter the way they view themselves, and decisively change their social behaviour. This view is avidly propagated by various types of liberationist, but it colours a good deal of current political thinking.

Freud was as interested in conscience as he was in social psychology. His reflections on large groups hold good, in many respects, for small groups too, especially if there is a charismatic leader with which the group identifies. He was particularly concerned about the disappearance of *individual* conscience in a group organisation that seeks to become a powerful social force,

---

[1] Formerly psychiatrist-in-charge, the Anna Freud Centre and Consultant Psychotherapist to the Psychiatric Unit at Watford General Hospital.

[2] I have in places drawn on a Radio 3 talk delivered in January 1986, the text of which was reprinted in *The Listener*. It was called Conscience and The Divided Self.

and one that *knows* it is always right. But the phenomenon is not restricted to the many kinds of social activists who are so intolerant of disagreement. And conscience can certainly be suspended in crowds: today we would perhaps first think of the seemingly mindless violence of some football team supporters; but the behaviour of some animal rights proselytisers is not always very different. When Freud once stated that 'social anxiety' is the essence of what we call conscience he had similar matters in mind; but, in emphasising the *historical* link between them (with the family or its substitute as the first society) he never confused the two.

The fact is that internal and external arbiters of conscience may be much more at odds with each other than some fashionable viewpoints allow. This was vividly brought home to me by a friend who works in a student health service. Some years ago, he told me that the permissive society might well have a lot to recommend it, but that it occasioned him more than a few problems. He repeatedly came across students who felt obliged to take part in sexual activity for which they felt unprepared and who could not understand why something everyone said was a joy brought, for them, so much inner anguish. He added that he spent some time with people who, intellectually, welcomed the principle of communal living in rebelling against the 'nuclear family' but who were surprised and dismayed when they discovered that the new social setting did nothing to subdue the pain of jealously.

Not all the suffering endured by students like these springs from the rebukes of conscience. Feelings of inadequacy, inferiority, ignorance, or the fear of the loss of a partner through a failure to comply with expectations, are among the more obvious examples of personal misery that readily spring to mind. But, for all the disparities between them, each one has some connection with what might loosely be called self-regard, and involves some degree of self-comparison with others. Once again, the states of feeling involved appear to have both internal and external points of reference. They are not to be equated with conscience, to be sure; but they may be sufficiently related to it to suggest a common ancestry.

Everyday experience, whether of ourselves or others, tells us that it is perfectly possible to have a strong sense of right and wrong, but that inner controls over impulse may be frail. Something snaps; restraint is lost; impulse spills over into action without further thought; and the result becomes a cause for profound regret. Conscience may be strong, but the power to respond to it less than adequate. So it cannot be that conscience alone, however great its strength, controls our actions. There must be something else – an internal system that keeps our impulses under control and makes our responses to conscience effective.

Children are not born with a ready made conscience, with a sense of guilt, of shame, and other internal deterrents; nor are they born with inner controls. They are, of course, born with needs, and very strong needs at that; and the satisfaction for which those needs cry out may feel far too imperative to wait on events without protest. So it seems worth looking at the way in which internal deterrents, internal controls, and for that matter internal guides, standards, aims and *ideals* may come into being, and to try to see how they become effective or sometimes fail to do so. For though it may be said that *internal* discipline is the only discipline really worth having, and perhaps the only one to be respected by its proprietor, no one can pretend it's easily acquired. And since human beings are enormously complex, what I say about these matters today will be limited by knowledge as well as the constraints of time and circumstance.

Even the most casual observer of children is bound to be impressed by the changes brought about in the first 5 years of life. (They may not add up to a miracle, but they come remarkably close to it.) In that short space of time, the infant is transformed. Helplessly dependent at the start, all need and *want*, his[3] existence is largely measured by rocketing need, satiation, and oblivion. By the time he starts school, he has embarked on an articulate social life, able to respond to, and relate with, teachers and schoolmates, able to work and play, to join in group activities, to undertake new tasks and obligations, able to leave the family behind for substantial periods, and, if all goes well, to get true pleasure from becoming part of this wider world outside. En route, complexities multiply in a developing world of emotional ups and downs, of fresh fears, frustrations, satisfactions and changing demands. If memory sprang from the drama of events, recall of these tempestuous times would indeed be vivid.

---

[3] His is used generically throughout, unless the context suggests otherwise, and can equally be read as Hers.

And yet ... that is exactly what it is not. Few people can bring to mind more than a hazy recollection of what is arguably the most formative part of their past. Childhood amnesia of this magnitude calls for explanation, and nothing as naïve as mere remoteness in time will do by way of it.

Montaigne does not help much here. Something more is needed than the notion that the mind is divided against itself. The mind, indeed, is *divided against its own past*. Only an internal division of a very special kind could make those vivid early years so inaccessible to consciousness. Nor can this be a simple matter of a mental divide which permanently shuts off one part of the mind from another. That would mean that those first eventful years had no influence or bearing on those that followed.

Freud's early awareness of this apparent anomaly – that much that defies the memory maintains a significant influence on early life and on its subsequent development – had an important bearing on many of his further formulations. The notion of a divide between events that *can* be recalled – albeit sometimes with difficulty – and events that, unlike the pangs of conscience, defy recollection – has long since passed into common currency under the term *repression*. But this is a term that is often misunderstood. It has nothing whatever to do with repression in a political sense. Nor does it mean *suppression*. We often suppress thoughts and feelings – or try to – but that is a conscious process. Repression, in contrast, is a process of which we remain unaware. It is of particular interest, in the present context, that Nietzsche, in one of his aphorisms, had already portrayed the process in terms which Freud found singularly impressive. The quotation may speak for itself. ' "I have done that," says my Memory. "I could not have done that", says my Pride, and remains inexorable. Finally, my Memory yields.'

It's surely worth noting that what Freud late called repression was, for Nietzsche, no mere matter of entertaining a memory in consciousness and then deliberately discarding it. 'Finally', he says, 'my Memory yields'. Awareness is now denied, but not as a matter of choice. It is no longer accessible to introspection. And it is striking that he invokes *Pride* as a motivator of very considerable power. Pride is the antithesis of shame. So Nietzsche's construction suggests that it is the preservation of self-esteem that can play a major part when memory is so decisively jettisoned.

But close observation of small children suggests that the role of pride and shame in the maintenance of self esteem is operative long before childhood amnesia sets in. The capacity to feel disgust, for example, and so to feel ashamed of whatever it is in oneself that gives rise to it, is generally acquired some time during the third year of life when an impressive interest in excreta and all things lavatorial gives way to feelings of aversion. But if shame springs from such humble origins, it later extends, as everyday experience confirms, to very different and diverse thoughts, fantasies and actions. And it is perhaps the *fear of shame* that is such a powerful motivator, that brings with it a fear of exposure and the wish to hide.

To start with, the child wants to hide from others, through fear of disapproval. Anna Freud – Freud's youngest daughter and the only one of his children to follow him into his profession – used to tell a story about Lisa, a little girl of two-and-a-half in a nursery school. The nurse was in the habit of offering the children fruit juice and chocolate by way of elevenses. Wisely, she kept the chocolates on a shelf out of the children's reach. One day she had occasion to leave the room unattended. The little girl at once seized a stool, dragged it to the wall, climbed onto it, reached for the shelf, and was just about to close her fingers on the chocolates when the nurse reappeared. With great presence of mind Lisa moved her hand to a more neutral object and climbed down with it. The nurse left the room again and the child climbed on the stool once more. This time, when the nurse reappeared, Lisa's hand had closed on a chocolate and seized it. Unruffled, she climbed down and graciously offered it to a somewhat surprised but appreciative little boy. The third time the process was repeated, the nurse returned in time to see the little girl stuffing the chocolate into her mouth.

Lisa is clearly at a moment of transition: she is approaching a point where a fear of shame is about to preside over actions with increasing effectiveness. But her behaviour is still, for the most part, a fear of disapproval, and not a fear of disapproval by her peers but by an adult authority. For all that, the child is on the road that leads from *external* to *internal* disapproval, to disapproval of herself. But she is not there *yet*.

But perhaps this little story will remind us that this discussion needs to be set in the context of the steps that lead from external to internal controls, and from external to internal *law*. And bearing in mind what has been said about Nietzsche and Freud, about shame and guilt, we have to try to trace the steps from external to internal *conflict*.

At the beginning of life the infant's needs and wishes are met by the mother's facilitation or restraint[4]. Within this interaction, *affective* (emotional) bonds are mutually established which open up new areas of gratification and well-being for the child and mark a departure from purely biological to psychological needs. In due course this interaction will modify the peremptory quality and urgency of the infant's demands, to that extent marking the beginning of a capacity to tolerate frustration. The way in which the mother exercises her functions as guardian and caretaker, the way she recognises and responds to her baby's needs, how she provides satisfactions and substitute satisfactions, and the ways in which she makes frustration more bearable – all these have a part to play in the building up of the child's inner world. Those experiences which enable the infant to tolerate delay in the face of mounting need, and which themselves become increasingly pleasurable in terms of the child's well-being, enable him to lay the foundations for inner controls, though it is axiomatic that for some time to come these measures will intermittently yield to the pressure of internal demands. In all these matters the influence of endowment, maturational factors, and of course experience itself, will together determine the individual variations in the way the mind develops in each child.

As the child becomes less dependent on his mother's body, as he grows more aware of the world around them both, and as he starts to explore it, learning to crawl and then to walk, his wishes and pursuits are increasingly interfered with by the mother or others in charge of him. The toddler is repeatedly frustrated by limitations imposed by what, to him, is an incomprehensible series of maternal interventions designed (unknown to him) to protect him from danger. He is driven by wishes that cannot always be granted and demands that cannot be met.

In order to adapt to these conditions the child has to develop new capacities. He has to learn to *remember* these experiences of wishes and activities that are tolerated (and often enjoyed) and those that are frustrated or forbidden (and often no less enjoyed). He has to learn to classify them in terms of the mother's approval or disapproval. But these new abilities do no more than reflect his mother's view of these different situations. He simply apprehends the models of 'goodness' or 'badness' which his mother holds up to him.

These models do not as a rule reflect his own wishes. Indeed they create formidable struggles which persist for some time and which can appropriately be called *external conflicts* – conflicts, that is, between himself and others. For example, a 3-year-old who particularly wanted to get her mother's approval repeatedly asked, 'Am I good?' As soon as she was reassured of this, however, she would add, with a certain immediacy: 'But I don't *like* doing what I'm told!' Another little girl, aged 4 at the time, clashed with her mother whenever she couldn't get her own way. In these circumstances the child would say, 'You don't love me or you wouldn't say "no". I don't love *you*'. Elements of these primitive barter systems can, of course, be detected much later in life. It is one thing to *understand* a prohibition and quite another to *accept* it. And without acceptance there is no possibility of making adaptations and modifying behaviour on the strength of *internal* resources alone. (Perhaps that is why we sometimes say that a law that no one obeys is bad law.)

There is, then, a line of development that leads from dependence on the mother as controller, through physical restraints, verbal restraints, interdiction or forbidding glance, to internal impulse control. External controls originally operate against a multitude of childhood wishes, not all of which are simple representatives of wishful impulses[5], but nevertheless endanger the child or, for that matter, the security of a brother or sister, the cat, or objects around the home.

FIFTH SESSION

---

[4] For 'Mother' read 'Mother or her substitute'. Some of this material appeared in a more academic form in a paper by my colleague Hansi Kennedy and myself published in 1982 in the Psychoanalytic Study of the Child (New Haven: Yale University Press).

[5] Freud referred to these basic impulses as instinctual drives, intrinsic to the organism, of which there were two main groups – libidinal and aggressive. In childhood the sexual drives are not to be equated with later genitality (of adolescence or adulthood) though genital wishes are recognisable very much earlier, normally passing into latency somewhere around the age of five. The drives go through various stages, rooted in bodily areas – to begin with the

While burgeoning achievements contribute to the child's capacity for inner control and self-regulation, the wishes that remain closest to these basic impulses are still the hardest to give up. It is these wishes which continue to mobilise anger with the restraining adult. Toilet training often provides some of the most striking examples. Tony, who at the age of 3¼ was excessively messy in his water-play and required repeated physical restraint, became very angry with his therapist whenever she interfered with his wishes. On such occasions he called her a 'bloody cow' and defied her in fantasy by pretending to be a fireman and dousing her with hoses. All the same, he was careful to emphasise that this was for her own protection! Another young patient repeatedly called his therapist 'naughty' whenever his own aggression was aroused and he anticipated her disapproval and retaliation.

Children have at their disposal a number of ways of dealing with these inner struggles. Some of these are still recognisable in the adult. It's easy to attribute something you don't like in yourself to someone else – to say *he* is mean, *she* is nasty, but not to indict yourself. If you want to hit somebody, but fail to recognise the fact, you may feel that this same person wants to hit *you*. And lots of people rationalise actions that they would otherwise find difficult to justify, and *for which they do not know the real reasons*. These defences against unwanted impulses are generally unconscious, though they are rather more accessible in children under five than they are in later life.

Nursery observations have furnished us with lots of examples of how children begin to internalise prohibitions. A first step is to deflect the adult's prohibitions by directing them against other children. Many a child who has not yet acquired bladder control points with indignation at puddles on the floor put there by others.

Until the child is able to identify with the ideal held up to him, and thereby turn against his own impulses, full toilet training cannot be achieved; and true *internal* conflict cannot be said to exist. In this respect, one of our Wartime Nursery children, Brigid, who had difficulty in acquiring control of her bladder, reached a turning point when she was able to announce, with feeling: 'No more wee-wee on the floor: Mummy doesn't like it; Nurse doesn't like it; *Brigid* doesn't like it.'

The crucial point that Brigid makes is that *she* doesn't like wee-wee on the floor; she takes an *affective*[6] attitude to unrestricted wetting and begins to find it repugnant, if not to hate it. Feelings play a considerable part in the defensive attitudes and inner controls that children build up and adults as a rule maintain.

Brigid has taken a step beyond that reached by Lisa in the story about the chocolates. Once Brigid had established true internal disappproval she would have been ashamed of herself had she relapsed into wetting. And if a child does something of which he is ashamed, he may not only hide his action from others; even the *thought* of the action may bring back the feeling of shame, and he may strive to hide the knowledge of it from himself. If Brigid's is an early step on the road to morality, it seems worth adding that not every adult has managed to take it. There are still many people for whom shame is experienced only when they are found out.

This is what Freud meant when he said that social anxiety is [historically] the essence of what is called conscience. The parents or their substitutes provide the social sanctions, and in some degree the sense of what is desirable, which form the foundations of internal authority. There is an internalisation of standards, as Brigid shows very well. The wish *to take pleasure* in wetting is no longer accessible to awareness. But it does not on that account cease to exist; it can

---

lips, mouth and skin. Pleasure derived from these various bodily areas can be recognised in the sexual foreplay of adults. The drives have various mental representations in the form of fantasies and wishes; many of these succumb to childhood amnesia, but others deriving and developing from them will find acceptable outlets. Others remain permanently unconscious. In adolescence there is a remodelling of drive derivatives as aggression and sexuality become capable of forceful expression, but the first five years or so of life, though for the most part inaccessible to memory, have profound influences on adolescent development. Man appears to be the only animal in which sexuality is bi-phasic. No one, I think, would dispute the reality of childhood aggression, though the force of it is limited by physical capability.

[6] Ie, emotionally charged. An affect is the general term for a state of feeling – happiness, sadness, anger, remorse or whatever else it may be. Some affects are complex, comprising mixed states of feeling; depression, for example, may contain, inter alia, a mixture of sadness and anger.

sometimes surface again when a new baby is born and a child who, until that time had no competitors, reverts to an early mode of behaviour. It can re-appear, too, in less normal circumstances – in certain cases of mental illness for example, or be put to deliberate use when the social approval and endorsement of a peer group overrides any individual scruples, and house-breakers express their anger on finding nothing of value by urinating and leaving excrement around the room.

These early moves from outer to inner seem quite insufficient to anticipate the massive childhood amnesia that sets in so decisively around the age of five. Pride and shame may help to make certain inclinations unavailable to consciousness, as Nietzsche recognised, and so make some contribution to the effectiveness of repression, but they cannot in themselves account for the effectiveness of a *repression barrier* of such a fateful kind. Something more is required.

Shame is not guilt. The two may co-exist; they may complement each other; in both, external origins precede an internal presence. But they are not the same. Freud came to regard guilt as a specific form of fear – fear of what he called the *superego*, using that term to extend the everyday notion of conscience to include its unconscious sources – sources which continue to operate beyond the level of conscious awareness, beyond the level of the sense of guilt that *is* accessible to introspection. We now have to address the question of how this *superego* – this conscience, *a powerful part of which is unconscious* and therefore operates silently – comes into being.

We have in fact already made a start. What have been described up to this point are early moves from the use of an external policeman to the use of an internal one, but it does not follow that both constables exercise identical functions, even though they recognisably belong to the same (parental) force. At first we see, internally, an incomplete representation of the external policeman, a mere cadet, who is able to discharge only limited functions, and who repeatedly needs reinforcements, orders, and support from outside.

Oddly enough, there is a similarity here with something I touched on earlier, with the state of affairs in children who develop a premature sense of guilt, a *kind* of conscience that is so harsh it gives the child no peace. It is as if the internal police cadet had been rushed through his training, qualified long before he was ready, was unable to use the power entrusted to him with any sense of fairness, and threw his weight about with excessive zeal. In such an instance, the child may repeatedly appeal to the real policeman, to the parents, seeking assurance and reassurance that he is really 'good', in order to deal with the sense of 'badness' that goes hand in hand with his failure to live up to the very high standards internally set for him and the severe and premature strictures of the internal cadet he has unwittingly imposed upon himself.

To pursue this matter further would take us too far into pathology, and we need to keep in mind a more normal state of affairs. More usually, in terms of our metaphor, the police cadet continues to rely for effective action upon external support. But harassed though he may be, he now draws strength from an unexpected quarter. *He draws it from the aggressive drive itself.* He turns to derivatives of that powerful force and uses them to re-enforce the internal prohibitions of the little person of whom he has taken charge. It is as if heavily armed ramparts bar the way to wishful impulses, thoughts, and fantasies that would otherwise get out of hand and threaten the small society in which the child is growing up and which he still needs for care and protection.

This remarkable advance in personal and social adaptation is presaged and reflected in certain changes to be observed in the fantasy play of children. Whereas, in the beginning, such play may tend to repeat, through imitation, the child's day-to-day experiences, he now begins to demonstrate a stand against powerful impulses to which, hitherto, he would have been tempted to give way. For example, one small boy who had always used dolls[7] to represent either himself or other children, and repeated with them the activities of his daily life around meal-times and bed-times, began to scold his dolls for their 'naughtiness' and 'dirtiness' , for doing 'wee-wees' and 'poos', and for being smelly or stinking. The dolls were dealt with harshly: they were often smacked and even thrown about. It would seem that the anger and humiliation aroused in the

---

[7] Child therapists often provide miniature dolls representing girls and boys, men and women, people in occupations of all kinds, for children to play with; often the child arranges the dolls in very informative ways that reflect their view of the state of the family, school-life as they see it, and so on.

child by external restraints and threats of punishment mobilised his aggression and the anxieties associated with it, so that they were defensively directed against the self.

It is impossible to understand the motivation behind these moves without giving due weight to *anxiety*. Indeed, it can be said that it is precisely the fear of loss of parental love which threatens the child with overwhelming anxiety, and which only appropriate internal measures can effectively keep at bay. Thus, on the one hand, the striving for pleasure makes it difficult for the young child to accept external prohibitions while, on the other hand, these selfsame prohibitions become an indispensable ally in the fight against his own pleasure-seeking demands.

How does it come about that the formation of the superego brings with it a sense of guilt? For its activities clearly go far beyond the exercise, conscious and unconscious, of simple checks and controls. Freud came to his views about guilt and its *unconscious power* by the fact of infantile sexuality and the instinctual life of childhood. He had to account for the manner in which the 'child's first great love affair', with its jealousy of the parental relationship, is banished from the memory as early incestuous attachments come to grief. If, in this context, the word 'incestuous' calls for justification, two points can be made. Firstly, *we are talking about impulses and fantasies, and not deeds* (except in the rarest instances where action is initiated by the parents). Secondly, in the early years of life the child's instinctual impulses, and the love and hate derived from them and through which they find expression, can *only* be directed against the family *because there is nowhere else for them to go*. It is only in the context of the family or its substitute that relationships have any meaning. Although counter-measures against these impulses and the wishes that strive to express them are, of course, set up, eventually such wishes have to be abandoned. The reasons for this are many and various: the impossibility that childhood incestuous wishes could ever be gratified; the fears of fantastic punishment or revenge; and even perhaps the fact that these childhood strivings were ordained to come to an end for constitutional reasons – all these, and others, could play a part.

But, if these sexual and destructive wishes are forbidden by the objects of the child's fantasies; if the child is compelled, for whatever reason, to abandon his aims; and if, too, he has to give up such aims in respect of others – then internal interdictions have to be replaced, or rather re-enforced, by the kind of internal policeman of which I have spoken and, to be successful, a policeman of impressive power. And there is one further point of cardinal importance. Just as the younger child fears loss of love, and punishment from the external arbiter of his conduct, so the older child possessed of an *internal parent or parents*, fears loss of love from that fantasy parent, and a fear of punishment known to us all as guilt.

If, to the adult, all this talk of a childhood love affair and its resolution has an air of unreality, it is important to remember that it is not just a matter of *real* events, of *real* threats, of *real* determinations and intentions. It is very much a matter of psychological realities, of psychological forces, where anything can happen because it can be thought, where fantasy and reality do not always recognise each other for the different forces that logic knows them to be. The internal police are therefore not simply police: they are *thought-police*. (The young child behaves as if he knows only too well the religious dictum that the evil thought cannot be distinguished from the evil deed, and may treat the one as if it were the other.)

It would not be true to say that the superego is simply an internal representative of the *real* parental precepts and prohibitions. Children of benign and understanding parents sometimes develop standards that are too harsh, too truly tyrannical, for their own good. Conversely, children who have been exposed to strict control and discipline sometimes achieve an unexpected degree of self-tolerance. There is no simple one-to-one correspondence: what is internalised is not an *objective* representation of the parents and their attitudes, but the parents as seen, consciously and unconsciously, through the child's eyes.

The child is not of course ruled internally simply by guilt or by shame and the fear of it. What is perceived by the child as loving and caring parental regard brings with it a wish for some degree of emulation. But it does more than that. It provides an *internal* source of love and self-esteem which helps to mitigate and modify the would be tyrant within. The child is no longer exclusively dependent on the approval of others for self-regard. But early idealisation of the parents and the wish to be like them is one of the ingredients of those ideals that provide the child with aims, guidelines and models in the conduct of his everyday life. To these may be added the way in which the child perceives the parental behaviour in its sexual and aggressive manifestations and the degree to which, in this respect, he will identify with the *real* parents; the manner in which the parents convey their concept of *their* ideal child, that is, the child they would like him to be; and whether father and mother convey *different* ideals and whether there are discrepancies between what they consciously or unconsciously convey. All these elements will be compounded in the formation of the child's *own* self-ideal, which will include, in addition, the attainment of his pleasure-seeking wishes, suitably modified by later developments to take full account of reality.

To return to the matter of guilt. The upheavals of adolescence are yet to come. Puberty brings with it a biological intensification of sexuality and aggression which puts a severe strain on the personality. For all its importance, childhood sexuality is a pale thing compared with its adolescent successor; and childhood aggression still lacks the physical means to inflict the damage it may entertain in fantasy. Existing checks and controls can no longer contain these drives without reinforcement. On the other hand, total instinctual suppression runs counter to the psychological tasks of adolescence: psychic health demands that the extensive restrictions imposed during latency[8] are modified. Sexuality must be freed, but only *outside* the family, now that the physical means exist to translate wish into action. Conscience is at a crossroads.

Unconsciously, the tyranny within is denounced; consciously, the uprising takes the form of the 'adolescent rebellion'. The tyranny is perceived once more as if it came from without – from the parents and the social values they are thought to personify. Sexuality may be acclaimed and aggresssion and war attacked – as it was so forcefully in the sixties but still is today – in the most belligerent terms. The loving side of the superego may find expression in youthful idealism; but the incest taboo generally remains unscathed. Indeed, since the attack on the superego is, at bottom, an attack on the parents, it fosters, in turn, the shift of sexuality towards the outside world. This indispensable part of growing up is naturally painful to many parents when they feel the force of their child's hostility and are unable to understand the strength of the love behind it.

The adolescent process modifies the tyrant, but it does not do away with it. In any case, its loving aspects have to survive in maintaining self-esteem. And the fight is far from one sided; the struggle may be long and intense but it does not end in total defeat. What results, if all goes well, is an agency that gives guidance, sets standards and gives aims. It fortifies the ability to co-operate and fit in, but its standards will not lightly be set aside simply by social manipulation. *Behaviour* may change, but the way one feels about it may not. Shame and guilt may not disappear. Up to a point, perhaps that is just as well.

Social psychologists and sociologists need to recognise that while many radical changes in society are necessary or desirable, these changes will not in themselves produce a revolution in internal harmony or disharmony. It is true that those whose superego is weak will take extra comfort from social approval, and that social disapproval may add to the discomfort of those whose superego is stronger than perhaps it ought to be. The danger is that, in considering the relationship between the internal and external, the importance of the one may be emphasised at the expense of the other.

A great deal that is militantly written and said today about important social issues such as feminism and sexuality makes precisely this mistake. It treats 'traditional' attitudes to these questions solely as the result of the social forces. Essentially, they fail to see that, unlike Pavlov's dogs, people may be more than a product of their environment. Such a view is thoroughly insulting both to children and to adults, but it is not difficult to see how it may have arisen. On the one hand, understandably, it ignores the existence of the repression barrier. On the other hand, unconsciously, it takes sides with it and regards what cannot be remembered as

---

[8] Latency is the period of relative sexual quiescence in childhood. It follows the ending of 'the first great love affair' when instinctual wishes are centred around the parents, when the superego is established, and when childhood amnesia sets in. The child's interests are generally turned outwards in this period, busily taking in the new and (generally) exciting new world outside the family. The period starts to come to an end in a time before adolescence proper, when sexuality returns with far greater force than it had before.

of no account. But the fears, fantasies and improbabilities of childhood will not be dismissed so easily. Unless we respect the child within, and the struggles he encounters, true social respect, and realistic attitudes based on it, may remain as elusive as ever. Perhaps the writers of fairy stories knew children better than we remember them through ourselves.

In children under five, access to the unconscious is not so impeded: the repression barrier is not yet fully formed and has not acquired the strength it has yet to achieve under the impact of the superego. The point may best be made through a true story. A little patient of mine, barely three years old, did not like some information about herself that I was trying to give her. Drawing herself up to her full height, she declared: 'Dr Yorke! I don't like you and I wish you were dead! Only you'd better not die just yet because next week I might have changed my mind.' No barrier, perhaps; and not yet conscience: but internal conflict, to be sure.

AFTERNOTE

This account is a generic one and does not address the complex issues of differences in superego formation in boys and girls, brought about by differences in sexual development. Nor have I examined the equally complex role of maternal and paternal contributions to superego formation – a difficult task in any case and one in need of further elucidation. These matters are undeniably important, but it is hoped that the general outline presented here will serve our purposes sufficiently well.

FIFTH PLENARY SESSION

This session took the form of questions and answers.

(a)   Were internal controls (conscience) innate or developed by social forces?

Dr Yorke said that internal controls of varying degrees of effectiveness were developed in every child, and it was hard to be sure to what extent they sprang from innate factors and to what extent they were moulded by upbringing. Sometimes, it seemed to him, constitutional factors were so strong that it was difficult for social and family (external) forces to bring about an effective and aim-giving conscience. In others, external factors seemed to play a predominant part. However, the superego was not simply an internal representative of **real** parental precepts and prohibitions but was also a product of parental standards and behaviour **as perceived by the child**. So the question of the comparative contributions of innate and social influences was not easy to answer. Although some attributes of the personality were built in rather than acquired, most seemed to him to result from the interplay between the innate and social forces. As all people develop a conscience of some kind, however imperfect or ineffective, innate factors evidently played a part: but the language spoken was that of the environment. To give an example by way of analogy, a child born into an articulate family learned to speak more readily (and with more skill) than a child born into an inarticulate family, but everyone develops speech. But the inarticulate were more likely to express themselves in action when they lacked the words. (Indeed, Freud said that the first person who was able to hurl abuse at his enemy instead of a spear had taken the first step to civilisation.) The answer was uncertain, but it would seem that conscience had innate roots but was developed by circumstances.

(b)   Could early childhood experiences 'smash' innate conscience?

Dr Yorke felt that enormous damage could be done if, for example, a child was subject to abusive behaviour. Inter alia, abuse could affect the development of the sense of shame and lead to intense feelings of worthlessness. There was also the question of 'shamelessness'. He said it was striking that people who had abused their children, and especially the children of others (paedophiles) often spoke about it without any sense of shame. Moreover, those many perpetrators of child abuse who had themselves been abused as children often had a very low self-esteem. This illustrated the complexities of the superego as an internal source of both criticism and self-regard. In essence, if a perpetrator did not think much of himself, he might not have the need to feel ashamed. The view of the self was affected by the manner in which the family operated – thus, if a sense of self worth had not been absorbed from the outset, and the love of the child had been absent then the individual's value of himself was skewed from the beginning.

(c)   Could psychopaths have a conscience?

Dr Yorke felt that though they behaved as if they did not, they often had some form of conscience, however atypical. But as psychopaths did not as a rule seek treatment, studies relating to their 'conscience' were not readily available.

(d)   What were the reasons for infantile amnesia?

Dr Yorke stated that memory of early life begins to retreat rapidly from the age of five years with the result that, within a short space of time, memory could only be reconstructed, not recalled; though family memory for the child's early life was often passed on, and this, together with the child's fantasies about it, could sometimes give the impression that more was remembered than was actually the case. He said that the loss of memory was not simply an unconscious 'defence mechanism', nor was it due to the fact that memory was not properly developed in a young child (for example, a 3-year-old child often has a remarkable memory of earlier events). But at the age of five or so, for complex psychological reasons and others unknown (and perhaps innate) something radical happens to affect memories of early life. Adults could to some extent 'reconstruct in a general way' instances of their early years but they could not remember (other than a very few) specific events. Such 'memories' had a 'portmanteau quality' in which a number of separate events might be telescoped into a single one. But if the precise reasons for the memory loss were unclear, the changes occurring in the first few years were momentous, with massive and rapid development taking place within a very short time. Moreover, much development occurred before language had been acquired and so earliest development made itself felt only through actions and sensations that had their origins in those years. For all that, the forces arising during the period of infantile amnesia continued to operate in the unconscious and profoundly affect attitudes and actions in later life. It was clear that many adults had a facility to behave as if they were in touch with whose first few years of childhood through actions (for an example, an ability to relate to, and play with, young children) or through sensual experiences (for example, smell evoking a memory) but there seemed to be a difference in the quality of verbal and non-verbal memories. Although pre-verbal memory was important its accuracy was difficult to assess (because of the impossibility of conversing with a pre-verbal child). Early traumatic events, even though masked by memory loss, could profoundly affect an individual throughout adult life and might often be the root of deviant behaviour.

(e)   Could early development in one family affect a later move to another?

Dr Yorke said it was almost impossible to change appreciably what had been built up in a child's inner world once it was firmly organised there. Although adopters had a natural wish to obliterate old memories – because they wanted a dream child of their own – they could not change the child's internal system of controls once these were well established. A study had been carried out at Yale University to discover if it was possible to lay down a time limit after which it was difficult or impossible to move a child to different caretakers with any degree of success. No definite conclusion was reached but, it *was* a fact that, early adoption had the best chance of success. In large measure, this was due to the adopters' better opportunity to influence the child through their own precepts, example and expectations and to develop a good adult/child relationship. If adoption took place at a later stage the child would seek to perpetuate its early relationships and, if these had been abusive, he or she would seek to recreate the circumstances of abuse.

In the light of this it was agreed that post-adoption help was required to assist adopters to know more about a child's early life and, where possible, its effects (sometimes assessed in treatment). However, it was recognised that there was a dilemma because many adopters might be afraid to proceed with adoption if they knew much of the child's detailed background.

SIXTH SESSION

Dr Jill Hodges and Dr Bryn Williams

INTRODUCTION TO PAPER

Dr Hodges pointed out that most studies of sexually offending behaviour towards children were of adults (who had organised paedophiliac fantasies). These studies were not necessarily appropriate to young abusers, because at this age their sexual organisation was more fluid. Accordingly, it was important to consider child offenders as 'children at risk/children in need' because this categorisation gave a better opportunity for preventative help.

TENSIONS IN TREATMENT

Together with a Senior Registrar, Dr Hodges interviewed a 13-year-old boy who had abused younger children. The initial reaction of the Senior Registrar was one of revulsion. During interview the 13-year-old boy gave a detailed account of his own victimisation/abuse at the hands of his step-father. He spoke of his feelings of being unable to avoid being like the abuser and there was a strong sense of the boy being pushed by factors beyond his control into damaging other children. At the end of the session, the Senior Registrar exclaimed 'Poor little boy'. Dr Hodges indicated that both reactions – revulsion and sympathy – were understandable/correct and that they illustrated the tensions which were present when dealing with child sexual abusers.

RISK FACTORS

An abused child could become an abuser, but this depended not only on the nature of the abuse suffered and the period over which the abuse had occurred, but on the presence of other adversities in the child's life. Factors which militated against this occurring included (1) The child had experienced continuity of care in its life; (2) There was no violence in the family scenario; (3) The child had established a good attachment relationship with someone during its life.

CONSCIENCE AND GUILT

In this study, the young abusers often had 'A vicious conscience', coupled with no inner sense of self worth. The result was that conscience was avoided and its promptings did not come into play to modify behaviour. For example, a young boy who had severely abused his sister was meanwhile ashamed and guilty. He had devised detailed plans for his own suicide but his 'severe conscience' had not stopped the abusive behaviour.

CHANGE OF CARER

A child acquired an internal system of values as a result of the experiences of its early years – the pattern of behaviour which resulted could not be broken easily. In reality, behaviour could only be changed if foster/adoptive parents had the necessary knowledge. There were courses for foster parents who had to deal with victims of abuse but, despite this, foster parents often could not cope because the pattern of destructive behaviour continued. There was often less support and assistance for adopters and it would be sensible if such education were available for them.

CHILDREN WHO SEXUALLY ABUSE OTHER CHILDREN

Hodges, J., Williams, B., Andreou, C., Lanyado, M., Bentovim, A., and Skuse, D.
Behavioural Sciences Unit
Institute of Child Health
University of London
30 Guildford Street
London WC1N 1EH

Intervention in cases of child maltreatment where the abuser is a parent or other adult tends to feel more straightforward than when the perpetrator, as well as the victim, is a child. Prior to the research we shall describe, over the past few years at the Great Ormond Street Hospital for Sick Children and the Institute of Child Health there has been a significant increase in the number of children and young adolescents, primarily male, who have sexually abused other children. Our emphasis has been to see the young abuser as a *child in need* and we have recently completed a preliminary investigation into the origins of sexually abusive behaviour in adolescent boys. Our approach is developmental and we have been able to build on our experience in the Child Sexual Abuse team of treating victims of sexual abuse and working with families and care workers to help children overcome the trauma of abuse. This paper sets out two questions which we believe are important to address based on our clinical experience and previous research. As well as describing and illustrating our initial conclusions, and outlining some of the likely psychological mechanisms, we shall discuss some of the implications of our research for those called upon to make judgments about young sexual abusers.

Since the early 1980s, it has become well established that adolescents are responsible for committing a significant proportion of all reported sex offences. Bearing in mind the fact that official statistics are unlikely to represent the full extent of abuse perpetrated by young people, figures indicate that 16% of all recorded sex crimes are committed by those aged 16 or younger (Home Office, 1992). The National Children's Home Report to the Committee of Enquiry into young sexual perpetrators suggested that many victims of abuse feel guilty and ashamed of the role they played in the abuse and are often reluctant to inform someone they trust and consequently many young abusers are not held accountable for their behaviour. Studies in the United States suggest that families often do not report abusive behaviour because it is common to regard such behaviour as experimental and exploratory (Ryan, 1986).

Establishing an unambiguous and comprehensive definition of sexually abusive behaviour, perpetrated by a minor is highly relevant. The National Children's Home report suggests that issues of coercion, abuse of power, consent and aggression are significant factors in any definition of adolescent sexual perpetration. The age disparity between the victim and the perpetrator has traditionally been considered important, although it is now thought necessary to examine the nature of the behaviour, the context in which the sexual act took place, and the developmental level of the children involved in defining abuse (Cantwell, 1988). The term 'sexual perpetrators' suggests a homogenous group and yet it is misleading to think of sexual perpetrating as constituting a single pattern of behaviour or having the same aetiological basis. This can be seen in the following examples drawn from cases referred to the Child Sexual Abuse Team at Great Ormond Street Hospital for Sick Children.

Two boys from the same family who were close in age, both had been abused by an older foster brother who had come to live in their home, and had subsequently been discovered engaging in masturbatory activity together. The boys were referred as perpetrators of abuse who had themselves experienced traumatic sexual abuse. It had not been established who the perpetrator was of the two. During psychotherapy it became clear that whilst the sexual behaviour between the boys was not healthy, it was difficult to describe the behaviour as abuse as it was more a consensual pattern of behaviour which emerged as a result of their own abuse.

A boy was referred as a perpetrator who was not known to have been sexually abused, but had experienced bullying and humiliation at school. On leaving school one day he assaulted a peer involved with the bullying, threatening him with a knife. During the assault, he found himself sexually aroused and the physical assault became a sexual assault.

A boy was referred as a victim of abuse. Through the process of psychotherapy he was able to tell his therapist that he experienced homosexual fantasies and later that his fantasies were of young boys. Although extremely painful he was able to say that he had begun cutting out pictures of young boys and looking at them whilst masturbating. There was no evidence that he had acted out these sexual fantasies. However, concern was raised that unless an effective intervention was made he represented a high risk of abusing young children in the future.

These examples illustrate the importance of examining the context in which the abuse took place, and establishing an index of risk. When one uses the term 'sex offender', 'adolescent abuser' or 'young perpetrator' consideration should be given to exactly what behaviour is being referred to.

Finkelhor (1984) suggests that in the general population between 2.5% and 8.7% of males have been sexually abused at some time. Around 50% of adolescent perpetrators of sexual abuse are reported to be victims of sexual abuse themselves, and this is widely recognised as an important factor in the development of sexually abusive behaviour (Watkins and Bentovim, 1992). However, when we consider the total number of male victims of sexual abuse it is clear that those who go on to sexually abuse others represent a minority. In other words, if we study a group of young sexual abusers retrospectively we would expect to find that around half were themselves victims of sexual abuse; conversely if we study a group of sexually abused boys prospectively, without intervention, we could not know at the outset how many are likely to become sexual abusers. In effect we do not know why some, but not all go on to abuse others (Hodges, Lanyado and Andreou, 1994).

The first question which is of interest to us is, **why a small proportion of victims of sexual abuse go on to become sexual abusers whilst others do not**. Key factors which may predict the progression from victim to perpetrator have been suggested as part of a model which conceptualises a risk index including: the relationship between victim and perpetrator, type of abuse, duration of abuse and the age at which the abuse occurs. In addition the victim's response by denying, blaming of others and aggressive acting out are also suggested (Watkins & Bentovim, 1992).

Given that only around 50% of adolescent sexual abusers are themselves victims of sexual abuse, our second question is, **what factors underlie the genesis of sexually abusive behaviour in the absence of sexual victimisation**. Two indicators have previously been suggested in evidence from North America. First, it is suggested that a proportion of young abusers display a more generalised pattern of antisocial behaviour. Becker (1990) postulates that sexually abusive behaviour is simply a feature of antisocial behaviour. She cites the example of an adolescent who breaks into a house with the intention of stealing property, who on finding a woman alone in the building rapes her. An alternative explanation for what makes some young people become abusers in the absence of sexual victimisation concerns other forms of abuse. Deblinger, McLeer, Atkins, Ralphe and Foa (1989) concluded that 17% of physically abused children display sexually inappropriate behaviour.

Much of what we currently know about the characteristics of young sexual abusers, their development and families is based on clinical reports and case studies. Whilst this provides us with important information which can be used to assess and treat the young abuser, there is a need to compare the young sexual abuser with other groups of normal and disturbed young people in order to gain a greater understanding about which factors are specific to this group. We know that around half of adult sex offenders report experiencing sexual arousal to young children and beginning their sexually abusive career during late childhood and early adolescence (Abel et al, 1987). This period when normally sexual orientation is not fully consolidated, might therefore provide the most valuable window of opportunity for working with the young sexual abuser in order to shift their sexual behaviour into a non-abusive path of development.

SIXTH SESSION

To outline how we investigated these questions we shall describe briefly the structure of the study. The sexually abused and abusing boys were referred to the Child Sexual Abuse Team at Great Ormond Street Hospital. Referrals of young people abusing within the family were already increasing: 15% of victims referred to the department had been abused by siblings or cousins (Monck et al, 1995). The research team was multidisciplinary, including child and adolescent psychotherapists, child psychiatrists, clinical psychologist and developmental psychologists[1]. The research was designed as a three year *hypothesis generating* study to investigate four groups of boys between the ages of 11 and 16:

Group 1 – Boys who were known to have been sexually abused but not known to have abused others (Victims).

Group 2 – Boys who were known to have sexually abused other children and known to be victims of sexual abuse themselves (Victimised Perpetrators).

Group 3 – Boys who sexually abused other children but were not known to be victims of sexual abuse themselves (Non-Victimised Perpetrators).

Group 4 – A comparison group of primarily behaviourally disturbed boys with no history of sexual victimisation or sexually abusive behaviour.

Referrals to the research project came primarily from Child Protection social workers across south east England. The boys were managed by the Child Sexual Abuse team at the hospital who ensured that all Child Protection issues were satisfied before the research assessment begun. All cases of boys matching the requirements of the research protocol on the basis of age and presenting problem were initially assessed by a child psychiatrist or child psychotherapist. The research comprised a two stage assessment, the first providing a broad investigation of the boy's developmental and cognitive functioning, and an examination of his familial and social adjustment. Stage two included 12 individual weekly sessions of a psychoanalytically informed 'psychotherapeutic assessment' which were conducted by the child psychotherapists.

Since recruitment of referrals of young male victims and abusers to the hospital in the summer of 1992, there were 160 enquiries, and from those 118 referrals until December 1994. Eighty-six boys were seen in stage one of the research assessment. This included an assessment of the boys' intelligence, psychiatric problems and psychological adjustment. In addition, detailed studies were made of the family through an interview with the boys' mothers, and of psychosocial adjustment through school based peer assessments. The majority of boys in all four groups were from white, lower socio-economic group families. Their experiences as victims of sexual abuse were severe. Many of the boys had been anally penetrated by fathers and step-fathers. The abuse in many cases had begun at a young age and had continued over a prolonged period. The sexual abusers in the study had typically abused children who were much younger than themselves and the abuse included a wide range of sexual behaviour, the most common being anal and vaginal penetration.

Of those cases 46 boys were taken into 12 weeks of the intensive psychotherapeutic assessment: the number of boys in each of the four groups was roughly equal. Six of the sessions were semi-structured, and during these a number of questionnaires and semi-structured interview methods were used to collect information about the boys, their childhood experiences and their internal mental state. These included structured psychological instruments to assess hostility, psychological trauma and anxiety. As the research was designed to be exploratory and hypothesis generating the research team have used a range of less conventional research methods to maximise the use of the psychotherapy sessions.

Another instrument used during the course of the psychotherapeutic assessment was a revised version of the Adult Attachment Interview (George, Kaplan and Main, 1985) adapted for use with adolescents. Themes raised by the boys during the course of the interview were extracted by independent raters in order to compare the early childhood experiences of victims and

---

[1] The research team included: Dr David Skuse (Professor of Behavioural Sciences), Dr Arnon Bentovim (Consultant Child Psychiatrist), Dr Jill Hodges (Consultant Child & Adolescent Psychotherapist), Chriso Andreou (Child and Adolescent Psychotherapist), Monica Lanyado (Child and Adolescent Psychotherapist), Michelle New (Clinical Psychologist), Dr Jim Stevenson (Reader in Psychology), Bryn Williams (Research Psychologist).

abusers. The psychotherapists also made clinical ratings on abuse related issues and other factors which they felt were clinically important in differentiating boys who sexually abused from those who did not. This process was crucial for identifying characteristics of the boys and processes involved in the development of sexually abusive behaviour specifically, above and beyond being a clinically referred population. In other words, all of the boys referred to the project were likely to display a certain degree of psychological disturbance; our aim was to isolate the characteristics of those boys who were at risk of either beginning, or continuing, sexually abusive patterns of behaviour. The use of psychoanalytically focused psychotherapeutic research assessments represents a unique approach in understanding the development of sexually abusive behaviour.

On the basis of standardised psychological questionnaires and the rich clinical material collected during the course of the psychotherapy the team has begun to highlight a number of possible characteristics associated with boys who become perpetrators of sexual abuse. These are in effect hypotheses for further research; they have been developed based on our work with the sample of boys referred to the hospital up to late 1994. Since in this exploratory stage the hypotheses are tested on the same group of boys from which they were developed, the preliminary findings cannot necessarily be generalised to other groups of abusers.

These preliminary findings indicate a number of risk factors. We were looking for characteristics which seemed to differentiate the perpetrating boys from the non-perpetrators, and in particular the victimised perpetrators from the victims who had not gone on to abuse sexually. We looked particularly at experiences which *preceded* their perpetrating behaviour, if abusers, or their own experience of being abused, if non-perpetrating victims.

Among the boys in this study, factors which seemed especially important included:

(1)   exposure to a climate of violence in the home,
(2)   experience of physical violence,
(3)   discontinuity of care,
(4)   a feeling of being rejected,
(5)   the mother having been a victim of sexual abuse. (This last item was based on an interview with the mother, and was not elicited from or discussed with the boys themselves.)

Other studies have identified a link between sexual offending and previous physical abuse and other adversities (see Watkins and Bentovim, 1992, Vizard et al, 1995, for review). Very broadly, we feel that the first four points may contribute mainly to whether or not a boy becomes an 'abuser-in-general', while the fifth has a bearing on why boys who have not themselves been subject to sexual abuse may go on to become sexual perpetrators. It is important to emphasise here that this study concerns young adolescents; we do not see them as having a structured sexual perversion and even without intervention we do not believe that all would go on to develop one. But intervention during this phase of development may go some way to reducing the risk, and we shall return to the question of protective intervention in the conclusion.

The occurrence and the psychological effects of the first four factors – exposure to a climate of violence at home, experience of physical violence, discontinuity of care, and feeling rejected – are interrelated. We shall take them in turn and outline some of the mechanisms through which they may have effects upon individual development and functioning. It will be evident that the effects can be considered along two broad dimensions, which are themselves related; those of developmental trauma, and of aggression.

Experience of physical violence, and exposure to a climate of violence within the home, were found in 83% and 78% of perpetrators, respectively, as compared to 39% and 43% of the non-perpetrating boys. Both experiences subject the child to fear, stress and trauma, often for long periods of childhood development, adversely affecting key developmental tasks and personality development (Pynoos, Sorensen and Steinberg, 1993).

Sixty-five per cent of the perpetrators had experienced another form of trauma, in the form of discontinuities of care during childhood (prior to their abusive behaviour) as compared to 20% of the non-perpetrators. They had lived in turn with various parents and step-parents and at times in Local Authority care. This, together with feeling rejected by the family, (70% of perpetrators, 27% of non-perpetrators) has a bearing on attachment and the lack of a secure relationship with an adult. Severe, unpredictable, early life stresses have been found to be related to the development of psychopathology in adulthood, while numerous studies have shown that a close confiding relationship is a protective factor (Rutter, 1987). The perpetrating boys in this study tended to have had the worst of both worlds.

Although, there was of course a range of severity in the traumas experienced, and only a minority of the boys showed behavioural signs of post-traumatic stress, we feel that it may be important to take into account the possible effects of a traumatising early environment upon development. We shall mention 'neurodevelopmental' effects upon brain chemistry and structure (for review see Perry, 1993), and the implications of recent work in attachment theory.

In outline, the neurodevelopmental approach examines how prolonged, intense or frequent stresses may alter brain development. 'Understanding the traumatised child requires recognition of a key principle of development neurobiology: *the brain develops and organises as a reflection of developmental experience*, organising in response to the pattern, intensity and nature of sensory and perceptual experience ... (T)he traumatised child's template for brain oganisation is the stress response' (Perry, 1993). As a result of developing in an unpredictable, stressful, frightening environment, the brain adapts on the basis that this is what the world in general has in store. Thus even if the environment alters, 'the traumatised child is walking around in a persisting fear state', hyper-reactive and hyper-sensitive to everyday stressors, and likely to show 'flight or fight' in response.

The discontinuity of care and sense of rejection prominent in the earlier histories of the young abusers suggest that in general they lacked secure early attachment relationships. Research in attachment theory suggests that if children show a 'secure' pattern of attachment behaviour in infancy, this tends to become internalised during development so that they have, as it were, a sense of security which they can carry with them into new situations. Attachment relationships in infancy have been found to have considerable continuities with later development, affecting among other things capacities for relationships, self-esteem, independence and affect regulation. Children showing 'insecure' attachment patterns in infancy are at risk for becoming victims or victimisers of peers by middle childhood (Holmes, 1993).

Recent studies have found that in samples of maltreating parents, about 80% of infants show 'disorganised/disorientated' attachment behaviour to a parent in the 'Strange Situation' assessment, while the proportion in normal populations is very much lower. Such behaviour appears to occur when the parent, as attachment figure and hence source of security, is also a source of fear, thus placing the child in an impossible dilemma where no organised response to the stress can be made. By middle childhood these children develop a pattern in response to separation of controlling their parents, either punitively or through solicitous 'parenting', while in contrast to this organised behaviour, doll play separations elicit violent, bizarre or catastrophic fantasies. This is unlike the representational play of children classified as 'secure' in infancy, who can acknowledge anxiety within a narrative but follow it with a happy ending; and also unlike the play of children who had been classified 'insecure' (Main, 1994). In other words, although children who had been 'disorganised/disorientated' were now able to show organisation at the level of behaviour, their emotional world still appeared frightening and disorganised.

In summary, the effects of early trauma and poor attachment relationships render children more likely to experience later events as stressful, threatening or frightening, and many of their responses are likely to be aggressive in nature. Quite apart from simple imitation or 'social modelling' of parental aggression, aggressive behaviour may be the 'fight' response of a traumatised child. Somewhat similarly, a number of psychoanalytic writers (eg Glasser, 1979) have emphasised the automatic nature of an aggressive or rage response when the individual experiences a threat to the self. This threat may not be a physical threat, but a threat for instance to self-esteem, produced by verbal criticism or aggression. A child threatened with loss of a parent is not only anxious but also intensely angry (Bowlby, 1988), although as this anger may not be safely shown towards the parent the child may displace its expression elsewhere.

For the boys who were victims, the particular traumatic effects of their own experience of sexual abuse must also be considered. Bentovim (1992) integrates many familial and individual processes in the model of the 'trauma-organised system'. Regarding traumatisation by sexual abuse he emphasises how flashbacks and memories, triggered by chance reminders of the trauma, may lead to abusive behaviour as part of the pattern of externalising responses which generally characterises male victims more often than female ones. Concurrent physical abuse, as well as the presence of conduct disorder, PTSD or a number of other psychiatric diagnoses, is seen as potentiating this externalising coping adaptation (Watkins and Bentovim, 1992). Of other aspects of 'traumagenic dynamics' (Finkelhor, 1987, Bentovim 1992) powerlessness may stimulate abusive behaviour as part of a compensatory aggressive dominating response; the sense of rejection may lead the boy to seek emotional closeness of a sexualised kind, while the sense of betrayal and stigmatisation may lead the boy to seek victims whom they can treat as they were treated, thus defending themselves against feelings of humiliation.

Compared to direct responses to trauma, these are more complex and integrated ways in which aggression may be passed on to others by its victim. The psychoanalytic concepts of unconscious identificatory and defensive processes, and of the role of fantasy, are important here. Identification with the aggressor, as a defence mechanism, has a foot in both of these camps. To avoid the terror of feeling the victim, the child identifies with the threatening aspects of the feared person, and acts (or imagines acting) like this aggressor. First described as a particular defence mechanism by A. Freud (1936), it can occur in response to various situations of threat – criticism, physical aggression, etc; and can occur before feared aggression as well as after actual aggression. Children who have been exposed to violent and threatening adults may well use this mechanism of defence against terrifying feelings and memories.

Another defensive manoeuvre often seen in children who have suffered traumatic and violent experiences, has been described as compensatory fantasy or escape into fantasy. In the particular situation of the traumatised child, it is in effect an identification with the aggressor in fantasy rather than in behaviour. Where the child feels endangered, but is vulnerable and powerless to fight back, he develops instead extremely aggressive 'revenge fantasies' (Pynoos et al, 1993) of power and invulnerability. These fantasies are found not only in abused and traumatised children but may also appear in other children who have unavoidably been subjected to painful and frightening experiences, accompanied by a feeling of helplessness and lack of protection by adults; for example, in children who have experienced much surgical or medical treatment when too young to understand the reasons and procedures.

Aggression is the core of the sexually abusive behaviour of the great majority of the boys seen in the study. For some, the sexually abusive behaviour appeared quite literally to be an attack on another child out of a sense of grievance at the privileged position they perceived their victim to have within the family.

Lenny was a young non-victimised perpetrator referred to the research having sexually abused his younger half brother (Robert), whom he perceived as the preferred child of his mother and step-father. He was a traumatised boy who had been subject to much violence and had lacked any experience of secure parental care. During the course of the psychotherapeutic assessment Lenny discussed his fear of becoming a (physical) abuser like his father and yet was unable to link his fear and denial of being an abuser with already having sexually abused and continuing to physically abuse Robert.

Another form of grievance may be particularly relevant to mention here as it concerns the symbolic role which the criminal justice system can play for the young victim in holding their abuser/s accountable. Successful prosecution of the abuser can act in a helpful therapeutic way in that the child feels the adult world has acted protectively, has made a clear statement that the abuser was responsible for wrongdoing, and has affirmed the child's own experience. Conversely, in some cases where despite the child's giving evidence, their abuser has been found not guilty, the boys' subsequent sense of grievance appears to have played a role in their own perpetrating behaviour. During the therapeutic sessions we found that it was not until the boys' own victim experience was addressed that they were able to think about and adequately acknowledge their own abusive behaviour.

SIXTH SESSION

Aggression, through these various psychological mechanisms, seems to play a major role in the development of sexually abusing behaviour. However, despite all their traumatic experience, it still remains to explore why those boys who have not themselves been sexual victims should sexually abuse others.

Campbell (1994) remarks that the 'burden of proof still lies with those who disagree with Freud's (1896) observation that children cannot find their way to acts of sexual aggression unless they have been seduced previously'. The group of boys we studied suggests an alternative route for the intergenerational transmission of sexual abuse or at least an indirect form of seduction. We found that among our group of perpetrating boys who had *not* themselves been sexually abused, a very high proportion had *mothers* who had suffered sexual abuse during their own childhood.

We see this as a key factor in explaining why the abuse perpetrated by the boy should take a sexual form. Our study could not itself address the mode by which the mother's history of abuse is transmitted to her son, in such a way as to increase the risk of his becoming a sexual perpetrator. However, it seems likely that the mother's mental representation of male figures and her relationships with them, as well as of appropriate generational boundaries, is altered by her own experience of abuse, and that her behaviour then reflects these representations in some way. One study (Sroufe et al, 1985) provides some evidence of this, in finding that women who suffered sexual abuse as children tended to behave in over-intimate ways with their young male children, including controlling them in seductive, over-intimate ways. This was specific to this relationship with their son, as evidenced by the finding that their relationships with their daughters were of a very different kind, distant and somewhat rejecting.

We do not know of systematic evidence on abused mothers' relationships with their sons after early childhood, nor of the role of fathers in moderating or exacerbating the effects of the mothers' behaviour to their sons. It may be that there is a particularly important time once the boy has entered puberty, when the fact of the boy's physical sexual maturity calls for a re-negotiation of relationships between mother (and father) and son as one of the normal tasks of adolescence. A mother who has herself been sexually abused may find particular difficulty in negotiating appropriate relationships with a son who is now sexually mature, so that the relationship continues to be one which transmits inappropriately sexualising messages to the boy.

The boy as a young child may also identify with the mother as a figure who is powerful and controlling in a way which is also seductive, and (especially in the absence of a father as an alternative identificatory figure) this may continue to influence the boy's relationships with younger children, and thus play a role in the development of abusive behaviour.

In summary, there may be various mechanisms which provide a pathway of transmission of the mother's own abuse to the boy in the form of an inappropriately sexualised representation of the self and of relationships. It seems likely that in interaction with aggression, this can lead to sexual perpetration by a boy who has not himself been sexually abused. The mother's history as a victim may also increase the likelihood of her giving in when faced with confrontation, with the consequence that she finds it difficult to set clear boundaries for the boy's behaviour.

Finally, we shall address the possible implications of research findings for those working with young victims and perpetrators of sexual abuse. With respect to the comparison between victims and victims who have become abusers themselves, the characteristics which discriminate between the two groups (experiencing violence in the family, witnessing violence, experiencing rejection by the family and discontinuity of care) indicate a long-term adverse family environment preceding the onset of sexually abusive behaviour. It emphasises how crucial it is for Child Protection Teams to do all that is possible to create a safe and secure environment within which the child who has suffered abuse can develop, with the intention of interrupting the progression from victim to perpetrator. There are likely to be a number of avenues available to create the appropriate environment for the child, and the choice is likely to be determined by the level of dysfunction in the child's family situation. In the first instance this may take the form of intervening within the family to remove the adult perpetrator and to enable a non-abusing parent to protect their child from further harm, although this may not be possible if the non-abusing parent continues to foster relations with a known abuser. For example, the Child Sexual Abuse Team at Great Ormond Street Hospital has established methods of working which emphasise individual and group therapeutic work with victims, and work with the family network, aimed at improving family relationships to reverse rejection and other negative processes. Work with the perpetrator is carried out separately. Rehabilitation is attempted only if there is acceptance of responsibility for the abuse.

A second avenue, and one which has been observed to provide a very important role in the lives of some of the boys seen in our study, is the option of foster placements.

Frank was a 13-year-old referred to the project having sexually abused his half sister. He was the victim of a paedophile ring, in which his father made him and his sister engage in sexual acts for the gratification of adults who would watch them. Frank's parents had divorced following a history of family violence which was exacerbated by drug and alcohol abuse by the father. Following Frank's abuse of his half sister he was placed in foster care during which he became very attached to his foster mother, in ways reminiscent of a much younger child, and with her support and care was able to begin to confront his own painful early childhood experiences and his own behaviour.

However, other boys, even when they were placed in safe and caring foster homes, experienced their new homes as a 'version' of their unsafe and violent home. Foster carers trying their best to provide a safe and secure base can easily to be perceived by the traumatised young person as unhelpful and potential abusers. Foster carers who are themselves subjected to aggression, and at times made to feel rejecting and abusive, will require more than good intentions and emotional strength to help these boys. They need training, preparation and support to enable them to sustain and keep these young people safe from further risk to themselves and others. Without this, the likelihood of the placement breaking down is strong. One of the boys we saw was severely traumatised from his early experiences of being brought up in a home environment of physical and sexual abuse and was consequently placed in foster care with a woman who had considerable experience of working with disturbed adolescents. His therapist observed:

> 'John used to cling to his carer, unable to let her out of his sight in case something happened to her or she abandoned him. At times, however, he would become very aggressive and used to run away for days at a time. The foster mother found she was unable to tolerate the level of anxiety she had to cope with. Furthermore the patience required and time John needed for his behaviour to change became too much for her and in the end she asked for him to be placed elsewhere. For John this confirmed what he expected to happen and was perceived by him to be brought about by his own destructive behaviour.'

Another risk factor during adolescence for boys like John is the lack of a good male role model:

> 'John used to run away to railways stations where he used to allow himself to be picked up by men who sexually abused him. It transpired during his assessment that in his mind railway stations were linked to the only happy memories he had of his father, who had abused him but whom he still longed for. It was not until he made this connection in his mind that he began to struggle with the reality of going to stations and placing himself at risk of further abuse.'

We raise this point in relation to the single foster mother mentioned above and the benefits of providing boys like John with alternative stable and caring male figures.

In summary, foster placements can provide a very good environment for the young abuser who cannot remain in their family in which the abuse took place. However, it is essential that given the specific needs of such young men, foster parents should receive appropriate preparation, training and support for the benefits of such placements to be recognised. Support for foster carers can also usefully be provided as part of therapeutic services for the child.

A further option for the young sexual abuser is placement in a therapeutic community which can provide therapeutic help, the boundaries and support, particularly for severely damaged children. Our experience of seeking placements in residential units suggests that there is an extreme paucity of resources for young sexual perpetrators, both in the juvenile justice system and mental health services. The limited places currently available for specialist work with young perpetrators are, not surprisingly, expensive and referrals are only made of the cases

SIXTH
SESSION

raising extreme concern (although resources are not always available for even the extreme cases).

There is growing clinical experience of a very wide variety of therapeutic models for intervention, both out-patient and residential, and a great need for evaluations of therapeutic outcome which would allow assessment of their effectiveness in halting the development of sexually abusive behaviour (Monck et al, 1995; Vizard et al, 1995). The need for evaluation of outcome is made more difficult by the recognition that a very long term follow-up of such cases would be needed in order to be entirely confident that the effect of treatment had been adequately assessed. The Research Unit at Dartington has played an important role in comparing the benefits of Psychoanalytically based interventions with more Cognitive/ Behavioural models (Dartington, 1989) and concluded that across a wide range of offenders the outcome of treatment on a psychoanalytic model tends to be better than for behavioural treatment. The form of therapy most helpful for one young offender is not necessarily the most helpful for another; and whatever the particular orientation of a residential setting it is likely to contain a number of different potentially individual and therapeutic components, for example: individual, group and family work, focused care, dynamic community therapy approaches and cognitive-behavioural work.

We note that, as yet, there is insufficient evidence available to assess the efficacy of treatment work with young sexual abusers and this should be considered when deciding on placements, and for policy makers and researchers is an area which requires urgent attention. There were hopes previously that brief forms of therapy could be developed which could be effective in working with young abusers. Clinical treatment experience now indicates that the level of disturbance and the therapeutic needs of this group are such that much longer-term work is required. In some cases 'pulsed' therapeutic intervention may be beneficial, with children reviewed at intervals in the knowledge that as they move through key developmental stages, issues may be revived in new ways and further therapeutic help may be required.

A further implication of the current ideas raised in the study concern male victims of sexual abuse, particularly young boys. Whilst we recognise, *and again emphasise*, that our study does not provide a definite nor exhaustive profile of the young victim who (with all factors being present) may become a potential abuser, it raises an important issue for child protection practice. Ultimately our aim is one of prevention. Therefore, our ability to identify the potential abuser before the behaviour actually occurs is fundamental, although in reality an ideal. Further research of the factors we believe to be associated with the development of sexually abusive behaviour will enable professionals to identify boys who are at high risk of becoming abusers, so as to make appropriate interventions.

REFERENCES

Abel, G G, Becker, J V, Mittleman, M Cunningham-Rathier, J, Rouleau, J and Murphy, W (1987) 'Self reported sex crimes in non-incarcerated paraphiliacs' *Journal of Interpersonal Violence*, 2, 3–25.

Becker, J V, 'Treating adolescent sex offenders'. *Professional Psychology Research and Practice* 21, 363–365.

Bentovim, A (1992) *Trauma Organised Systems: Physical and sexual abuse in families* London, Karnac Books.

Bowlby, J (1988) 'Violence within the family'. In *A Secure Base: Clinical Applications of Attachment Theory*, London, Routledge.

Campbell, D (1994) 'Breaching the shame shield: thoughts on the assessment of adolescent child sexual abusers' *Journal of Child Psychotherapy*. 20, 3, 309–326.

Cantwell, H B (1988) 'Child sexual abuse: very young perpetrators' *Child Abuse and Neglect*. 12, 579–582.

Deblinger, E, McLeer, S V, Atkins, M S D, Ralphe, D and Foa, E (1989) 'Post traumatic stress in sexually abused, physically abused and non-abused children' *Child Abuse and Neglect* 13, 403–408.

Finkelhor, D (1987) 'The trauma of child sexual abuse; two models' *Journal of Interpersonal Violence*, 2, 348–366.

Finkelhor, D (1984) 'Boys as victims: review of the evidence'. In: Finkelhor, D (Ed), *Child Sexual Abuse: New Theory and Research* New York: Free Press.

Freud, A (1936) *The Ego and the Mechanisms of Defence* London: The Hogarth Press.

Freud, S (1896) *Heredity and the aetiology of neurosis*, Standard Edition Vol 3 141–156.

George, C, Kaplan, N and Main, M (1985) *Adult Attachment Interview*, Department of Psychology, Berkeley, California.

Glasser, M (1979) 'Some aspects of the role of aggression in the perversions'. In: Rosen, I (ed) *Sexual Deviation*, (2nd edition), Oxford University Press, 278–305.

Hodges, J, Lanyado, M and Andreou, C (1994) 'Sexuality and violence: preliminary clinical hypotheses from psychotherapeutic assessments in a research programme on young sexual offenders', *Journal of Child Psychotherapy* 20, 3.

Holmes, J (1993) *John Bowlby and Attachment Theory* London, Routledge.

Home Office (1992) *Criminal Statistics for England and Wales* London, HMSO.

Main, M (1994) *A Move to the Level of Representation in the Study of Attachment Organisation: Implications for Psychoanalysis* Annual Research Lecture to the British Psycho-Analytical Society. London July 6, 1994.

Monck, E, Sharland, E, Bentovim, A, Goodhall, G, Hyde, C, and Lwin, R, *Child Sexual Abuse: A Descriptive and Treatment Study* HMSO. 1995.

Perry, Bruce D (1993) 'Neuro-development and Neuro-physiology of Trauma 1: Conceptual Considerations for Clinical Work with Maltreated Children' *The APSAC Advisor* 6.1, 1–18 American Professional Society on the Abuse of Children, Spring 1993.

Pynoos, R S, Sorensen, S B, and Steinberg, A M (1993) 'Interpersonal Violence and Traumatic Stress Reactions'. In: Goldberger, L, Breznitz, (eds). *Handbook of Stress: Theoretical and Clinical Aspects*. (2nd Edition) New York: Free Press 573–590.

Ryan, G (1989) 'Victim to victimiser' *Journal of Interpersonal Violence*. 4, 325–341.

Rutter, M (1987) 'Psychosocial Resilience and Protective Mechanisms' *American Journal of Orthopsychiatry* 57 (3) July 1987.

Sroufe, L A, Jacobvitz, D, Mangelsdorf, S, De Angelo, E, and Ward, M J (1985) 'Generational boundary dissolution between mothers and their pre-school children: a relationship systems approach' *Child Development*. 56, 317–325.

Vizard, E, Monck, E and Misch, P (1995) 'Child and adolescent sexual abuse perpetration: a review of the research literature' *Journal of Child Psychology & Psychiatry* 36, 5, 731–756.

Watkins, B, and Bentovim A (1992) 'The sexual abuse of male children and adolescents: a review of current research' *Journal of Child Psychology and Psychiatry* 33 (1) 192–248.

SIXTH SESSION

CONFERENCE REVIEW

Chaired by The Rt Hon Lady Justice Butler-Sloss

Lady Justice Butler-Sloss stated that the Conference had been a unique experience because, although psychodynamic practitioners may have been accustomed to attending conferences of this nature, it was 'a first' for all the members of the judiciary present.

There was universal acceptance that the Conference had been a great success on every level, not only because the participants had learnt a great deal about each others' disciplines but because barriers had been broken down, consequently there was no longer any question of a 'them and us' mentality. The level of debate had been of the highest and it was recognised that each group of professionals had much to contribute the other.

Lady Justice Butler-Sloss drew the analogy of all Conference participants travelling along the same road (albeit joining at different places) with the same goal in mind – viz, the best interests of the child within a family context (even if not within the natural family). Often the difficulties which faced professionals, were the intermediate destinations along the road and how best to deal with them. Questions such as – where do we go?; what is the best way to get there? and what are we seeking to achieve? – needed to be answered in a spirit of constructive co-operation. Thus, a mutual understanding of the separate (but complimentary) roles of all those involved in child care work was essential if the needs of the family were to be served.

There was a general recognition that the scope of the Conference should be broadened to include other professionals, for example – family therapists and advocates.

There was unanimous agreement that the Conference must not be a 'one off', but must lead to further meetings of a similar nature in the future. A great deal had been (and needed to be) learned through this inter-disciplinary approach. The good work which had already been accomplished should be disseminated and the papers which had formed the basis of the Conference would be published. Furthermore, a *Users' Guide* would be brought into being, listing all the psychodynamic expertise and other child-oriented services available in any given area. This type of directory would be useful for, inter alia, members of the Bar, the Official Solicitor, Guardians ad Litem and Judges. The preparation of such a practical guide would also highlight the areas where services were not available.

It was agreed that practical steps had to be taken encourage the funding of therapy/treatment for children in need and their parents (even if, at its most basic level, this meant the provision of fares to enable families to attend treatment sessions/assessments). Particularly, as the use of resources at an early stage might lead to vast saving of costs in the longer term.

The future structure of the Conference was discussed in detail and it was agreed that:

(1)   the working party should be retained with input from the judiciary, mental health practitioners and social workers/guardians ad litem. It was hoped that the President of the Family Division would be prepared to chair the working party – which would henceforth be known as 'The President's Inter-Disciplinary Committee'. The working party should, if at all possible, plan another Conference in 2 years' time.

(2)   the Conference should be kept 'small' because this enabled the participants to get to know one another and to exchange views frankly. Although the scope of participants might be broadened.

(3)   there should be more focus on case studies – with specific input from a judicial/medical/social work point of view.

(4)   the amount of material should be reduced, because participants felt that there had not been enough time to deal with all the information which had been made available on this occasion.

SIXTH SESSION

Lord Justice Thorpe brought the meeting to a close. He thanked all those who had been involved in the preparation of the Conference listing in particular the Steering Committee, all those of the medical profession who had attended the conference, the Social Research Unit of Dartington, all those who had written papers for the Conference, the Judicial Studies Board and the Department of Health. In particular he thanked, his clerk, Roger, who had spent a great deal of his free time making sure that the administration ran smoothly.

Lord Justice Thorpe remarked that an excellent camaraderie had developed during the Conference. He drew the distinction between the new-found understanding which had been engendered by the exchange of views, as opposed to the cautious approach present at the start of the meeting. This was summed up by the limerick by James Wigmore printed at the end of this book. (He is also responsible for the final quotation from *Macbeth*.)

To roars of laughter the Conference ended.

FOOTNOTE

The President's Inter-Disciplinary Committee had its first meeting on 30 April 1996 in the President's chambers at the Royal Courts of Justice. Sir Stephen Brown, the President, presided. Membership of the Committee comprises the following:

Rt Hon Lord Justice Thorpe (Committee Chairman)
Rt Hon Lady Justice Butler-Sloss
The Hon Mr Justice Wall
The Hon Mr Justice Kirkwood
Mr Gerald Angel (Senior District Judge)
Mr Peter Harris (The Official Solicitor)
Mr Arran Poyser (Social Services Inspectorate, Department of Health)
Ms Ann Gross (Department of Health)
Ms Deborah Cameron (Director of Social Services, London Borough of Newham)
Mr Michael Leadbetter (Director of Social Services, Essex County Council)
Ms Tessa Duncan (Panel Manager, Surrey Panel GALs)
Ms Gillian Schofield (University of East Anglia)
Dr Anne Zachary (The Portman Clinic)
Dr Judith Trowell (The Tavistock Clinic)
Dr Claire Sturge (Northwick Park Hospital)
Dr Marion Myles (The Medical Centre, London W9)
Dr Brian Jacobs (The Maudesley Hospital)
Ms Jenny Stevenson (NE Worcestershire Community Healthcare)
Ms Florence Baron QC (the bar)
Mr Iain Hamilton (child care solicitor)
Mr Michael Tester (Assistant Secretary at the Principal Registry: Secretary to the Committee).

ADDITIONAL PAPER

BAD PARENTING AND PSEUDO PARENTING[1]

Patrick Gallwey[2]

Before discussing the assessment of parents who are involved with the family courts, I am going to start by looking briefly at the general problem of giving expert evidence in Court as a Psychiatrist.

Expert is rather a grand word because it means you are expected to say things which are true and reliable. This is where any psychiatrist really has to be pretty humble because although psychiatry wants to be an objective science it is really a long way from being so. As you all realise, you cannot do many reliable tests which will support or refute your points of view. Of course, that can be an advantage in some ways because you can get away with an awful lot if you want to sound clever. When the issues are very grave as they are in legal proceedings of all kinds, then one really has to be rather careful about what one says and what one puts forward as a matter of fact. Most of my work in Court, certainly before I retired from the NHS as a Forensic Psychiatrist, was in the Criminal Court. I had experience of family work along the way, and nowadays, I find myself involved more and more in Family and Civil Courts. It really is remarkable the difference in the atmosphere between the Family Courts and the Criminal Courts. Criminal Courts have an awe about them which I think can only be called 'paranoia inducing'. They carry all the history and all the awful history of the power of the state. Ultimately, criminal law is about controlling people's behaviour, deterring it when it is inclined to err and punishing it when it has done so. If one looks at the history of criminal law it is frightening the length to which the law went to control people not so long ago and I think one still gets the feeling of that in the atmosphere of the Criminal Court.

Still engraved on my memory is a moment in a trial of the serial murderer Neilson in which I was giving expert evidence for the defence to support his plea of diminished responsibility. He had done some terrible things and the trial attracted a lot of attention especially from the media. After some fairly amazing revelations about his behaviour, the Court adjourned for lunch and I was approached by a member of the Press who tried to get more details from me in regard to this. I told him I was on oath and I could not talk and tried to get away, but he would not leave me alone. Eventually, the Clerk of the Court had to come and take him away and this news got to the learned Judge. After lunch the Court was very crowded and there was a lot of what one might call 'the Quality' present, friends of the Judge who no doubt had lunched with him, as well as members of the public and lots of reporters. Before the jury was called in the Judge asked me what had happened and he listened very gravely to what I had to say. He asked if the person was in Court and if he was, to stand up. There was a palpable hush and a very lonely looking man from a tabloid newspaper stood up at the back of the Court. The Judge told him that he had committed contempt of Court and the worst kind of contempt, namely in the face of the Court and what it was possible for the Judge to do. There is a sword in number one Court at the Old Bailey over the Judge's throne and one could feel the power of the criminal law and the terrible authority of it. It was quite a moment. Of course I was in the right you see and the Judge went on to thank me very much for handling it as I had. It was a gratifying moment to feel so full of righteousness, not often to be repeated.

But to return to the Family Court, the situation is so different because the imperative to punish is replaced by concern for children and for understanding the deeper nature of the issues. When I am in a case relating to a child I am always enormously grateful that I do not have to make the

[1] Dr Gallwey's paper was given to a conference for the Circuit Judges on the Western Circuit at Dartington on 18 September 1995.
[2] Consultant Forensic Psychiatrist, Nuffield Hospital, Exeter.

SIXTH SESSION

final decision. I try to give my best opinion and I always think how dreadful that must be in cases in which it is hard to weigh the rightness or wrongness, the safety or otherwise of the outcome of the Judge's deliberations. This realisation certainly makes one want to give as much help as one can and I will try to describe how I approach the problem of assessing parents and their suitability to care for children.

As I am not a child psychiatrist, I do not have to give views on children and whether or not they are going to be damaged or likely to be damaged if they stay with one or another parent or if they should be adopted or put into care. I am asked to give an opinion on the parents' mental state, on their behaviour and their capacity to care for or even have contact with their children.

Basically, there are two issues and they form the title of my talk: firstly, are they good parents in spite of appearing bad, in other words is their manifest bad behaviour of the sort which is likely to damage children and second, is their apparent good behaviour concealing something not so good, in other words is there a goodness, a pseudo-goodness behind which lies something more sinister. Both questions are difficult, but at least with the first a Psychiatrist feels on more familiar ground.

Psychiatric diagnoses such as mental illness or personality disorder are made on the findings of fairly gross phenomena. However, in the domestic environment many forms of subtle behaviour such as an unremitting disguised cruelty, sexual perversity or mental undermining are much harder to detect and impossible to fit into the standard psychiatric nosologies. I am going to concentrate on problems of personality rather than look at mental illness because paradoxically mental illness is a less perplexing area. It is not without its uncertainties in relation to child care, but at least the nature of the psychological and behavioural problems for someone who is mentally ill are fairly well known. The psychiatric role is therefore much more certain. Somebody who is depressed, for instance, may be too retarded, too preoccupied with morbid self reproach to actually be able to care for a child. They may even be a danger to themselves and to the child. On the other hand, although apparently able to function quite well, they may be over-conscientious, so frightened of doing anything wrong they actually over-mother their child and produce psychological damage that way. These are the kind of problems upon which a Psychiatrist with the help of a Social Worker and the relatives may be able to conduct a good assessment.

In most cases that I see there is not a mental illness and one is usually looking at neurotic problems and questions of personality. When it comes to personality, psychiatrists talk of personality disorder. These are enduring aberrations of behaviour and social relating often with distressing emotional states which go right back to childhood. To make the diagnosis one has to be able to demonstrate satisfactorily whether these factors apply. Sometimes one sees a Psychiatrist making the diagnosis because the patient is over-aggressive, attacking, uncooperative and touchy. Sometimes it appears to be made because the Psychiatrist disapproves of the kind of life the person leads without their way of life being necessarily maladaptive or destructive. Personal antipathy should not be the basis for making a diagnosis, yet for many years a condemnatory bias has adulterated the term so a pejorative labelling is now almost inevitable. It is an awful thing for anyone to lose their child and disturbed people are less able to manage the stress of having their child removed than those with a stronger personality. Sometimes the fact that a mother becomes very upset, angry, persecuted and attacking because she has lost her child into care is then used as a reason for recommending a continuation of the Care Order and even removing the child from contact with the mother. It is particularly hard for parents who are rather simple and lack the tactical ability to say the sort of things which will reassure the professionals that they are putting the child first. Under those circumstances, what one really needs to know is how specific is the emotional disturbance of the individual concerned with the situation of losing their child and how much is it an habitual pattern that appears far too often and is unlikely to be treatable. If it is habitual, longstanding, present in a variety of different situations and triggered by a number of different life events, one can be more certain that one is dealing with a personality disorder. Then one is on much safer ground in making judgments about continuing possibly untreatable, maladaptive or bad behaviour.

However, in the Family Court standard psychiatric diagnoses are often of limited value. The factors to be considered are less gross so a psychiatric diagnosis cannot be easily made. This is one reason why psycho-dynamic thinking and concepts are more commonly used by professionals working in this area. As a Psychoanalyst, of course, I welcome this and hope that my special training gives me an extra dimension to assessing and understanding the problems that family work entails. However much one wants, particularly as a pschoanalyst, to understand each case individually because of the time limit it is very important to have a scheme in which one can categorise different types of individual in a way which allows one to make some judgments on their behaviour, treatability and their safety fairly quickly. Once one dispenses with the standard psychiatric nosology, then one needs something else to put in its place which will include those who are more subtly and covertly disturbed. Some years ago, I developed a rough and ready guide of this kind with six simple categories which are not far removed from psychiatric diagnosis categories but which represent in very broad ways how different individuals manage their emotional turbulence and conflicts. These different ways of organising mental defences can be identified fairly easily and have some practical value in making the sort of judgments that are needed regarding safety, vulnerability and treatment. I will describe this guide and try and relate the question of bad and pseudo parenting to the various categories[1].

The categories are:

1. Well adjusted delinquents.
2. Poorly adjusted delinquents and frail neurotic personalities.
3. Over defended personalities.
4. Psychotic personalities.
5. Pseudo-normal personalities.
6. Those with a primary diagnosis of mental illness or organic disorder.

You may be puzzled by the first category which appears to be a contradiction in terms since delinquency by definition is social maladjustment. However, here I am referring to psychological adjustment within the individual for, in my view, much delinquent behaviour can be explained as a compensatory mechanism, a defence against anxiety and conflict which enables the individual to function without breaking down into neurotic turmoil or psychotic confusion. You will be aware that almost all criminals, particularly habitual criminals, have appalling family and early histories. Emotional buffers acting through largely unconscious phantasy (defence mechanisms) are essential psychological tools which enable us to maintain psychic equilibrium in the face of stress. These defences rely for their creation upon good parenting, so that a mobile repertoire of imagination as a buffer against stress reflects the mobility and sensitivity within the framework of good and loving nurturing.

When the parental figures are harsh, violent, inconstant and unyielding then the individual grows up not only with a harsh view of life, but with a grave deficiency in their capacity to modify experience through imagination. Instead of being able to alter harsh realities within their fantasy world thereby mitigating them, they attempt to rearrange reality itself by direct manipulation of social structure and other people. Instead of being able to lessen their sense of deprivation by dreaming that they are helping themselves to what they want, they have to actually help themselves through burglary, stealing or physically defeating someone they experience as a bad figure. Of course other things enter into criminality as well, but the essentially fantasy driven nature of it can sometimes be startlingly clear when one looks behind the purely hedonistic or sensation seeking elements. Provided that such individuals can, through their manipulation of the world, make up for the absence of a defensive imagination then they will feel psychologically 'safe'. Their lives may be dangerous, uncertain, full of contradiction and threatened with loss of liberty and yet they have an emotional equanimity which belies their perilous situation. If they try and behave better they may become disturbed. This is a frequent finding in the treatment of habitual delinquents and a real stumbling block when they attempt to settle down into family life. Often they manage to keep their criminality going as a separate split off activity. Since they rely on their delinquency as a means of emotional adjustment then if they try to give it up completely they become frightened, violent

SIXTH SESSION

---

[1] For a fuller account of the way the nosology can be used, refer to two previous papers of mine. The first, a chapter on Social Maladjustment in a book edited by Jeremy Holmes called 'A Textbook of Psychotherapy in Psychiatric Practice' and the other which is more brief and perhaps more readable, named 'The psychotherapy of Psychopathic Disorder' in 'Criminal Behaviour and Mental Health' published in 1992.

or behave catastrophically. In this state they represent an almost certain risk of harm to a child especially when their criminal adjustment is unsafe so the risk of violence or hazardous accident is very real. This takes us to the second category of poorly adjusted delinquents and frail neurotic personalities.

Poorly adjusted delinquents are really a menace. Some of the worst cases of child neglect and child cruelty derive from delinquent individuals who are constantly decompensating into neurotic turmoil with rages and catastrophic behaviour. It may seem unfair to link them with the neurotically disordered but the common denominator is their liability to emotional disorganisation. It is also the case that when neurotically disordered individuals become too disorganised, they may move into delinquent acting out, or into a depressed state in which they are quite unable to care for a child or even collapse into violence. Attacks of self harm explosions of rage and emotional paralysis cause rapid emotional damage and sometimes physical damage in young children. They are often manipulative and over demanding within their social relationships thus alienating their spouses, friends or relatives. When the social support collapses, for example through separation from a partner, then the emotional stress is too much for their frail resources, some may act out with delinquent behaviour and in others catastrophic behaviour results. Individuals in this category may very well be able to respond to help and support, but they can be very demanding and require a great deal of input by way of social work time and therapeutic care. They form quite a large proportion of those parents with whom the Social Services and the Courts become concerned. They are often single parents and the extent of their emotional instability, the frailty of the defensive organisation and the poverty of social supportive arrangements may mean that they inevitably lose their children. A history of episodic delinquency is also a bad sign for the maintenance or support and treatment.

The third category are the over defended personalities. In this category the defensive organisation is very rigid, attempting to control emotions and figures both in the internal and social world of the individuals. Harm can arise in two ways: firstly, because of their need to control, they are rigid and often authoritarian in their attitude to parenting. Secondly, they may have compulsive behaviour patterns which are harmful to others including children such as compulsive sexual deviancy or other rituals. Even if the rituals are not directly harmful, the amount of time spent on, for example, washing, checking, mental rumination or compulsive thinking, means that there is little time left over to look after children let alone to look after them in a dedicated and flexible way. The pressure of children and the tension of the compulsive life of the individual results in panics or rages. This behaviour may be very hidden and a pseudo-parenting aspect can hide some quite dreadful things.

Some over-defended personalities who do not have clear obsessional features, and who therefore appear less ill can nevertheless under exceptional stress break down into catastrophic violence. Often they are rather passive individuals with poorly integrated aggression who tend to be somewhat compliant and have over-dependent features in the way they relate to others. They respond to stress, characteristically by becoming depressed. They contain a great deal of unconscious violence towards internal figures and this may erupt in catastrophic homicidal violence if the external stress becomes too great. Homicide and suicide can result and these are cases who often successfully plead diminished responsibility when charged with the murder of their spouse. The question is then whether or not they may be allowed to return to care for their surviving children. There are many complex issues in this situation including the question as to whether or not the children would be harmed by living with a parent who has killed their mother or father, but since the trigger for this violence is usually exceptional they may be safe to do so. These matters will of course be decided in the Family Court when the individual is able to re-enter the community.

Often one feels it would be important for the Judge in a criminal trial to look at this question when deciding on a sentence for a successful plea of diminished responsibility. I was very dismayed recently when giving evidence on sentencing and mitigation in a homicide by a mother of her husband, when the needs of the 11-year-old surviving child of the family, who was very dependent on his mother, were not taken into account in sentencing. I was told that the welfare of her child had no bearing on the sentencing process and she was given two years imprisonment, when a probation order would have protected the frail mother–child relationship. Very often it is the children of convicted people who may suffer the most and it is the preoccupation with punishment of the Criminal Courts that prevents the welfare of children being taken into account in relation to sentence.

My fourth category concentrates on individuals who, although not mentally ill, nevertheless use psychotic mechanisms as a way of managing their emotional turmoil. Psychotic mechanisms are different from neurotic mechanisms in that through a process of omnipotent phantasy they cut the individual off completely from their own dependency needs. As a result, they live in a strange world of artificial self-sufficiency technically called narcissism. Such narcissistic fantasies are expressed by grandiosity, by the projection of disturbance into others as a way of getting rid of it or by the operation of splits within the mind to deny the existence of the disturbed areas.

The term 'borderline personality disorder' has become more frequently used of late and may indicate someone with a tendency to psychotic defence mechanism. However, it is defined in a way which includes many different types of psychopathology so individuals who have acquired this label need some clear assessment to see to what extent they are using psychotic defences as part of their personality problem.

Psychotic personalities may be very hard to assess in terms of their safety in relation to others, including children. Paranoid personalities who rely heavily on projection of bad feelings into others are highly suspicious and antagonistic to the world, can particularly, if they are intelligent, sustain a somewhat beleaguered way of life within the framework of their grandiosity and hostility to others. They of course make bad parents, they might be cruel or violent, but it may be very difficult to show that this is the case.

I treated a young man who was brought up by a very paranoid father who was near the edge of mental illness, but who was able to sustain himself in a very isolated and strange way of life with the help of his compliant and rather depressed wife. My patient, as a child, was treated in an enormously controlled and emotionally deprived way so that he was hardly allowed to develop an identity. He grew up thinking he was a ghost and that he mattered to no one except in so far as he was able to be academically successful. He had the greatest difficulty thinking and after he had tried to take his life at University, he was admitted to a psychiatric hospital where he was felt to be psychotic. He responded extremely well to analytic treatment where it became clear that he had been prevented from developing his own identity and personality because of the tyranny of his paranoid father. His teachers recognised there was something very wrong with the father, but he never seemed bad enough for Social Services to be involved. Because he had money and education, he was able to erect a wall against those who were concerned about his son. Many paranoid individuals are another example of pseudo parents. They may not be violent or physically abusive, they may present as socially correct and moral but the rigidity of their thinking, the inability to criticise or examine their own behaviour and the coldness of their emotional make-up make them very poor candidates for parenthood.

Another group who rely on psychotic mechanisms are those who operate on the basis of very profound splits within their personalities. This schizoid group lead double lives so that some highly abnormal, destructive, perverse or dangerous behaviour is carried on in a clandestine way. They present a convincing picture of normality and represent par excellence the pseudo parents. When their perverse behaviour comes to light, as is the case with many sexual offenders towards children, they manage to appear regretful and express shame, but at the same time convey a self-congratulatory, high moral tone about themselves in the same breath. They quite subtly convey that although it is not right to have sex with children and maybe that on this occasion they went too far, nevertheless at the time their intentions were good and the whole thing grew out of their love and concern for their victim. They have a great capacity to deceive themselves as well as others and have very often managed to find their way into a way of life in which they have much contact with children or are in positions of trust like Clergy, Teachers or youth workers. They often seem to have a powerful influence as if they are able to hypnotise people into believing their pseudo-goodness and the denial of what they have done, so that they are once more able to insinuate themselves into the situations where they can continue their abusive needs.

SIXTH SESSION

Things have improved in the last 15 years or so because we have begun to listen to children more and to be ready to challenge the integrity of those in official positions of trust. It can be very difficult to uncover perverse traits in short assessments, but such individuals find it very hard not to be drawn by their deviance into perverse discourse if one gives them the opportunity. As an example, some years ago, I was asked to assess a man whose wife felt sure he was a risk to her children and had found amongst his possessions some pornography which contained photographs of naked children. He denied that he was a paedophile, maintaining that he had bought the magazines as a job lot and had simply neglected to throw away the photographs of the children. He presented at interview as very self-satisfied, very sure of himself and quite adamant in a disdainful way against suggestions that he had perverse problems in relation to children. I had with me the photographs that were the cause of concern and after asking him to speak about one or two of no great significance, I selected one of some Asian children, all girls of around six or seven sitting naked in a row. It was clearly one of those photographs deriving from the appalling sexual exploitation of young children in parts of the world such as Thailand and to any normal person it would have been a depressing and miserable reminder of that awful reality. I passed it to him and asked him to comment. He looked at it and on handing it back to me he said with a smile endeavouring to involve me in his joke, 'peas in a pod'. I was fairly sure then that he was deeply deviant. It is the absence of real concern for the other person that is the hallmark of perverse relating.

I have moved without realising it into the next category which is that of pseudo-normality. These are individuals who have apparently normal lives with no obvious history of distress or maladaptive behaviour who nevertheless are deeply disturbed. Many of those individuals whom I have been describing merge into this category of pseudo-normality and the falsity of their apparent mental health will include the likelihood of presenting an adequate parents; in other words, individuals who seem to lead apparently normal lives, but have either habitual pathology which they disguise or whose adjustment collapses into catastrophic or dangerous behaviour under certain conditions. We have already discussed this to some extent with the over-defended personalities, but there are a group in whom one cannot make a diagnosis of personality disorder or detect any clear pathology, but in whom encapsulated areas of high disturbance may erupt under certain conditions precipitating brief psychotic episodes or violence, perverse or even homicidal behaviour. Such encapsulated disturbance is rather like an aneurysm in the brain which may suddenly rupture causing physical catastrophe to the individual, but which was previously completely silent and therefore never detected. Encapsulated psychopathology is equally hard to detect although certain features of over-compliance and anxiety usually discovered only in retrospect after the occurrence of the catastrophe may indicate the hidden encapsulated disturbance.

A similar pseudo-normal group are those with very inadequate over-dependent personalities who rely on a very structured or strong environment in a parasitic way to get by and appear untroubled within the context of this pathological collusion. The 'host' of such parasitic personalities can be a strong and resourceful individual who, for their own reasons, needs a dependent invalid for a partner, or institutions such as the Armed Services or prisons which provide a very structured and authoritarian environment in which personal initiative and responsibility for decisions and the management of daily problems are abrogated in those in charge. Under these conditions the individual may appear normal, compliant and helpful. However, their lack of resourcefulness and vulnerability to collapse is completely hidden until their partner goes off with someone else or they are demobbed or discharged from prison. They are highly suspect as parents and again may abuse the children in their care with whom they are strongly identified[1].

I am going to end by introducing a word of caution into the use of psychoanalytical formulations. Because they refer to unconscious processes which can only be inferred, psychoanalytic concepts are best used in the situation for which they are designed, namely psychoanalytic psychotherapy. In the treatment situation, one has the chance, albeit a very difficult one, of supporting or refuting one's view of what is going on in the patient's mind. Their

---

[1] I describe these two groups more completely in a chapter in Gunn and Farrington's book on *Violent Offenders and Dangerousness* published in 1985 by Wiley.

use in brief assessments is much more difficult. I sometimes find myself somewhat worried when reading reports when psychoanalytic terminology is used somewhat freely and judgments on future behaviour based on these formulations. As I mentioned earlier, when parents lose their child it may very well be that they become paranoid and persecutory and it can be very unfair to pick up the projections and suggest that these are necessarily long term psychological problems. Although, psychoanalysis provides a platform and a set of theories, a way of looking at people which can be of great use to those trying to evaluate the quality of interpersonal behaviour between parent and child, in the end the quality of the conclusions must be judged on the experience of those using the concepts and not just the concepts themselves.

I remember once having given evidence, again in a case of diminished responsibility, when I had used some psychoanalytic concepts. The Counsel for the Prosecution, encouraged no doubt by his own expert, suggested that anyone who walked into my consulting room would emerge with a full set of psychopathology for such was the nature of my discipline that I could find illness in anyone. There is something important in this criticism. Psychoanalysts very often use psychological mechanisms observed in very ill patients to describe phases in normal development in everyone. This can lead to a sense of universal psychopathology and a blurring of the distinctions between healthy and pathological states of mind. Over recent years, I have tried in my own theoretical work to get away from this tendency and to give descriptions of healthy development as quite different from those mechanisms which cause illness but that would require another paper to describe.

I trust what I have said has given some glimpse of the way I try to work, with the shortcomings and advantages of the psychiatric and psychoanalytical ways of approaching the assessment of individuals and the great problem of knowing, because of the complexity and unpredictability of human nature, what the future may hold.

SIXTH SESSION

APPENDICES

APPENDIX I

CONFERENCE PROGRAMME

Friday 22 September 1995

16.00–17.00	*Arrival, Registration and Tea*
17.00–17.10	WELCOME
	Lord Lloyd of Berwick
17.10–17.15	INTRODUCTION TO PAPERS
	Mr Justice Thorpe and Dr Jacobs
17.15–18.15	SYNDICATE DISCUSSION
18.15–19.00	PLENARY DISCUSSION
19.30	*Dinner*

Saturday 23 September 1995

08.00–09.00	*Breakfast*
09.00–09.10	INTRODUCTION TO PAPERS
	Mr Justice Wall and Dr Trowell
09.10–10.10	SYNDICATE DISCUSSION
10.10–10.45	PLENARY DISCUSSION
10.45–11.15	*Coffee*
11.15–11.25	INTRODUCTION TO PAPER
	Dr Kennedy
11.25–12.25	SYNDICATE DISCUSSION
12.25–13.00	PLENARY DISCUSSION
13.00–14.00	*Lunch*
14.00–15.45	*Recreation*
15.45–16.15	*Tea*
16.15–16.25	INTRODUCTION TO PAPER
	Dr Campbell
16.25–17.25	SYNDICATE DISCUSSION
17.25–18.00	PLENARY DISCUSSION
19.30	*Dinner*

Sunday 24 September 1995

08.00–09.00	*Breakfast*
09.00–09.10	INTRODUCTION TO PAPER
	Dr Yorke
09.10–10.10	SYNDICATE DISCUSSION
10.10–10.45	PLENARY DISCUSSION
10.45–11.15	*Coffee*
11.15–11.25	INTRODUCTION TO PAPER
	Dr Williams and Dr Hodges
11.25–12.25	SYNDICATE DISCUSSION
12.25–13.00	CONFERENCE REVIEW
	Chaired by Lady Justice Butler-Sloss
13.00–14.00	*Lunch*
	Departure

APPENDIX II

LIST OF PARTICIPANTS
(As at 28 July 1995)

The Right Honourable The Lord Lloyd of Berwick — Conference Chairman
The Right Honourable Lady Justice Butler-Sloss
The Right Honourable Lord Justice Thorpe — Conference Director
The Honourable Mrs Justice Bracewell
The Honourable Mr Justice Connell
The Honourable Mr Justice Holman
The Honourable Mr Justice Johnson
The Honourable Mr Justice Kirkwood
The Honourable Mr Justice Stuart-White
The Honourable Mr Justice Wall
The Honourable Mr Justice Wilson
Her Honour Judge Darwall-Smith
His Honour Judge David Davies
His Honour Judge Evans
His Honour Judge Fricker QC
His Honour Judge David Gee
His Honour Judge Hart
His Honour Judge Jones
His Honour Judge Lees
His Honour Judge Mahon
Her Honour Judge Norrie
Her Honour Judge Palin
Her Honour Judge Pearlman
His Honour Judge Sleeman
Her Honour Judge Tyrer
His Honour Judge Wigmore
His Honour Judge Wilcox
His Honour Judge Wilson
Florence Baron QC — Reporter
Jim Baker — Deputy Official Solicitor
Debbie Cameron — Director of Social Services, LB of Newham

Dr Hamish Cameron — St George's Hospital
Donald Campbell — Portman Clinic
Carol Edwards — Guardian ad Litem, London
Dr Trian Fundudis — Fleming Nuffield Unit, Newcastle
Dr Judith Freedman — Portman Clinic
Dr Danya Glaser — Great Ormond Street Hospital
Dr Rob Hale — Portman Clinic
Peter Harris — Official Solicitor
Rina Herbert — Guardian ad Litem, Cambridge
Dr Jill Hodges — Great Ormond Street
Dr Brian Jacobs — Maudsley Hospital
Dr Robert Jezzard — NHS Executive HQ
Dr Carol Kaplan — Fleming Nuffield Unit
Dr Roger Kennedy — Cassel Hospital
Trudy Klauber — Director, Donald Winnicott Centre

Professor I Kolvin — Tavistock Clinic
Dr Michael Little — Dartington Research Trust
Professor Mervyn Murch — Cardiff Law School

Arran Poyser — Social Services Inspectorate, Department of Health

Gordon Read — Chief Probation Officer, Devon
Dr John Shemilt — Consultant Child Psychiatrist, Glasgow

Kathleen Taylor — Department of Health
Carola Thorpe — Psychoanalytic Psychotherapist
Dr Judith Trowell — Tavistock Clinic
Brian Waller — Director of Social Services, Leicester

Dr Bryn Williams — Institute of Child Health
Peter Wilson — Director, Young Minds
Dr Jill Woodhead — Guardian ad Litem, Oxford
Dr Clifford Yorke — Anna Freud Centre
Dr Anne Zachary — Portman Clinic

Administration

Roger Kinnerley — Clerk to Lord Justice Thorpe
Len Williams — Clerk to Mr Justice Wall

APPENDIX III

A SOCIAL SERVICES VIEW OF THE DARTINGTON CONFERENCE

Brian Waller[1]

A conference held at Dartington Hall on 21–23 September 1995 brought together professionals who make decisions about children and families. The two largest groups were judges and children psychotherapists/psychiatrists and, inevitably, this combination influenced both the content and focus of the discussion. Social workers were less well represented, with two Guardians and two Directors of Social Services being present. This made it difficult to incorporate a social work perspective into the debate. The observations of those from a social work background on the conference as a whole may, therefore, be helpful in highlighting qualifications that need to be made about the conclusions reached. Three examples are offered.

The danger of generalising from individual cases

Judges and psychotherapists have a mutual interest in individual cases, an emphasis that can elevate the significance of exceptional situations for the development of general ideas. A single judgment can alter interpretations of law and many examples cited by the therapists, although very interesting, were untypical. Examples are children who kill or are victims of 'stranger rape'. Social Services work with a wide range of young people and families and are rarely able to select only those cases that are likely to respond well. Thus, social workers have a wide view of anti-social behaviours and may be less prone to generalise from extreme cases.

An example occurred in discussions about juvenile offending. Each year Social Services deal with a quarter of a million adolescents who break the law. It soon becomes clear from such an involvement that delinquents vary, in their background, presenting behaviour and prognosis for change. There are sub-groups within the larger group of offenders, such as temporary delinquents, persistent offenders, dangerous offenders, disturbed offenders, etc, but generalisation about them all is difficult. Few social workers would subscribe to simple explanation of the causes of delinquency, such as stress, unemployment, boredom or psychological disturbance although those undoubtedly contribute to the problems posed by particular individuals.

Judges and psychotherapists tend to deal with particular groups of offenders who are referred to them; for example, the judiciary regularly encounter the persistent and serious, therapists help disturbed and dangerous young people. There is a danger that the lessons from this specialist work may be applied too generally. Thus, some of the statements made at the conference on the nature and causes of juvenile delinquency need qualification in the light of evidence based on samples representative of all young people who offend. This would provide an estimate of the numbers who need specialist help.

There was also a tendency in the conference discussion to concentrate on the psychoanalytic process which, although underpinned by sophisticated theory, does not offer an exhaustive causal explanation of young people's problems. To do so it would need to display predictive powers when applied to new cases, a quality that some social workers would doubt. This limitation can lead to a simplistic view of a complex social problem. A wider perspective would help clarify the factors that influence human behaviour.

The importance of taking a broad view of young people

A further contrast between a social work perspective and the conference discussions concerns the importance of taking a broad view of children and families. While many of the case studies

---

[1] Director of Social Services, Leicestershire County Council.

described the psychological characteristics of the individuals concerned, the social workers present felt that the young people were sometimes viewed in isolation, as someone to be treated over time in short sessions. Social work plans tend to be broader, involving contributions from several agencies and incorporating the strengths in the child's family. They consider the child's long term social, educational and economic career. These aspects of the young people's lives complement rather than contradict the psychological development emphasised in the conference, social workers would agree that treatment is most useful if it is incorporated in a social care plan. A common frustration, however, arises when difficult clients are deemed unsuitable for therapeutic help.

Concern with outcomes

Social Services are under increasing pressure to evaluate their work and produce data on the outcomes of interventions. This demand comes from the growing significance attributed to scientific knowledge in court hearings, where estimates of successful adoption or parental access are regularly argued, and from the requests of auditors and politicians to justify value for money. While individual judges may have a natural curiosity about the outcomes of their judgments, they are less likely to be concerned with the clinical results. The legal system is mostly concerned with decisions which, if found to be incorrect, can be overturned. None of the psychotherapists attending the conference provided evidence to show that their work was exceptionally effective when compared with alternatives. The tradition of empirical clinical research was little acknowledged, making it difficult for those from different backgrounds to judge the value of the psychotherapeutic approaches described.

It would have been helpful, therefore, to have had more people working with children and families in contexts other than psychotherapy. Also, it would have been beneficial to have had a wider range of professionals undertaking therapeutic work with children.

These comments are provided in good faith to indicate changes that might be considered when further meetings of the group are planned.

APPENDIX IV

MEMBERS OF THE PRESIDENT'S INTER-DISCIPLINARY COMMITTEE

Chair

The Rt Hon Lord Justice Thorpe — Royal Courts of Justice

Secretary

Michael Tester — Secretariat, PRFD, Somerset House

Members

Ann Gross — Department of Health,
Wellington House, 133–155 Waterloo Road,
London SE1 8UG

Arran Poyser — Social Services Inspector,
Department of Health,
Wellington House, 133–155 Waterloo Road,
London SE1 8UG

Dr Anne Zachary — Portman Clinic,
8 Fitzjohns Avenue,
London NW3 5NA

Dr Judith Trowell — The Tavistock Clinic,
120 Belsize Lane,
London NW3 5BA

Deborah Cameron — Director of Social Services,
Newham Council
Social Services Department,
99 The Grove, Stratford,
London E15 1HR

Brian Waller — Director of Social Services,
Leicestershire County Council,
County Hall, Glenfield,
Leicester LE3 8RL

Michael Leadbetter — Director of Social Services,
Essex County Council
Social Services Department,
PO Box 297 County Hall,
Chelmsford CM1 1YS

Gillian Schofield — Lecturer in Social Work and GAL,
University of East Anglia,
Norwich NR4 7TJ

Tessa Duncan — Panel Manager,
Surrey GALRO Panel, PO Box 52,
Guildford,
Surrey GU4 7WL

Dr Claire Sturge — Department of Child and Adolescent
Psychiatry,
Northwick Park Hospital, Watford Road,
Harrow,
Middlesex HA1 3UJ

Dr Marion Myles	The Medical Centre, 7e Woodfield Road, London W9 3X
Jenny Stevenson	North East Worcestershire Community Healthcare, Department of Clinical Psychology, Smallwood House, Church Green West, Redditch, Worcs B97 4BD
Dr Brian Jacobs	8 Maberley Road, Upper Norwood, London SE19 2JB
The Rt Hon Lady Justice Butler-Sloss	Royal Courts of Justice
Florence Baron QC	Queen Elizabeth Building, Temple, London EC4Y 9BS
District Judge Angel	The Senior District Judge, PRFD, Somerset House
The Hon Mr Justice Wall	Royal Courts of Justice
The Hon Mr Justice Kirkwood	Royal Courts of Justice
Peter Harris	The Official Solicitor, 81 Chancery Lane, London WC2A 1DD
Iain Hamilton	Jones Maidment Wilson, 5 Byrom Street, Manchester M3 4PF
The Director	The National Council for Family Proceedings, University of Bristol Centre for Socio-Legal Studies, 3 Priory Road, Bristol BS8 1TX
Her Honour Judge Pearlman	The Crown Court Office, 1 English Grounds, Battle Bridge Lane, Southwark, London SE1 2HU
David Hill	The Chief Probation Officer, South East London Probation Service, Crosby House, 9–13 Elmfield Road, Bromley, London BR1 1LT
Trudy Klauber	The Tavistock & Portman NHS Trust, Child & Family Department, Tavistock Clinic, 120 Belsize Lane, London NW3 5BA

Jenny Kenrick

The Tavistock & Portman NHS Trust,
Child & Family Department,
Tavistock Clinic,
120 Belsize Lane,
London NW3 5BA

A J P Butler

Chief Constable, Gloucestershire
Constabulary,
Police Headquarters,
Holland House,
Lansdown Road,
Cheltenham GL51 6QH

Dr Danya Glaiser

Department of Psychological Medicine,
The Hospital for Sick Children,
Great Ormond Street,
London WC1N 3JH

William Arnold

Family Policy Division,
Lord Chancellor's
Department,
Selborne House,
54–60 Victoria Street,
London SW1 6QW

'A psychiatrist (given the chance)
Her theory would always advance
That her patient's replies
Were not really lies
But a different cognitive stance.'

HH Judge Wigmore

'Bring me no more reports . . .'

Macbeth, Act V, Scene III, line 1.